SERIAL MURDER AND MEDIA CIRCUSES

SERIAL MURDER AND MEDIA CIRCUSES

DIRK C. GIBSON

Foreword by DENNIS L. WILCOX

PRAEGER

Westport, Connecticut
London

Library of Congress Cataloging-in-Publication Data

Gibson, Dirk Cameron, 1953–
    Serial murder and media circuses / Dirk C. Gibson.
        p.   cm.
    Includes bibliographical references and index.
    ISBN 0-275-99064-8 (alk. paper)
        1. Serial murders—History—Case studies.   2. Serial murderers—Case studies.
    3. Serial murder investigation—History—Case studies.   4. Murder in mass media—
    Case studies.   5. Mass media and crime—Case studies.   I. Title.
    HV6513.G53 2006
    070.4'4936415230973—dc22   2006015394

British Library Cataloguing in Publication Data is available.

Library of Congress Catalog Card Number: 2006015394
ISBN: 0-275-99064-8

First published in 2006

Praeger Publishers, 88 Post Road West, Westport, CT 06881
An imprint of Greenwood Publishing Group, Inc.
www.praeger.com

Printed in the United States of America

The paper used in this book complies with the
Permanent Paper Standard issued by the National
Information Standards Organization (Z39.48–1984).

10 9 8 7 6 5 4 3 2 1

CONTENTS

FOREWORD

—•◦•—

CRIME IS A basic staple of news coverage. And the old cliché, "If it bleeds, it leads," has more truth than most journalists would care to admit. A single murder generates its share of local news stories, but a series of killings not only causes public panic, but a virtual media circus.

Journalists and editors cover murder, and particularly serial killings, for several reasons. First, murder satisfies many of the basic criteria for what is considered news, such as the unusualness, drama, conflict, human interest, and magnitude of the event. On occasion, the prominence of the murder victim or the killer also enters into the equation. There is, however, no equality in murder. The abduction, rape, and murder of a white, attractive teenager from suburbia generally gets more coverage than the murder of a black prostitute from the "other side of the tracks."

The media, on occasion, do engage in hype and sensationalism depending on the magnitude of the murder. Serial killings, for example, get more attention for valid reasons. One is the public interest. A serial killer continues to strike and be a threat to society. Second, the media does pander to the public's curiosity and thirst for titillation. Readers and viewers enjoy the vicarious experience of learning all the horrifying details in the safe confines of their own home. And the media, of course, often benefits financially with spikes in newspaper sales and higher audience ratings.

The junction and interaction between serial murder and how the mass media covers such events is the subject of this book. Dirk Gibson, a professor of mass communication at the University of New Mexico, posits that "American media plays a multidimensional and integral role in serial killings and the investigation into serial killings." He does so in such a way that the crime buff, interested in the gory details of strangulation, stabbing, torture, dismemberment, and even instances of cannibalism, will not be disappointed.

This book is entertaining in a morbid sort of way because Gibson has assembled a dozen case histories of serial murderers over the past century. He has methodically researched a number of resources to give the readers a complete "MO" on the killer, beginning with their childhood (most had rotten ones) and proceeding through the crimes committed to the police investigation, the arrest, and the trial.

The reader meets such interesting characters as Henry Desire Landru, known as the French Bluebeard, who killed at least ten women by meeting them through matrimonial ads, to Dorothea Puente (only 20 percent of serial killers are women) who operated a boarding house and managed to kill up to twenty-five of her eld-erly tenants for the purpose of keeping their state social services checks. Of course, there are also profiles of more famous serial killers such as Charles Manson (the Sharon Tate murders) and Jeffrey Dahmer who, over three decades killed at least seventeen men and kept their body parts around the house as souvenirs.

At the end of the each case history, Gibson critiques the positive and negative aspects of the media coverage that these serial killers generated. On the positive side, he points out that media coverage was useful in alerting the public about tak-ing high-risk situations (women who owned boarding houses were warned about a Bible-toting, mild-mannered man who used the pretext of looking for a room to rent and then strangling them), and publicizing the details of a suspect and gen-erating tips that lead to the killer's arrest (Dorothea Puente was caught because a potential victim recognized her face on a television news broadcast). Indeed, the author also explores the use of public relations tactics by law enforcement agen-cies in various cases. Such tactics as press conferences, hotlines, posters, fliers, and even media kits are used by police to inform the public and generate leads.

On the negative side, the media gets brickbats for a number of "misbehaviors." Often, aggressive reporters hinder police investigations by revealing too many details about the crime, harassing the families of victims, contaminating the rec-ollections of witnesses, destroying evidence at a crime scene, and even "blowing" stakeouts by police. In the case of the Green River murders, in which fifty or more women were murdered, a news helicopter buzzed the police stakeout of an area and told everyone, including the killer (Gary Ridgway), what the police were doing. On other occasions, the media have made a killer somewhat of a celebrity. Andrew Cunanan, who killed five people including clothing designer Gianni Versace, even collected press clippings about himself and his exploits.

There will always be a synergy between serial murders, police investigation, and media coverage. Gibson ultimately concludes that there needs to be more study and analysis of this synergy so that the public can be better served. He, for example, says police should pay more attention to communications (in the form of notes, letters to the editor, or even messages written in blood on walls) so they better understand the mindset of the killer. At the same time, the media must continue to better understand the dynamics of serial killers because "the media motivates some killers, and enables others."

In sum, the author has written an informed, useful book that will further a better understanding of the media/killer/police interaction. It's a good read, but because of the subject matter, it may not be ideal bedtime reading.

Dennis L. Wilcox

ACKNOWLEDGMENTS

ANY STUDY LIKE mine, which uses integrative research methods, is inherently and deeply indebted to the work of others. My book organizes, analyzes, and integrates the findings of numerous authors into a cohesive narrative. Thus, without those prior contributions, this book would not be possible. I wish I could recognize each book of value to my study.

A considerable number of sources need to be acknowledged. James A. Fox and Jack Levin have made four substantial contributions by their 1985, 1994, 2001, and 2005 books: *Mass Murder: America's Growing Menace, Overkill: Mass Murder and Serial Killing Exposed, The Will to Kill: Making Sense of Senseless Murder,* and *Extreme Killing.* Elliott Leyton also has produced three important works: *Compulsive Killers: The Story of Modern Multiple Murder* (1986), *Hunting Humans: Inside the Minds of Mass Murderers* (1986), and his edited compilation of journal articles, *Serial Murder: Modern Scientific Perspectives* (2000).

Similarly, Ronald M. Holmes offered a trio of valuable studies. He co-authored *Serial Murder* with James DeBurger in 1988 and *Murder in America* (2001) with Steven T. Holmes. He also co-authored "Female Serial Murderesses: Constructing Differentiating Typologies," in *The Journal of Contemporary Criminal Justice* with Steven T. Holmes and Eric Hickey. John C. Douglas and Mark Olshaker also have written three noteworthy books: *Obsession* (1998), *The Anatomy of Motive* (1999), and *The Cases That Haunt Us* (2000). Brian Lane similarly has produced three important books. He co-authored *The Encyclopedia of Serial Killers* with Wilfred Gregg, and he wrote *The Butchers: A Casebook of Macabre Crimes and Forensic Detection* (1994) and *Forces from Beyond* (1995).

Three books by Michael Newton should be mentioned. I used his 1990 book, *Hunting Humans: An Encyclopedia of Modern Serial Killers,* the 2000 revision, and *Silent Rage: The 30-Year Odyssey of a Serial Killer* (1994). I frequently cited Joel Norris's 1988 *Serial Killers,* Gini G. Scott's *Homicide: 100 Years of Murder in America* (1998), Joseph C. Fisher's *Killer Among Us: Public Reactions to Serial Murder* (1997), and Eric Hickey's *Serial Murderers and Their Victims* (1997).

Other books were nearly as important to my study. Specifically, I used Colin Wilson and Donald Seaman's *The Serial Killers: A Study in the Psychology of Violence* (1992), Jane Caputi's 1987 work, *The Age of Sex Crimes,* Robert K. Ressler and Tim Schachtman's 1992 book, *Whoever Fights Monsters,* and David Everitt's *Human Monsters: An Encyclopedia of the World's Most Vicious Murderers* (1993).

The twelve serial murder cases discussed in my book have already been the subject of excellent previous studies, upon which I relied. For instance, in the Henri Landru case, Dennis Bardens's historical biography *The Ladykiller* (1972) was an important work. I also used the work of Trivia-Library.com, Court TV's CrimeLibrary.com, and Biography.ms.

I did not use a case-specific book on the Axeman of New Orleans chapter. However, I took advantage of several excellent Internet sources. These included Troy Taylor's "Dead Men Do Tell Tales," AmaZon, "Axeman of New Orleans," and the CrimeLibrary.com.

The Earle Nelson case chapter was facilitated by Harold Schechter's valuable 1998 book, *Bestial: The Savage Trail of a True American Monster.* I also used "The Strangler" by John Burchill of the Winnipeg Police Service, and "Earle Nelson," by Serial Killers A-Z. Other valuable sources were "Earle Nelson the Gorilla Murderer," by FortuneCity.com, and Mark Gribben's "Descent to Madness," at CrimeLibrary.com.

The Moors Murders of Ian Brady and Myra Hindley were well-described in Emlyn Williams's *Beyond Belief* (1968). Also useful were Greg Taylor's Internet study, "The Moors Murders," a British Broadcasting Corporation article attributed to Chris Summers, and a study by Murder in the UK. Similarly valuable were other Internet pieces by Ananova, UKOnline, and FortuneCity.com.

The crimes of Charles Manson and his "Family" have been the subject of numerous books, periodical articles, and Internet studies. Probably the most important such work was Vince Bugliosi and Curt Gentry's *Helter Skelter* (1974), although I also made extensive use of Ed Sanders's 1971 book, *The Family.* Important Internet sources are in abundance, and include, among others, The Zodiac Manson Connection and CharlieManson.com. The law school at the University of Missouri at Kansas City has made major Internet-based contributions, as has The Internet Crime Archives.

The "Hillside Strangler" murders of Angelo Buono Jr. and Kenneth Bianchi have been well-chronicled, as well. The two books I relied upon the most were Darcy O'Brien's *Two of a Kind: The Hillside Stranglers* (1985), and *The Hillside Strangler: Inside a Murderer's Mind* (1981), by Ted Schwartz. I also used a number of Internet sources, such as TrueCrime.com, Kari & Associates, bbc.co.uk, and the New Criminologist. Two basic resources on this case are the site at www.hillside-strangler.com, and the CrimeLibrary.com.

Jeffrey Dahmer's thirty-year reign of serial murder and more sordid crimes has been the subject of several important studies, to date. I relied greatly on *The Man Who Could Not Kill Enough* (1992), by Anne Schwartz, and *The Milwaukee Murders* (1991), by Don Davis. Valuable additional sources included Newton's *Hunting Humans* and the encyclopedia by Lane and Gregg.

Dorothea Puente's social services scam and serial slayings were well researched and covered in Daniel Blackburn's *Human Harvest* (1990). Also very useful in this chapter were *Murder Most Rare: The Female Serial Killer* (1998), by Michael D. Kelleher and C. L. Kelleher, and Newton's *Hunting Humans*.

The Green River murders were recently traced to Gary Ridgway. The most valuable information source on that case might well be *The Search for the Green River Killer* (1991), by Carlton Smith and Tomas Guillen. I also used Antonio Mendoza's *Killers on the Loose* (2001). Among the many important recent information sites were *New York Times* and *Washington Post* stories.

Andrew Cunanan's serial murders and related events have attracted numerous authors. Maureen Orth's *Vulgar Favors* (1999) was an important resource, as was *Three-Month Fever* (1999), by Gary Indiana, *The Evil That Men Do* (1998), by Roy Hazelwood and Stephen G. Michaud, and Wensley Clarkson's *Death at Every Stop* (1997).

Canadian husband-and-wife serial killers Paul Bernardo and Karla Homolka have also elicited considerable media interest. Most useful was *Deadly Innocence* (1995), by Scott Burnside and Alan Cairns. I also used a wide variety of excellent Internet sources in this chapter, including Biography.ms, Serial Killers A-Z, CBC News Online, and All Serial Killers. Equally useful to my research were Joe Chidley's article in *Macleans*, and other Internet sources like Wikipedia and Nationmaster.com.

The Westley Dodd case is the subject of a valuable book. I used Gary C. King's work, *Driven to Kill* (1993). In addition, I also used several Internet sources extensively. These included the CrimeLibrary.com, Answers.com, The Explore Dictionary of Famous People, and Nationmaster.com.

INTRODUCTION

———•◦•———

THE AXEMAN OF New Orleans specialized in killing grocers of Italian descent in New Orleans in the 1910s, apparently to promote jazz music. Dorothea Puente was an elderly landlady who murdered her tenants, but continued to cash their government checks. The Manson "Family" terrorized California in the 1960s, as did the Hillside Stranglers a decade later.

This book examines a dozen cases of serial murder. Included are: Henri Landru, the Axeman of New Orleans, Earle Nelson, the Manson Family, Ian Brady and Myra Hindley, Angelo Buono and Kenneth Bianchi, Jeffrey Dahmer, Dorothea Puente, Gary Ridgway, Andrew Cunanan, Paul Bernardo and Karla Homolka, and Westley Dodd. A total of fifteen individuals in all.

Each of these very different serial murder cases represents one of eight decades between the 1890s and 1990s. They all had one thing in common: the significant presence of the mass media. These might seem an unlikely combination at first glance—serial killers and mass communication. In fact, there is a complex and deep-seated interrelationship between these two important factors in contemporary American life, as this book will make abundantly clear. It will soon become apparent that the American media plays a multidimensional and integral role in serial killings and the investigation into serial killings.

This role is not generally a positive one. Serial murder cases motivate the media in unfortunate ways. The result is that even typically respectable media organizations like the *New York Times* can be involved in serial murder document theft, while CBS News interferes with a seventeen-year FBI serial murder investigation and forces a premature arrest when the FBI had hoped to wait and catch their suspect in the act of mailing an explosive device. Law enforcement officials conducting serial murder investigations have referred to the media personnel assigned to their cases as "drunks" and "dickheads."

This book occurs at the intersection of two important phenomena in twenty-first century America: serial murderers and the media. This linkage between multiple murderers and mass communication is not accidental or coincidental. Rather, the relationship between the press and serial killers is one of extraordinary importance to both parties, as we shall soon learn.

Serial murderers use the media; Dodd did, as did the Axeman of New Orleans. In some cases, the media interferes in the investigation, as it did in the Green River murders case, the Hillside Stranglers case, that of Canadians Bernardo and Homolka, and Cunanan. The media has helped apprehend serial killers, as have law enforcement public information efforts in the Nelson, Puente, and Dodd cases. But in the Manson case, prosecutors protecting an important witness led the media on a high-speed freeway chase, until the media won and took photographs. This book analyzes the media/murderer relationship through consideration of a dozen serial murder cases.

THE KILLERS

The choice of which cases to include was difficult, as there were many deserving candidates. An attempt was made to achieve some balance, so there are three women and twelve males in our group. The cases span a century; there was one each in the 1890s, 1910s, and 1920s, followed by two cases from the 1960s. There was one 1970 case, two from the 1980s, and three from the 1990s. One case included the 1970s, 1980s, and 1990s.

Killers from four countries were included: the United States, Canada, Great Britain, and France. Eleven cases were solved; only the Axeman of New Orleans defied certain identification. Eight of the cases involved lone killers, with four others being the result of teamwork. Roughly half of the cases are relatively unknown today—Landru, Axeman of New Orleans, Nelson, Brady and Hindley, Puente, and Dodd.

These cases are typical, or representative, of the one thousand such cases I have examined. Their rhetorical behavior and the mass media coverage of the events are important factors in the majority of these crimes. The specific rhetoric and precise mass media varies from case to case, yet are present in some manner most of the time. That is because serial murder is rhetorically motivated much of the time, and such crimes typically elicit strong media interest and aggressive behavior.

PURPOSE

Serial murder is an important issue in contemporary America, deserving of our best efforts at understanding and combating this criminal menace. The mass media play a critical and largely ignored role in serial murderer cases. So, the general purpose of this book is to enhance our understanding of serial killers and serial murder investigations, through a comprehensive consideration of the media/murderer relationship. Four specific sub-purposes might be considered, as well:

1. The role of the media in serial murder cases needs to be explored and exemplified; this book does so.
2. The body of knowledge on serial murder should be expanded to include the mass communication dimension; this book begins that effort.
3. The effectiveness of the law enforcement response to serial murderers might be improved if the mass communication causes and consequences

of serial murder were better understood. I hope this book initiates that enhanced understanding.

4. The public needs to understand and appreciate the magnitude of the serial murder problem, as well as recognize and comprehend the interaction between the media, serial killers, serial murder investigators, and other stakeholders. This book promotes those understandings.

CONCLUSION

In closing, it would be appropriate to consider a conceptual preview. At the risk of making the rest of this book unnecessary, five central facts might be asserted at this time. Much of this book's content will involve these five fundamental facts.

1. Serial murder is a significant social phenomenon in contemporary America. There is a large but unknown number of serial killers (probably in the hundreds) accounting for a large but unknown number of victims (probably in the thousands). The qualitative consequences of serial murder are equally severe.
2. The interrelationships between serial killers, law enforcement, the media, and the public are complex, multidimensional, and probably affect all salient stakeholders.
3. Media coverage of serial murders influences the killer(s).
4. Media coverage of serial murders influences the serial murder investigation.
5. Serial killers and serial murder cases influence the media.

There is much more to be considered, of course, and there are exceptions and caveats concerning even these fundamental facts. Nevertheless, as a general rule these five facts consistently appear in case after case of serial murder.

This book is the second in my series of studies of serial murder. The first, *Clues from Killers: Serial Murder and Crime Scene Messages* (Praeger, 2004), explains the rhetorical behavior of serial murderers. Hopefully, these books will stimulate serious discussion of the role of communication in serial slayings.

1

HENRI DESIRE LANDRU

HENRI LANDRU WAS called the "French Bluebeard" because his wives had a way of dying soon after the wedding. Very soon. Within five years he killed ten women, a teen-age boy, and two dogs. And quite possibly a cat, as well.

His motive was monetary. Eleven lives were spent so that Landru might attain a little wealth, such a terrible waste of humankind.

It is uncertain how he killed his victims, but poison and strangulation are two methods mentioned by authorities. It is known that after he killed his victims, he dismembered and burned the corpses.

Communication played an extremely important role in Landru's crimes. He placed ads in newspapers soliciting victims, and he wrote them letters. He kept detailed records of his crimes in his *carnet,* or little notebook. He wrote letters to friends, relatives, and work associates of his victims, covering up the fact that their significant other was already dead.

Mass communication was extremely important. He obtained his victims through the mass media. The Landru crimes depended entirely upon mass communication.

Nine main topics will be discussed to enable us to understand the Landru crimes and their communication elements. They include the criminal and his crimes, along with the investigation, arrest, and trial of Landru. Public and media interest in this case will be described as will the communication-based nature of Landru's offenses and his communication. The negative effects of media coverage will also be explored.

THE CRIMINAL

Landru was a cunning and creative criminal. He had a long criminal record, and an even longer record of romantic exploits. He was truly a French serial killer.

Landru was not called by his proper name, of course. He had a nickname, "The French Bluebeard."[1] Another source added, "After the fairy-tale character who kills his wives, Henri Landru was called, 'Bluebeard.'"[2]

Landru was born in Paris in 1869.[3] One study noted that, "His parents were honest and forthright."[4] Another account reported, "Born of parents of modest means in 1869 during the middle of France's Third Republic, Landru's childhood and early years were as nondescript as he was." His father worked at the Vulcain Fireworks in Paris as a fireman, and his mother was a housewife.[5]

All indications are that Landru enjoyed a relatively normal childhood. "Born in Paris, his childhood and early years are thought to have been fairly uneventful," one source noted.[6] Another study confirmed the normalcy of Landru's childhood and family life.[7]

Landru was reportedly quite intelligent. According to the *Crime Library*, Landru "was considered a bright lad." He was allowed to take courses in engineering at the prestigious School of Mechanical Engineering.[8] "He did well in school," confirmed *The News of the Odd*, which also mentioned his coursework at the engineering institute.[9]

One unhappy factor in Landru's life was his father's suicide. One source said that "distressed by his son," the senior Landru committed suicide in 1912.[10] The role Henri Landru played in his family's misery was made clear by the *Crime Library*, "He had already driven his father to suicide and left his family penniless and humiliated."[11]

Like many young men, his adult life began with a stint in the armed forces of his country. "After leaving school he spent four years in the army."[12] Adding detail, another study noted that he was drafted by the military at eighteen, and young Landru excelled in the French armed forces, being promoted to the rank of sergeant by the time of his discharge.[13] Another source suggested that "when he was drafted into the Army at the age of 18, he succeeded there, too."[14]

The warm side of Landru was aptly characterized by one study. "Henri Landru had been a sunny child who grew up to be a mercurial, intelligent adult. A sensualist, he loved roses, so much so that when the police were spading up his yard trying to find bodies, his main concern was for the flowers."[15]

There was a sincere spiritual substance to Landru. He went to Catholic schools, and he "was admitted as a sub-deacon in the religious order of St. Louis en l'Isle."[16] On the other hand, Colin Wilson called him "a callous ruffian who deserved to be guillotined."[17]

His criminal career was extensive and varied. Initially, he received a two-year prison term for a fraud conviction in 1900.[18] In 1900, when Landru was thirty-one, he was jailed for three years for swindling an elderly widow over a marriage settlement. From then until his arrest for the murders, he was sentenced five times for extortion and cheating elderly women out of their savings.[19]

"He had been convicted seven times for fraud," claimed Publications International Ltd.[20] A second study noted that in a span of ten years, Landru was in and out of prison on seven occasions.[21] After his initial incarceration in 1900, Landru was imprisoned seven more times, for a total of eight terms in prison.[22]

He reportedly attempted suicide while serving his first prison sentence. Some doubted the sincerity of the suicide attempt.[23] Perhaps he was contemplating his lifelong deportation to New Caledonia.[24]

There is a popular tale that Landru confessed, in writing. He painted a picture in prison while awaiting trial. On the back of the drawing, inside the frame, Landru wrote, "I did it. I burned the bodies in my kitchen oven."[25] An encyclopedia also recorded this incident, claiming that Landru's daughter's attorney discovered the incriminating inscription, forty years later.[26]

Was Landru an irresistible charmer? There are two sides to this story. But first, we should consider his relationship to his cousin, Remy. Kissing cousins they were, and much more.

"At 22, he had impregnated his cousin," recalled one source.[27] "He seduced his cousin," agreed another source.[28] A more detailed version was provided by the *Crime Library*, "In 1891, he seduced his cousin, Mademoiselle Remy, who became pregnant and bore him a daughter."[29]

Landru was a womanizer. Bardens noted that in Landru's home, references were found to 283 women, and he met at least 169 of them. Bardens observed that Landru had romanced and made love to a rather considerable number of women.[30]

One account reported that Landru had a full and bushy red beard, a pleasant speaking voice, courteous and generally excellent manners, and hypnotic black eyes with long silky lashes. But could those traits mesmerize more than two hundred women? "By his own accounting, he had been the lover of 283 women," Bardens noted in quantifying Landru's sexual prowess. According to the *Crime Library*, "He was probably a romantic man, able to sweep lonely women off their feet, and since his physical appearance was more comical than handsome, he must have been a smooth, fast-talker. His sexual appetite reportedly was ravenous."[31]

Others disagreed. One source reported, "By physical appearance, Henri Landru was not the type of man that one would suspect of being able to romance more than 300 women out of their life savings." According to another study, "Landru was not particularly handsome."[32]

THE CRIMES

The Landru serial murders pre-dated the existence of the very term used to describe them. In this section, we will learn about the crimes, through examination of five subjects. The number of deaths will be examined, as will the manner of death. Landru's motive and modus operandi will be considered and the victims identified.

The Number of Deaths

There is a small variation in the estimates of how many people were killed by Landru. We will consider several such estimates. This will give us an idea of the scope of his serial murder spree.

"At least nine French women" were murdered by Landru, according to one estimate. He was "sentenced to death for the murder of eleven women," another source suggested.[33]

"Between 1914 and 1918 Landru claimed 11 victims: 10 women plus the teenaged son of one of his victims," one source noted. According to the *Crime Library,* "In all, at least 10 women and one boy (and two dogs) had disappeared after meeting Landru." Another source concurred, noting that "Between 1914 and 1918, Landru claimed 11 victims." A third study added that "The enterprise necessitated the deaths of 10 women, a young boy, and two dogs."[34]

The Manner of Death

Considerable disagreement exists over how Landru killed his victims, largely because the bodies were never found, only bone fragments and ashes. We will consider several different accounts of the method of murder.

"How they were killed was still a mystery," contended the *Crime Library.* The same source added that "His method of killing is unknown." Others authorities disagreed, and offered causes of death.[35]

"He used poison to kill them," one recent study concluded. Another account reported another murder method, "Landru would seduce the women who came to his Parisian villa and, after he had been given access to their assets, he would kill them—probably by strangulation—and burn their dismembered bodies in his oven."[36]

He dismembered the bodies prior to disposal. According to one study, after he killed the victims, "Then he cut up the bodies with a handsaw."[37]

Saw marks on pieces of charred bone incriminated Landru. At his trial, it became clear that the victims had been dismembered. "The President of the court asked Landru to explain the saw marks on the bones, reminding him that his notebooks indicated the purchase of several saws."[38] Landru remained silent.

After murder and dismemberment came incineration. In the ashes, police discovered small pieces of human bones. Landru had disposed of his victims by dismembering and then burning the corpses, one study claimed. Landru "incinerated the pieces in his stove," reported another study.[39]

"Very curious now, the police investigated his stove at Gambais. When they sifted the ashes from it, and examined the outhouse and the garden, they found hundreds of human bone fragments, some teeth, and some hooks-and-eyes." Another study recalled that Landru would kill victims, "then burn their dismembered bodies in his oven."[40]

There is some uncertainty about Landru's body burning. Bardens reported that the French criminal and civil authorities did not believe that Landru had cremated all eleven bodies in his home stove. The incineration facilities for disposing of victims at Vernouillet were considered to be inadequate; how could Landru have dismembered and burned eleven bodies, in town, under the very noses of his nearest neighbors?[41]

Modus Operandi

How did Landru accomplish his murders? Although we have some indications of his methods, at this point we will specifically consider his modus operandi. Bardens gave a detailed description. The similar disappearances, believed to be murders, of ten women in quick succession had established Landru's rubber-stamp system for homicide. Each killing was virtually identical. A matrimonial advertisement, in the name of Diard, Fremyet, Guillet, Forest, or Petit, with more or less the same language, attracted similar victims, and led to the same type of meeting, whirlwind romance, engagement, and the removal of the property from the victim's homes, followed by a one-way visit to Landru's villa at Gambais. Then the victim disappeared forever.[42]

A similar but more concise summation of Landru's methods was provided by another source, "Landru specialized in seducing lone rich women, abusing their confidence to obtain a *procuration* (power of attorney) for their financial dealings, strangling them, then disposing of the corpses by burning the corpse and burying the remains in his garden."[43]

According to Publications International Ltd., Landru was consistent, using the methods previously described. "Once he married a mark, Landru would assume all her accounts and property. He would either sell her furniture or store it at one of his villas. A small outdoor stove on the property of one villa was used by Landru to burn the bodies of his victims."[44]

The Motive

Landru was not a crazed psychotic killer; to the contrary, his crimes were calculated and very well planned. Nor was he acting from insane sexual lust, or a similar sensual stimulus. He only murdered his victims "after he had been given access to their assets."[45] His murders were motivated by money.

He managed through murder and manipulation to be named custodian of his victims' treasures, Bardens recalled.[46] Another account bluntly observed that "Henri Landru enticed women with offers of marriage and killed them after he had stripped them of all their assets." Landru specifically sought the legal power of procuration, comparable to the American concept of power of attorney, over his victim's estate.[47]

"He planned to seduce a wealthy respondent, con her out of her fortune, and kill her. It worked like a charm, and proved to be extremely lucrative," one source noted. The *Crime Library* concluded that "Landru killed for money or to rid himself of a tiresome or inconvenient lover."[48]

The Victims

Serial murder victims deserve recognition and respect. They were killed before their time, and perhaps they suffered terribly. In this section, we note those killed by Landru, including: Anna Colomb, Celestine Buisson, Jeanne

Cuchet (and her sixteen or eighteen-year-old son Andre), Therese Laborde-Line, Madame Heon, Marie Angelique Desiree Pelletier, Andree Babelay, Louise Jaume, Annette Pascal, and Marie-Therese Marchadier.

THE INVESTIGATION

Never before in the history of France had the civil authorities and the French police investigated a criminal so adroit, secretive, tireless, and audacious, Bardens contended. This was indeed a most difficult investigation. During the search of Landru's estate, it was with a sense of near-desperation that officers Riboulet, Dautel, and Brelin searched the property.[49]

The main reason for the investigative lack of progress was the lack of bodies and clues. One source claimed that the French authorities were totally baffled by the lack of clues. Where had Landru disposed of the bodies? What had he done with the bodies?[50]

Ironically, while one major investigative hurdle dealt with the scarcity of clues, another problem with the probe resulted from abundance. There were lots of leads and numerous documents.

Nearly one hundred French police and detectives attempted to unravel the complex story of Landru's crimes. M. Bonin, the Paris examining magistrate, initiated one of the lengthiest and most expensive investigations in French history, according to Bardens. He added that investigators followed the often difficult trail of the 283 women who had corresponded with Landru, and the 169 women he had selected to receive his amorous and homicidal attention. In addition, "There was the endless list of witnesses to be seen." And there was paperwork; "Bonin was plagued by a superabundance of documents," also referred to as "the sheer deadweight of the paperwork."[51]

A final investigative hurdle proved most formidable—penetrating Landru's labyrinth of aliases. Jean Belin was a Paris police official investigating the Landru crimes. At first he thought he was following different people until he realized that M. Fremyet, M. DuPont, and Lucien Guillet were all false identities for the same criminal, who turned out to be Landru.[52]

The police conducted numerous searches in an attempt to locate Landru's victims' bodies. The water reservoir at Landru's estate was drained, and the cesspool, well, and pump examined. The large pond at Bruyeres was drained, and each piece of the mud was sifted and searched. The police were everywhere, digging in the garden, pulling up the paving in the basement, constantly searching.[53]

"The variety of handsaws" found at Landru's Gambais residence interested investigators. A billhook was also discovered. Landru refused to explain why he owned such a large number of saws and the hook device.[54]

It was believed that Landru dismembered and burned the bodies of his victims. For this reason the police carefully examined the special stove Landru added to his residence. It used coal, not the local wood, and it was modified "so that it would ensure a powerful draught." The result was exceptionally hot burning for brief periods of time.[55]

Police gathered affidavits from a variety of witnesses. One person swore to smelling burning meat on a number of occasions, the odor emanating from Landru's stove. Another witness saw two of the women who disappeared in Landru's company.[56]

Police conducted an experiment to see if Landru's stove could incinerate flesh and bones. A sheep's head was reduced to ash in fifteen minutes. A leg of mutton was completely burned up in an hour and a quarter's time.[57]

THE ARREST

The victims' relatives played a major role in Landru's apprehension: this is not unusual in serial murder cases. "Henri Landru was finally caught by the persistence of his victims' relatives," according to Publications International Ltd.[58]

The sister of Madame Buisson had tried without success to contact or even locate her missing sister. Then, on April 11, 1919, she encountered Landru strolling down the Rue de Rivoli in Paris. She notified the police, and Landru was arrested the next day. A similar tale was told by another source. In 1919, the sister of a Landru victim, Madame Buisson, tried to locate her vanished sibling. She did not know Landru's real name, but she recognized him when she encountered him, and after much effort she finally persuaded the police to arrest him.[59]

When the police learned of Landru's whereabouts, Belin ordered twenty-four hour surveillance on the premises. Then he set off to obtain a warrant for M. Fremyet's arrest.[60] Fremyet was Landru's alias at the time.

Belin gained entry into Landru's lodging by subterfuge. He pretended he was there about an advertised automobile for sale. Once inside, he addressed Landru and his mistress, Mme. Fernande Segret, "Inspector Belin, Surete Generale. We need to question you on various matters. Please get dressed and come with us."[61]

At his arrest, Landru was overheard being addressed by his real name by Segret. Belin then checked Surete files on Landru, and discovered the true identity of his suspect. He confronted Landru with his discoveries, and Landru admitted his true identity. Because Landru was still serving a suspended sentence from 1914 for previous crimes, he was placed under arrest for violating the terms of the suspended sentence.[62]

THE TRIAL

Landru had a preliminary hearing on December 8, 1920. The preliminary court remanded Landru for trial at the Assizes of the Seine. He appealed, the appeal was accepted, but a subsequent hearing in May 1921 reaffirmed the previous judicial opinion.[63]

The trial started on November 7, 1921. The prosecutor was Maitre Godefroy, the Advocat General, who was assisted by M. Brouchot, the assistant judge of the Civil Tribunal of Versailles. Landru's defense counsel was Maitre de Moro-Giafferi, a colorful and well-known defense attorney.[64]

The trial began with the traditional Act of Indictment. Here the Clerk of the Court read a report summarizing the accusations and evidence against the defendant. This monotonous narration lasted for more than two hours. Then the list of 150 witnesses was called in court, with each witness indicating his or her presence.[65]

Landru's demeanor was one of the most memorable aspects of the proceedings. He was noncommittal and seemingly uninterested in his trial, and he maintained a calm, unworried, and almost professional appearance in court. "It was really Landru's demeanour and personality that dominated the proceedings from start to finish," Bardens contended.[66]

The President of the Court was the presiding judge at the trial. On the fifteenth day of the trial, he began the court session by inquiring, "Landru, how did you carry out your crimes?" Landru characteristically remained silent and refused to answer.[67]

Landru refused to answer most questions. But he did offer a few statements. At the beginning of the trial, he stated: "I simply want to say a few words, to protest my innocence. From the very first day I have held to my protest. I have asked for proof, and have had but words proffered to me, never any proof. I acknowledge the eloquence of the Public Prosecutor, but I am also aware of the great impartiality of the Judge, and that I can count on the devotion of my defending counsel. Thus, I trust that these discussions will finally prove my innocence."

Landru kept his composure during the trial, for the most part. On one occasion, though, he slipped. Irritated by the prosecutor, he said, "Always the same question! I fully realize, M. l'Avocat General, that you are after my head. I regret that I have not got more than one head to offer."

At the conclusion of the trial, before the jury deliberations, Landru declared that "I affirm, on the love that I have for my wife and my children, feelings which have been testified to in these hearings that I am innocent of the crimes that I am accused of." After being pronounced guilty, before being taken from the courtroom, he claimed, "I have only one thing to say, Your Honor. I have never committed murder. This is my last protest."[68]

As the trial progressed, Landru seemed to deteriorate. After expert evidence on bones and Landru's stove seemed especially incriminating, he seemed depressed. Later, he looked "deathly pale."[69]

Landru's attorney defended him as best he could. DeMoro-Giafferi emphatically pointed out that Landru's silence could not be held against him. "That man has a right under our law to remain silent! Who shall deny him this right?," he asked rhetorically.[70]

The jury deliberated for just two hours. They found Landru guilty, but requested that he not be executed. The judge disagreed, and sentenced him to death by guillotine.[71]

COMMUNICATION-BASED OFFENSES

It is my belief, and the evidence clearly supports the notion, that these crimes were based on communication. The ads were placed in the French mass media of the day, newspapers. The subsequent letters between Landru and his victims, and from Landru as part of his cover-up, were rhetorical acts. And his notebook was a communicative behavior.

The communication aspects of the case were recognized by one source. Landru preyed upon vulnerable widows. He placed matrimonial ads in newspapers, thereby collecting responses from hundreds of interested women. Between 1914 and 1919, Landru claimed to have received hundreds of applications to marry him, and he murdered ten of the women.[72]

PUBLIC AND MEDIA INTEREST

The Landru trial attracted significant public interest, in France and worldwide. The media, both national and global, were similarly stimulated. In this section, we will examine both the significant public interest and major media interest.

In France, around the time of World War I, Henri Landru created quite a sensation. It was bitterly cold outside when his trial began, well below freezing. Hundreds had cheerfully risked illness to be seated at the trial, which was the main topic of conversation for the last three years. Everyone wanted to see Landru, "Old Bluebeard."[73]

"There is little doubt that Landru's trial captivated his countrymen," the *Crime Library* claimed. Besides, in 1919 there was no term "serial murder" and such killings were "still a novelty." In fact, there was some clandestine respect paid to Landru. "The people of his native France didn't condone the killings, but they secretly admired his prowess as a seducer and lover," according to one source.[74]

His trial stood as an indication of how popular the Landru case had become. "Fashionable women with lunch baskets and dogs flocked to the trial, fighting for seats in the courtroom," reported a recent source. Bardens added that even the current darlings of the Paris social scene were forced to fight their way through crowds to be seated at the most popular show in France.[75]

Media Interest

There was considerable media interest in Landru, just as there was public interest. We might briefly consider the extent of this media passion for Landru. We will find that it mirrored that of the French people.

"Landru's belated trial was front-page news around the world," according to Publications International Ltd. Bardens echoed this perception of substantial media interest. France's most reputable reporters and cartoonists, along with the cream of the world's newspaper staffs watched the trial, with media representatives from America, Britain, Spain, and Italy.[76]

Landru attracted so many journalists to cover his trial that "The hundred journalists are appallingly cramped," noted a contemporary report. According to another source, Landru's trial was a front-page news item around the globe.[77]

THE COMMUNICATION

Landru's criminal operation depended entirely upon communication. In addition to the advertisements that he placed to solicit his clientele, communication played two other central roles in these crimes. Landru wrote letters to those who responded to his ads, and he wrote letters to conceal their death, in addition to keeping detailed notes in a notebook.

The Advertisements

The advertisements were at the very heart of Landru's serial murder system. He solicited likely victims through the ads. No ads, no victims.

Landru placed small classified matrimonial advertisements in Paris newspapers. He quickly became a master at crafting effectively worded notices that brought elderly women flocking around him in great numbers, Bardens recalled. The intrinsic importance of the ads to Landru's schemes was described by the *Crime Library*, "Each woman in the ledger had met Landru through his marriage advertisements and had disappeared."[78]

The advertisements were effective. "Over five years, Landru received more than 300 inquiries from interested women." A different source offered a less specific quantification; between 1914 and 1919, Landru received what he claimed were hundreds of applicants to finally woo, marry, and murder ten women. Another study also found that Landru's ads were effective at eliciting responses.[79]

Landru had practiced this scheme in 1908, in the case of Mademoiselle Izore. He placed a matrimonial ad, and she responded with payment of a 15,000 franc dowry. The payment of this dowry left her penniless and destitute, and Landru received a three-year prison term.[80]

We might assess a few of these ads, to conclude this section. Three of Landru's ads will be examined. They were relatively similar in content and style.

Here is one of Landru's ads from the matrimonial section of a contemporary newspaper, "Widower, with two children, aged forty-three, possessing comfortable income, affectionate, serious, and moving in good society, desires to meet widow of similar status, with a view to matrimony."[81]

A second ad differed slightly in information, but the basic content and structure were the same as in the last ad. "Single gentleman, aged 45, pound 400 per year, desires to marry homely lady of similar age and income." *La echo de Paris* was where Mme. Louise Jaume read this Landru ad, "Gentleman, aged fifty, for many years a widower, with no children, skilled and educated with frs. 20,000 capital and a good job, seeks marriage with like-minded lady."[82]

The Letters

One of the most prolific serial killing letter writers, Landru wined and dined his victims, which he obtained through correspondence. Letters figured prominently in his murders in other ways, as well. He wrote to the police and tried to conceal the demise of his deceased pen pals with a stream of phony letters.

Landru wrote to widows, and he killed many of those whom he met in this manner. Bardens quantified Landru's literary behavior. Landru was determined to be corresponding with at least 283 women, whose letters to him were frequently written in relatively uninhibited and romantic language.[83]

Bardens described Landru's letter-writing modus operandi. Landru wrote to Mme Buisson from the Hotel de France et d'Angleterre at Beauvais, claiming that he was a successful businessman who had escaped from Lille when the Germans invaded. It was agonizing for him to abandon his possessions there, to leave his family and friends. He was lonely and wanted a woman to share his life. The response from Mme Buisson was predictable. She pledged to love him well, and make him forget his unhappiness in face of the German invaders, she passionately replied.[84]

The letters he wrote to eventual victims, and those he received from them, were incriminating evidence at his trial. The judge asked Landru to explain why he corresponded with so many women, whom he had met through his matrimonial advertisements, and why he kept the letters.[85] But Landru refused to do so.

Landru sent a second sort of crime-related letter, one with decidedly sinister overtones. Friends and relatives of women who went to meet Landru, under his various aliases, sometimes received postcards and letters that did not seem quite right. Bardens described one such experience.

After meeting Landru, neither Mme Pascal or her cat were ever seen again. Her sister received one postcard from her in Toulon, with the original date altered. The real date could still be made out—April 4—the night of her arrival. It had been changed to correspond with the postmark, which was April 19.[86]

"Landru obviously took great pains to cover up his crimes. He sought to avoid detection and make it look like his victims were still alive," reported the *Crime Library*. How did he accomplish that? By sending fraudulent reassuring letters to the significant others of those he had killed. The *Crime Library* added, "Two of Guillin's friends received postcards from Landru, saying that Guillin was unable to write herself. He forged a letter from Buisson to her dressmaker and another to the concierge of her Paris apartment."[87]

Landru wrote to the police in his hometown of Mantes, to explain why he failed to keep an appointment. Alerted by the stench of decaying bodies, neighbors had called the police to investigate Landru's home. When the police called on him, he brushed them off, saying he would come down to the police station shortly. Instead, he left town as soon as his visitor was out of sight. He departed immediately for Lyons where he wrote to the Brigadier of Police at Mantes from the Terminus Hotel. Landru wrote that he had been required to travel on business, which would keep him from his home in Vernouillet for several weeks. He had made an appointment with the Mantes policeman who had called upon him and his wife, he said, but his wife was suddenly called to London on an urgent family matter. He would let the Mantes police know when she had returned, he wrote, adding that since the complaint involved was a small one, he trusted that no one would care about the delay in following it up.[88]

Landru maintained the correspondence received as a result of his ads. They were filed in categories like "Reply later," "File," "Reply immediately," and "Ignore." Landru maintained an exact index of each woman's name with numerous little biographical details as to their physical and moral qualities, their family situations, their work, interests, and style of living.[89]

The Carnet

A meticulous note-taker, Landru kept a small notebook, or *carnet,* with him at all times. At his trial, the notebook would be used to incriminate him. In 1917, very soon after Andree Babelay disappeared, Landru began to pursue Mme Buisson with intensity and passion. In his small black notebook he wrote next to her name the number Seven. Why was that important? Because six of his previous "fiancées" had mysteriously disappeared. Mme Buisson was the seventh.[90]

This notebook contained frank appraisals of the women he was considering victimizing. Landru had written about Mme Pascal in his notebook, "Widow for five years, young appearance, without children, 2 Villa Stendhal, Paris, wearing a tailor-made costume and sombrero hat." Mme Pascal was never seen alive again after April 5. The prosecution contended that the time inscribed in Landru's *carnet* indicated the time of her death at his hands.[91]

The *carnet,* important as it was to Landru, was vital to the police. At first, it was all they had. According to one source, "All the police had to go on was a cryptic memorandum book where Landru had meticulously recorded his income and expenses."[92]

Landru's *carnet* figured prominently in his trial, as well. One recent analysis asserted, "Even more damning was the notebook Landru kept," because "the names of missing women appeared again and again in his calendar." "The notebook alone was sufficient evidence to convict Landru of all ten murders, and it suggested his involvement in many others," according to another study. Bardens candidly contended that the most incriminating evidence at trial was Landru's notebook.[93]

"As evidence the police took his notebook," according to one study. It explained why this was important: "It was incriminating enough that the names of the missing women were penciled on the inside front cover; it was even more incriminating that train tickets to his villas (the latest one in Gambais) were recorded often as 'one single. One return.'"[94]

Landru needed his notebook. He was involved in so many scams and crooked deals, under so many different names, he needed to keep careful records. "Often, Landru operated under several names with several appointments a day. No wonder he needed a notebook to keep it all straight." Another source agreed, adding that "Landru used a wide variety of aliases; so many, in fact, that he had to keep a ledger listing all the women with whom he corresponded and which particular identity he used for each woman."[95]

According to Publications International Ltd., Landru was caught attempting to get rid of a relatively small black notebook after his arrest. It contained detailed records of all of his expenses and assets relating to his marriage and murder schemes.[96]

NEGATIVE EFFECTS OF THE MEDIA

In some serial murder cases, the media plays a negative role. That was true of the Landru case. Two negative effects of media coverage will be examined, the creation of celebrities and the creation of media zones.

The Creation of Celebrities

In France at the time of World War I, Henri Landru's serial murders and the subsequent investigation and trial resulted in a sensation. The Landru serial murder crimes were an international cause celebre, which was daily reading for a world horrified by the endless carnage of World War I and badly in need of diversion.[97]

Others besides Landru became celebrities. Take the case of Mlle Fernande Segret. As a result of her dalliance with Landru, she became a celebrity. Bardens recalled that Mlle Segret became considerably more in demand in concert halls and nightclubs than she was before. The sudden celebrity and even notoriety attached to her name made her desirable for public appearances.[98]

Creation of Media Zones

During the time of Henri Landru's crimes, the early 1900s, there were large crowds of reporters and photographers in attendance at every Landru court appearance. During Landru's trial, the press gallery was so packed that the media representatives sat elbow to elbow, and other journalists even packed into the aisles.[99]

There were other Landru-induced media zones, as well. When the news broke, it quickly led to local media zones. Bardens observed that after the Landru story was disseminated around the world, throngs of journalists and photographers descended on previously unknown Gambais and the typical suburb of Vernouillet.[100] Landru maintained small villas in both towns.

CONCLUSION

Landru killed for money. He was willing to end at least eleven lives in order to enrich himself. He was a merciless and insensitive person.

Communication was at the core of the Landru crimes. Mass communication, in the form of his ads, was the manner of obtaining victims. Letters to these victims were the mechanism for beginning to seduce the women and setting up meetings. Other letters were sent to relatives and employers of the victims, and to the police, in an attempt to cover up the murders. Finally, Landru's *carnet* was necessary for record keeping, but it proved to be highly incriminating at his trial.

The Landru crimes were very popular at the time. They elicited substantial public and media interest. This resulted in numerous instances of media conduct resulting in undesirable consequences. These negative effects included the creation of celebrities and media zones.

2

---•◦•---

THE AXEMAN OF NEW ORLEANS

THE AXEMAN OF New Orleans terrorized the residents of New Orleans in the 1910s with one and maybe two sets of axe murders. Most of the victims were Italians, several being grocers and storeowners. The crime scenes were bloody messes.

Considerable controversy exists over whether or not the mysterious Axeman murdered anyone in 1911. Some authorities claim that there were two or three such early murders, while other experts argue that the first real Axeman murder was the 1918 killing of Catherine Maggio and the attempted slaying of her husband Joseph. Throughout the rest of 1918 and 1919, the Axeman terrorized the city of New Orleans, and the media contributed to this state of fear.

The elusive criminal engaged in only two acts of mass communication, but both were important; one was a crime scene outdoor message, and the other was in the mainstream mass media of the day. The crime scene rhetoric was brief, enigmatic, and possibly an attempt to implicate the 1918 axe murderer for similar crimes committed in 1911. The Axeman's other use of mass communication was very interesting. In it he claimed to be an evil spirit from outer space and his mission seemed to be to popularize jazz music, which he professed to liking a great deal. He threatened to kill all New Orleans residents not listening to jazz. Word of this threat was leaked through the media, and it created a sensation, possibly helping to popularize this form of music more than before.

THE CRIMINAL

Joseph Mumfre has been the leading (and only publicly identified) suspect in the Axeman of New Orleans murder case. Circumstantial evidence and an eyewitness identification by one victim's widow led to Mumfre's murder—and the assumption by many that he probably was the Axeman. We will consider opinions that Mumfre was the Axeman, as well as contrary opinions. We will discover why Mumfre was a suspect. Theories about multiple Axemen will be examined, along with the invocation of the supernatural in these crimes.

Mrs. Mike Pepitone gave the name Mrs. Esther Albano when Los Angeles Police Department (LAPD) officers arrested her for shooting Joseph Mumfre on December 2, 1920. A heavily-veiled woman dressed in black shot Mumfre on a sidewalk, then waited for police to arrest her.[1] "He was the Axeman. I saw him running from my husband's room," she reportedly told LAPD.[2] LAPD noted, "There is some evidence he killed Mike Pepitone."[3]

"Was Joseph Mumfre really the Axeman of New Orleans? There is some reason to believe so. A habitual criminal, Mumfre had been in and out of jails for the past ten years, and all the periods he had been at large coincided with the times of the Axeman attacks. . . . the epidemic of New Orleans ax murders came to a halt after his death," Everitt reported.[4] A similar assertion was advanced by Wilson and Wilson. Was Mumfre the Axeman? they asked. He might have been. He was released from prison shortly before the 1911 murders, then was re-incarcerated for the next seven years. He was released again immediately prior to the first of the 1918 murders, and he was back behind bars during the interval between August 1918 and March 1919, when the killings resumed. He left New Orleans immediately after the murder of Mike Pepitone.[5] Respected criminologist and serial murder expert Eric Hickey lists Joseph Mumfre as being responsible for the Axeman of New Orleans murders.[6]

The identification of Mumfre as the Axeman by the last victim's widow was powerful proof for many. She got a good look at the assailant. When she heard the attack on her husband, Mrs. Pepitone hurried to that room, "She rushed in, nearly colliding with a man fleeing the scene."[7] Another source agreed, adding that "when grocer Mike Pepitone was murdered at home, his wife glimpsed the killer."[8] According to Schechter and Everitt, "Although the killer was never identified, some believe he was an ex-con named Joseph Mumfre. . . . Mrs. Pepitone claimed she had seen Mumfre flee the crime scene."[9]

Mrs. Pepitone went on trial for killing Mumfre, who was described as "a hoodlum and thief."[10] She was sentenced to a ten-year prison term.[11] She was released about three years after her incarceration.[12]

One explanation for Mumfre's motives, if he was the Axeman, was suggested by Taylor:

> The police began working to try and untangle the mystery that probably linked Mumfre's murder to the Axeman case. Some curious circumstances were revealed during the investigation. Mumfre had once been the leader of a band of blackmailers in New Orleans who had preyed on Italians. He had also been (for a separate matter) sent to prison just after the first axe murders in 1911. In the summer of 1918, he was paroled—at the same time the Axeman appeared again. Immediately after the Pepitone murder, Mumfre had left New Orleans for the coast and strangely, the Axeman had vanished as well.[13]

Despite the circumstantial evidence implicating Mumfre as the Axeman, not everyone is convinced of his culpability for the crimes. No direct evidence connects him to the crimes, and some doubt that he was involved. In addition, the eyewitness identification may be flawed.

"Does that mean Mumfre was the killer? There are many who think he was not," Lane and Gregg noted.[14] Schechter and Everitt agreed, adding that "whether Mumfre really was the Axeman remains in dispute."[15] There was no direct evidence tying Mumfre to the crimes. According to Everitt, "Unfortunately, beyond this circumstantial evidence, there is nothing to link Mumfre *directly* to all the attacks."[16]

One theory holds that Mumfre was an assassin for organized crime, a hit man for the mob. Newton recalled, "In 1973, author Jay Robert Nash 'solved' the case by calling Mumfre a Mafia hit man, allegedly pursuing a long vendetta against 'members of the Pepitone family.'"[17] According to the Crime Library, "Newton points out that author Jay Robert Nash, in *Bloodletters and Badmen,* fingered Mumfre as a Mafia hit man, but then identifies the flaws in his theory."[18]

Mrs. Pepitone's crime scene identification of Mumfre as the Axeman was probably the most convincing evidence against him. However, she may not have been the most reliable witness. In fact, her initial crime scene statement seems a bit odd.

"Mrs. Pepitone claimed that she had seen two men in her home, not just one, and both had been large. After attacking her husband, both had fled, taking nothing with them. Oddly, there were eight people in the house at the time, yet the attackers had not been intimidated by the possibility of being identified," according to one report.[19]

Was there just one person acting as the Axeman of New Orleans, or was more than one person involved? Many believed the multiple killer theory, while others insisted that there was only one individual behind the crimes.

"Another theory is that there may have been more than one culprit responsible for the Axeman terror, the evidence being that the modus operandi was not exactly the same in all the attacks," Everitt suggested.[20] Lane and Gregg concurred, adding that many people believe that there was more than one Axeman.[21]

The salient, on-point question was articulated by Taylor. He asked, "Was Joseph Mumfre the Axeman? Or were there actually several killers, all working together to terrorize the Italian community?"[22] Some New Orleans law enforcement officials tended toward the conspiracy or multiple killer theory, "Police wondered if this was all the work of a single 'degenerate' or several different people."[23]

The public concern over these serial murders was extreme and very understandable. The police seemed unable to apprehend the culprit. Perhaps that is because they were dealing with a criminal that seemed almost supernatural. As one study reported, "One of the most mysterious and still unsolved frenzies to grip the city of New Orleans came in the early 1900s with the arrival of the enigmatic 'Axeman.' Who was this strange and terrifying creature? Ghost, ghoul or something worse?" This same document offered this speculation:

> The police were once again stumped and rumblings began to suggest that perhaps the Axeman wasn't really a man at all. Some claimed that he might be a woman, or a midget, enabling him to slip through the small space that he cut in the doors. But others maintained he was a creature from the world beyond. How else, they questioned, could all the witnesses describe the killer as being a "large man," when only a small person could have slipped through the chiseled panels of the rear doors? The killer had to come in through supernatural means as each door was still locked when the attacks were discovered.[24]

New Orleans Police Department Detective Joseph Dantonio was assigned to the Axeman case. He remarked, "In fact, there seemed to be something almost supernatural about his ability to get in and out of places, and even to be seen without a single victim recalling any details."[25] Another report recalled that it was not surprising that several New Orleans citizens began to refer to the Axeman as some sort of spirit, a demon in their midst.[26] After the Romano murder, one of the witnesses said the attacker "vanished as if he had wings."[27]

THE CRIMES

The murders of the Axeman of New Orleans were frightening and violent events. Yet there is disagreement over the precise number of Axeman slayings. Some authorities contend that the Joseph Maggio case was the initial slaying.[28] Others believe that there were two Axeman killings prior to the Maggio attack.[29] One authority decided that there were three Axeman cases prior to the Maggio case, while another thought there were either two or three.[30]

The initial consensus attack by the Axeman of New Orleans occurred on May 23, 1918. Joseph Maggio was seriously injured, and his wife Catherine was killed by an axe-bearing intruder.[31] Police discounted robbery as a potential motive, as money and other valuables in plain sight had been left behind by the killer.[32] The murderer did not bring his own axe—he used Joseph's.[33]

The most severe injuries were suffered by Catherine Maggio. Mrs. Maggio's head was almost completely severed from her shoulders.[34] She endured a virtual decapitation.

On June 28, 1918, Louis Besumer and his live-in girlfriend Anna Lowe were the next Axeman victims. Most accounts credit the discovery of the dying Lowe and seriously injured Besumer to a baker, John Zanca, who was making his morning deliveries.[35]

But Lowe did not die immediately after the attack; she lived for seven weeks.[36] Wilson and Wilson described her statement to the police. She said she was attacked by a large white man brandishing a hatchet. She died a short time later, and her lover Besumer was charged with her murder.[37]

Mrs. Ed Schneider was pregnant when attacked by the Axeman on August 5, 1918. Her husband found her nearly dead when he returned from work that afternoon. She survived a savage assault. She was discovered by her husband "with her head savagely battered."[38] Despite her injuries, Mrs. Schneider gave birth a week after the attack.[39]

Taylor explained her injuries, and the attack upon her, "A woman named Mrs. Edward Schneider awakened in the night to see a tall, phantom-like form standing over her bed. She screamed just as the axe fell. A few minutes later, her neighbors found her unconscious with her head gashed and bloody and several of her teeth knocked out."[40]

Mary Cortimiglia was the infant daughter of Rose and Charles Cortimiglia. Mary was killed by a savage axe attack on March 10, 1919. This attack differed from the others in that it took place in Gretna, a suburb of New Orleans. As in the Maggio slaying, the Axeman used the homeowner's own axe in the assault.[41]

Mrs. Cortimiglia awoke to find her husband struggling with a large white man armed with an axe. Taylor recalled, "As her husband fell in a bloody heap to the floor, Mrs. Cortimiglia held her two-year-old in her arms and begged her attacker for mercy, at least for the child. But the axe came down anyway, killing the little girl and fracturing the skull of her mother."[42] Both parents survived. The Cortimiglia crime scene was discovered by a neighbor who lived across the street, named Jordano. He said he was alerted to trouble by the sounds of screaming. He and his son would later stand trial and be convicted of the murder and assaults, based on Mrs. Cortimiglia's testimony.[43] This miscarriage of justice was eventually overturned.

Joseph Romano was killed by the Axeman on August 10, 1919. Romano was discovered by his nieces covered with blood, and his skull was fractured.[44] Pauline and Mary Bruno woke to the sounds of struggle in the adjacent room occupied by their uncle, Joseph Romano. They rushed next door to find him dying of a head wound, but they caught a glimpse of his assailant, described in official reports as "dark, tall, heavy-set, wearing a dark suit and a black slouch hat."[45] According to Taylor, Romano was a grocer.[46] Wilson and Wilson described his occupation as barber.[47] Lane and Gregg agreed with Wilson and Wilson.[48] Romano did not die immediately; he lingered for two days before he died.[49]

Steve Boca became the next Axeman victim on August 10, 1919. Although he was not killed, he was badly hurt when attacked in his home.[50] According to Wilson and Wilson, Boca awoke to see the dark figure of a large man beside his bed wielding an axe, before losing consciousness. When he reawakened, he was bleeding profusely from a skull wound. He staggered to the home of a friend named Frank Genusa. The frantic police showed up—and arrested Genusa—then released him with great embarrassment.[51] Lane and Gregg added that Italian grocery store owner Steve Boca had his head split open by an axe as he slept. Boca survived, but never regained his memory.[52]

Another unsuccessful assault attributed to the Axeman occurred during August or September 1919. According to Lane and Gregg, Sarah Laumann was found in her bed on the evening of September 3, 1919, suffering from severe wounds.[53] Jeffers suggested that Laumann was attacked two weeks after the Boca assault, and that she was struck once by an axe. Her attacker supposedly entered through an open window.[54]

A slightly different version was recalled by Wilson and Wilson. They observed that her neighbors found the nineteen-year-old Laumann unconscious. She had been viciously attacked with an axe and had three teeth knocked out. She had no recollection of the crime events when she regained consciousness.[55]

The final Axeman victim was Mike Pepitone, an Italian grocer, who was brutally murdered in his bed as he slept. His wife and six children were sleeping next door to Pepitone's room, but were left untouched.[56] Another account differed in the details. His wife, who was asleep in a separate room, heard the noises of a fight and entered his room just as a large man disappeared. Her husband was killed by an axe blow so forceful that blood splattered high up the wall.[57]

"In the early hours of the morning of 27 October, Mrs. Pepitone awoke to hear a struggle going on in her husband's room next door," according to Lane and Gregg.[58] This was the last known attack by the unknown killer.[59]

The Motivation

It is difficult to speak with certainty of the motives behind the Axeman of New Orleans murders. Since the killer was never caught, we have no confession or public admission. Speculation is possible, however, and the Mafia was part of the public rumors at the time and subsequently. So was sex.

"What was his motive?" asked criminologists Colin and Damon Wilson. Their answer to their question involved sex: they asserted that the Axeman was probably a sadist who sought women victims, not men. Joe Maggio was left alive, but his wife was killed. Louis Besumer was only knocked unconscious, while his wife died of severe injuries. Most of the later victims were women, and it is probable that he only attacked men while searching for women.[60]

Others saw the Mafia behind the murders. "It wasn't long before people in the Italian community began to talk about a possible connection with the Mafia," the Crime Library recalled.[61] Because several of the Axeman's victims were Italian grocers, a theory developed, wholly without substance, that the Axeman of New Orleans was a Mafia enforcer and "hit man."[62] Another source reported, "Some writers have speculated that the Axeman murders may have been part of a Mafia extortion scheme."[63]

One motivation seldom mentioned is the promotion of jazz music. In the letter to the New Orleans newspaper that was supposed to be from the Axeman, he said he would spare the lives of those listening to jazz. This was a clear attempt to motivate people to listen to jazz, but this fact does not appear prominently in any of the accounts of the case.

Modus Operandi

While the identity of the killer is a mystery, along with his motives, we have a clear picture of the modus operandi (MO) used in the crimes. In most cases, the back door of a home was smashed, resulting in a relatively small hole. One or more residents were then attacked, with an axe and/or a straight razor. Nothing was taken from the crime scene by the killer.

The similarity in crime scene behavior at Axeman sites was noted by Everitt, "All were perpetrated by an unknown, ax-wielding assailant who struck in the middle of the night, gaining entrance to the victim's homes by cutting a panel out of the back door."[64]

Jeffers confirmed Everitt's perceptions about MO similarity. "The common thread in the 1911 and 1919 killings was the Axeman's method of breaking into homes through a door panel and leaving the bloody axe behind."[65] Schechter and Everitt added their expert description of the Axeman methods. His MO varied. Lurking in the darkness, he would select a victim's house, chisel out a back-door panel, enter the home, and make his way to the bedroom. There, he would slink toward his sleeping victims, raise the axe, and strike with superhuman fury.[66]

Public Consequences of the Murders

The most immediate public consequences of the Axeman murders were panic and terror. The crimes were detailed in the media of the day, and people could read about them and discuss them in alarming detail. Residents of New Orleans were aghast at the prospect of having a serial murderer in their midst. As one source realized, New Orleans was in a state of public panic similar to that which had captivated London during the Jack the Ripper crimes. As a result, practically all of New Orleans began to take elaborate emergency precautions to ward off and protect against the Axeman.[67]

"By this time, hysteria was sweeping through the city. Families divided into watches and stood guard over their relatives while they slept. People went about with loaded shotguns and waited for news of the latest 'Axeman sightings,'" Taylor recalled.[68]

It is difficult now to fully appreciate the depth of the emotions felt then by the frightened residents of New Orleans. The Axeman was "The most fear-provoking axe killer in the annals of American crime, however—one who kept a whole city in a state of panic for over two years," according to Schechter and Everitt. Jeffers concluded that "Still unsolved are a group of murders lumped together as the work of the 'Axe-man of New Orleans.' Committed between 1911 and 1919, they created a panic."[69]

THE INVESTIGATION

Since the Axeman was never apprehended and convicted, we might conclude that the investigation was ineffective. In this section, we will analyze claims that the 1918–19 crimes were related to the 1911 New Orleans murders, the investigation into three of the murders, and police conclusions about the Axeman.

There is considerable controversy over whether there were Axeman slayings in 1911. One source noted, "Committed between 1911 and 1919, the first two victims were two Italian grocers and their wives," according to Jeffers.[70] Many authorities claimed that there were three such early axe assaults, not two.

When police looked for similar crimes, "to their surprise they discovered that three murders and a number of attacks against Italian grocers had already taken place in 1911." Lane and Gregg contended that in 1911 an axe-bearing intruder killed three Italian grocers and their wives. They were the Crutis, the Rosettis, and the Schiambras.[71]

Other authorities emphatically deny that there were any such murders in 1911. According to the Crime Library, "In 1911, seven years earlier, there had been either two or three incidents of horrendous axe murders (depending on whose account one reads. Michael Newton claims that there is no record of any of these deaths)."[72]

"Examination of contemporary documents reveals that no such crimes were noted in newspaper obituaries, coroner's records or police reports for the year 1911," Newton claimed. He tallied sixteen axe murders committed in Louisiana that year, but all of the victims were black and none lived in New Orleans. No one named Crutis or Schiambra died in New Orleans in 1911.[73]

Joseph Maggio's brothers were initially suspected in his murder. Jake and Andrew Maggio were jailed after the discovery of the crime, but Jake was released the next morning. Police believed that a razor used in the assault belonged to Andrew, but he was released a few days later. The police concluded that an axe had been used to chisel out a panel of the back door to gain entry. The murder weapon was an axe that had been left in Maggio's home and was covered with blood and body fragments. Robbery was ruled out as a motive, as plenty of valuables had been left in plain sight, but were not taken.[74]

Anna Lowe, Louis Besumer's live-in lover, was fatally injured by the Axeman. Before dying, she told police that Besumer was a Nazi spy, and her attacker. A jury deliberated for approximately ten minutes on May 1, 1919, before acquitting Besumer. In her first story, she claimed to have been assaulted by "a mulatto." (An account of the crime by Lane and Gregg differs slightly; they indicate that Lowe's first name was Harriett, and Besumer was acquitted in April 1919.) Suspicion then fell on a recently-hired black employee of Besumer's, who told conflicting stories to the police, but was nevertheless released.[75]

Rose Cortimiglia, who lost her infant daughter in an attack, accused Iorlando and Frank Jordano of the attack. However, her husband Charles said the Jordanos were not involved in any way. The Jordano's trial started on May 21, 1919. Both were convicted, with Frank sentenced to death and Iorlando receiving a life sentence. On December 7, 1920, Rose admitted that she had committed perjury and recanted her testimony. Both Jordanos were then released.[76]

Law enforcement officers arrived at some conclusions about the Axeman of New Orleans. For instance, the crimes were the act of one individual, acting alone. "The police stated that they believed all of the crimes to have been committed by the same man."[77]

Other generalizations were agreed upon. "From what they could determine, this intruder left no fingerprints (it is not clear from accounts whether they actually used a forensic method or looked for prints with the naked eye) and there was no clear pattern to the crimes," the Crime Library suggested. The authors concluded they "seemed to have been picked at random."[78]

MEDIA INTEREST

There was substantial media interest in this case. In the absence of known facts, the media conjectured and reported whatever it could. For instance, "A newspaper, The States, offered speculation about the killer, wondering whether he was a fiend, a madman, a sadist, or some supernatural entity."[79]

This media interest translated into frightening stories. The Crime Library concluded, "When the newspapers ran the story, they spread fear in the populace by asking in bold headlines, IS AN AXEMAN AT LARGE IN NEW ORLEANS?"[80] After the Maggio murder, "The Times-Picayune newspaper ran the story on its front page that morning, including a photograph of the death chamber."[81] Another newspaper reported, "At least four persons saw the Axeman this morning in the neighborhood of Iberville and Rendon. He was first seen in front of an Italian grocery. Twice he fled when citizens armed themselves and gave chase."[82] The contemporary newspaper reports linked the 1918–19 murders to the 1911 crimes: "The local press revealed that New Orleans had been rocked by an epidemic of unsolved ax murders of Italian grocers in 1911."[83]

CRIME SCENE MASS COMMUNICATION

There were two significant mass communication acts in this case. Both were by the killer, purposive elements of the serial murder act. The Axeman had something to say, and he said it in public using mass media on two occasions, once at a crime scene and the other time on the front page of the New Orleans Times-Picayune.

The initial incident involved a message written in chalk near a crime scene. Soon after the attack on Joseph Maggio and his wife, a strange message was noticed one or two blocks from the Maggio crime scene, discovered by the

New Orleans police. Written in chalk on the sidewalk, it read, "Mrs. Maggio is going to sit up tonight just like Mrs. Toney."[84]

An Internet Axeman site, "Dead Men Do Tell Tales," had the wording of the message different. It reported that the single and solitary clue that police found was a mysterious message that had been written in chalk close to the Maggio home. It read, "Mrs. Joseph Maggio will sit up tonight. Just write Mrs. Toney."[85] Court TV's Crime Library noted the verbal variation, "different sources report the wording differently."[86]

The Crime Library offered this informed perspective on this rhetorical incident:

> About a block away from the small grocery store where the Maggios were mur-
> dered, two detectives came across a strange message, written on the sidewalk in
> chalk: "Mrs. Maggio will sit up tonight just like Mrs. Toney." They carefully
> copied it (although different sources report the wording differently. One says,
> "Just write Mrs. Toney," but the newspapers report it as the former statement).
> The writing resembled that of a schoolboy and it seemed an important clue, but
> at the moment, no one was sure what to make of it. Some said that it had been
> written by an accomplice to warn the killers that Mrs. Maggio was on guard. After
> some digging, they eventually spotted a possible connection to earlier crimes in
> the area.[87]

Wilson and Wilson noted the possible significance of the message, "On the pavement two streets away someone had chalked on the pavement: 'Mrs. Maggio is going to sit up tonight, just like Mrs. Toney.' It reminded the police that seven years earlier there had been four axe-murders of Italian grocers including a Mrs. Tony Schiambra."[88]

What are we to make of this terse, laconic, and enigmatic crime scene message? It most likely referred to the Axeman murders. It seemed to be an explicit attempt to tie the 1918 murders to those committed in 1911. It is not uncommon for serial murderers to take credit publicly for their crimes, so it is very possible that the chalk message was actually from the Axeman of New Orleans, in an informal use of outdoor communication.

It is believed that the Axeman of New Orleans, whoever he was, wrote to a local newspaper during the serial murder campaign. The letter was both shocking and amazing.

The *Times-Picayune* printed the letter on March 14, 1919, four days after an Italian grocer's infant daughter was killed, and two others hurt, in an attack. The letter, whose author was self-described as being "A fell demon from the hottest Hell," declared that he would tour New Orleans on March 19 (St. Joseph's night) and leave untouched any home where jazz could be heard.[89]

"One thing is certain, and that is that some of these people who do not jazz it (if there be any) will get the axe," the letter threatened.[90] Obviously the city's musical medley met the Axeman's expectations, "On the appointed night, already known for raucous celebration, New Orleans was even noisier than usual. The din included numerous performances of 'The Mysterious Axeman's Jazz,' a song composed for the occasion, and the evening passed without a new attack."[91]

Wilson and Wilson recalled a similar situation. Soon after one attack, the city newspaper received a letter from "The Axeman," datelined "From hell." In it he declared that he would come to New Orleans on a specified Tuesday at 12:15, but would spare the people in any house playing jazz music.[92] German researchers have arrived at identical conclusions: "Meanwhile, on March 14, the Times-Picayune published a letter signed by 'the Axman' [sic]. Describing himself as a 'fell demon from the hottest hell,' the author announced his intention of touring New Orleans on March 19—St. Joseph's night—and vowed to bypass any home where jazz was playing at the time."[93]

Here is the full text of the letter, which was dated "Hell, March 13, 1919" at the top of the first page:

Esteemed Mortal:
They have never caught me and they never will. They have never seen me, for I am invisible, even as the ether that surrounds your earth. I am not a human being, but a spirit and a fell demon from the hottest hell. I am what you Orleanians and your foolish police call the Axeman.

When I see fit, I shall come again and claim other victims. I alone know who they shall be. I shall leave no clue except my bloody axe, besmirched with the blood and brains of him whom I have sent below to keep me company.

If you wish you may tell the police not to rile me. Of course I am a reasonable spirit. I take no offense at the way they have conducted their investigation in the past. In fact, they have been so utterly stupid as to amuse not only me but His Satanic Majesty, Frances Joseph, etc. But tell them to beware. Let them not try to discover what I am, for it were better that they were never born than to incur the wrath of the Axeman. I don't think there is any need for such a warning, for I feel sure the police will always dodge me, as they have in the past. They are wise and know how to keep away from all harm.

Undoubtedly, you Orleanians think of me as a most horrible murderer, which I am, but I could be much worse if I wanted to. If I wished, I could pay a visit to your city every night. At will I could slay thousands of your best citizens, for I am in close relationship to the Angel of Death.

Now, to be exact, at 12:15 (earthly time) on next Tuesday night, I am going to visit New Orleans again. In my infinite mercy, I am going to make a proposition to you people. Here it is:

I am very fond of jazz music, and I swear by all the devils in the nether regions that every person shall be spared in whose home a jazz band is in full swing at the time I have mentioned. If everyone has a jazz band going, well, then, so much the better for you people. One thing is certain and that is that some of those people who do not jazz it on Tuesday night (if there be any) will get the axe.

Well, as I am cold and crave the warmth of my native Tartarus, and as it is about time that I leave your earthly home, I will cease my discourse. Hoping that thou wilt publish this, and that it may go well with thee, I have been, am and will be the worst spirit that ever existed either in fact or realm of fantasy.

The Axeman.[94]

The newspaper publicity accomplished quite effectively the promotional and behavioral goals of the Axeman. According to the Crime Library, "Whether a prank or the real thing, people took the letter seriously. It's been said that, while the residents of the 'Big Easy' will use any excuse for a party, there has never been a louder, more raucous evening than that St. Joseph's Night on March 19. One host issued the Axeman an invitation, promising him 'four scalps,' but insisting he abide by protocol."[95]

A similar public response was described by another source, "The people of New Orleans did their best to follow the Axeman's instructions to the letter. Restaurants and clubs all over town were jammed with revelers. Friends and neighbors gathered in their homes to 'jazz it up,' and midnight found the city alive with activity."[96] The theme song for the evening, "The Mysterious Axeman's Jazz," was written by Joseph Davilla.[97]

What did the letter mean? We can disregard the writer's claim to have originated on the planet Tartarus and to have supernatural powers. Two content themes dominated this letter; it attempts to frighten readers, and promote jazz music. The rhetorical style of the letter could best be characterized as eerie.

CONCLUSION

The Axeman of New Orleans was never officially caught. And it is possible that Mrs. Pepitone incorrectly identified her husband's killer. That is why the Axeman case is officially called unsolved. "The killer was never identified," recalled Schechter and Everitt.[98]

What can we say with certainty about the Axeman of New Orleans? Is there anything we can assert with confidence about the crimes, his communication motivation, and the criminal? Despite the uncertainty surrounding an unsolved case, we can draw some conclusions. One is the importance of mass communication to the Axeman.

The murderer must have been very intelligent, to murder repeatedly and escape apprehension. He was also highly motivated, as he killed on at least seven occasions and attempted numerous other murders. We just do not know what those motives were. But they involved mass communication, that much is clear.

The Axeman's communication was enigmatic and playful at times, then threatening at others. His crime scene message about Mrs. Maggio was possibly vague and apparently meaningless, on the literal level. Or was it a statement by or to the killer linking the 1918–19 axe murders to those of 1911? It is also possible, but far less likely, that the killer was communicating a general message of defiance and disrespect for law enforcement and society.

The crimes and communication caused public panic and terror, which was most likely the rhetorical purpose or motive behind both sets of acts. The killer used the mass media of the day, a newspaper, to publicize a bizarre message about his ability to return to New Orleans and kill everyone, and the necessity of listening to jazz music to avert such a grim fate.

The letter was multidimensional. The author's claim to be a spirit from outer space was probably a joke, and meant to confuse and frighten New Orleans residents. The overall content of the letter was typified by outlandish threats and exaggerated, hyperbolic expressions of the dangerousness and violent potential of the Axeman. He bragged about his criminal and homicidal prowess, while taunting the police for their inability to apprehend him. And he threatened death to those who did not listen to jazz.

Much like the Zodiac, the Son of Sam, and Ted Kaczynski Jr. (the Unabomber) in later years, it is safe to say that the killings were the platform used by the Axeman to wage his communication campaign. The murders forced the *Times-Picayune* to print the killer's letter, and the murders also cast a sinister context and meaning on the crime scene chalk message. The Axeman of New Orleans deliberately and purposefully manipulated the media of New Orleans into publishing his letter from outer space. Only one thing is certain in this puzzling serial murder case: the murderer intentionally promoted jazz.

3

EARLE NELSON

EARLE NELSON WAS a man with many nicknames. At various times, he was called "The Dark Strangler," "The Phantom Killer," "The Beast Man," "Jack the Strangler," and most often "The Gorilla Killer." As a youth, his Uncle Willis referred to him as "The Wild Man of Borneo," in critical reaction to his eating habits.

He had a difficult life. His mother died of syphilis before he was one, and his father succumbed to the same disease about six months later. He was expelled from Agassiz primary school in San Francisco before the age of seven because he could not control his behavior.

Clara Newman was his first known murder victim, on February 20, 1926, in San Francisco. Emily Patterson of Winnipeg, Manitoba, Canada, was his last official victim, on June 10, 1927. However, in addition to the twenty-two confirmed Nelson victims, there are probably that many unsolved cases that bore his murderous modus operandi (MO) and for which he was the sole suspect.

A more apt nickname for Nelson would have been "The Landlady Killer," because that is what he was. The majority of his victims were elderly landladies. He killed them while posing as a Bible-toting prospective tenant.

He began his serial murders in California, moved north to Portland and Seattle, then headed east. He killed in Missouri and Iowa en route to the East Coast, where he visited and killed in Philadelphia and Buffalo before returning north. His victims in Detroit and Chicago made it easy to trace his path to Canada, where he was eventually apprehended.

Nelson was the celebrity killer of his day, a phenomenon not unknown to us in contemporary America. He created a media frenzy with each new crime. His trial was a media windfall. It is difficult to overstate the role of the media in this case. Nelson was caught because of the media; on the other hand, he might have been caught sooner had it not been for the media.

We will consider nine main topics in this chapter to assist in understanding Nelson, his crimes, and the mass communication milieu within which he killed and by which he was apprehended. They include the criminal, the crimes, and the investigation, apprehension, and trial. Public interest in the case will be documented, and we will consider both positive and negative effects of the media, along with public relations tactics used in the investigation.

THE CRIMINAL

He was born as Earle Leonard Nelson on May 12, 1897. His birth name was actually Earle L. Ferral.[1] He was married twice—more about his wives later.

Nelson was a very different sort of person. To better comprehend him, we might examine six topics, including his difficult childhood, his bad and strange behavior. His intellect, his use of the Bible, and his alcoholism will also be covered.

Nelson had an unusually bad childhood. This may not explain his subsequent behavior, but his life began quite poorly. Three different aspects of his youth deserve mention. He was orphaned, suffered a serious accident, and had a stern upbringing.

"Earle Nelson never had a chance to know his mother or father. He was just a little over nine months old in 1898 when his mother died because of a syphilis infection," Gribben contended. Others offered similar recollections. By all accounts, Earle Leonard Nelson was orphaned as a youth when both of his parents died of syphilis, Scott suggested. Schechter and Everitt noted that because he was orphaned as a baby when his parents both died of syphilis, Nelson was taken in and he grew up with his maternal family.[2]

A serious accident seemed to affect him. One study observed that as a result of a severe head injury that occurred when his bicycle ran into a cable car, his behavior worsened. Scott added that this occurred when he was ten years old,. Afterward his mood swings increased, and he experienced intense pain.[3]

Nelson's injuries were severe. Burchill asserted that "at the age of ten, while riding his bicycle, he ran into a streetcar and was carried home unconscious with a hole in his temple. He remained unconscious for six days and while he seemed to return to normal he suffered frequently from headaches and would complain of lapses in memory." Everitt agreed, calling Nelson's injuries "a life-threatening head injury."[4]

Another source arrived at similar conclusions. According to Wilson and Wilson, he was unconscious for six days, due to a slight concussion.[5]

There was a final challenging dimension of his childhood—the stern upbringing he received. Scott put it bluntly. He was reared by a Philadelphia aunt who was obsessed with religious zeal and fanaticism. Burchill claims that Nelson lived with Lars and Jennie Nelson, his maternal grandparents. According to Burchill, "Earl's [sic] grandparents had very puritan views and brought Earl up in an atmosphere which regarded sex as dirty."[6]

A slightly different version of Nelson's childhood was suggested by Gribben. "Nelson was raised in San Francisco by his grandmother, a widow, who had two pre-teen children of her own. She was a devout Pentecostal." When Earle's grandmother died, he went to live with an aunt and her husband.[7]

Nelson was exceptionally delinquent. In this section, three aspects of his bad behavior will be described and documented, including sexual misbehavior, criminal behavior, and necrophilia. Nelson engaged in criminal and immoral sex on numerous occasions. As a youth, he engaged in voyeurism behavior directed at his cousin Rachel. He began frequenting the prostitutes near Fisherman's Wharf at the age of fifteen. Everitt provided an apt analysis of Nelson's sexuality. He had achieved a lengthy history of sexual violence by the time he was twenty. His animal-like appearance truly reflected the primitive, savage impulses that lay within him.[8]

Nelson ran afoul of the law on numerous occasions. He got in trouble for burglary, sex crimes, and shoplifting. Was there a natural progression to murder? In 1915, before his eighteenth birthday, Nelson was arrested for burglary and received a sentence of two years in San Quentin.[9]

As a youth he was increasingly rough and violent with girls, and this violent sexual misconduct toward women would increase later in his life. He began to engage in criminal behavior at the age of twenty-one. In May 1918, Nelson attempted to sexually molest a twelve-year-old girl, "but her screams brought her brother to her aid and Earl [sic] fled the house after a short struggle."[10]

This diverse criminal even resorted to shoplifting as a youth. Gribben claimed that "More than once, an irate shopkeeper who had caught Earle stealing trivial items from the store summoned his grandmother."[11]

We might consider a third element of Nelson's bad behavior. It is perhaps the worst. Nelson engaged in necrophilia with several of his victims. "The killer necrophiliac" is what one source called Nelson.[12] He had initiated a way of life that was devoted to only two things, murder and necrophilia, Everitt claimed. Nelson had a bad habit of "killing landladies, sometimes violating their bodies after death." Another source recalled that, after lulling landladies into a false sense of security with his Bible and gentle demeanor, "He would then strangle them and rape their corpses at the first opportunity."[13]

Nelson murdered Mrs. Olla McCoy on October 18, 1925, in Philadelphia. On November 6, he killed Mrs. Mae Murray, and three days later he murdered Lillian Weiner. All three women had been sexually violated after death. Similarly, "Clara Newman had been sexually assaulted, but not until after she was dead." In another case, "It soon became common knowledge that Ollie Russell had been sexually violated after she was dead." In March 1928, Nelson killed Mrs. Lillian St. Mary. "After she was dead, her assailant raped her," Gribben concluded.[14]

In addition to criminal behavior, Nelson sometimes acted strangely. This was noted in his childhood, and again in his later years. This behavior was interesting. Nelson would frequently lock himself in his room and quietly mutter to himself, without stopping for lengthy periods, as if intoning some sort of magical chant. Bible passages were included in this litany. So were unusually vulgar, foul-mouthed obscenities, according to Everitt. There might have been some kind of behavioral problems. Gribben noted, "He was at times hyperactive, at other times, profoundly depressed. Growing up he had little regard for hygiene or manners." He was repeatedly but unsuccessfully criticized for his table manners.[15]

Maybe the strangest aspect of Nelson was his clandestine clothes changing. According to Gribben, "Besides his strange eating habits and bipolar personality, Earle demonstrated a number of other peculiar behaviors. He would often leave for school in one set of clean clothes and return home wearing a completely different outfit, most of them much more shopworn and filthy than those he set out wearing." Schechter and Everitt corroborated Gribben's strange tale, "Among his other peculiarities, he would regularly set off for school in neat, freshly-laundered garments and return in foul rags, as though he'd swapped clothes with a derelict."[16] Nelson's clothes swapping continued in his later years. "Just as he had as a young boy, Earle would often leave home in work togs only to return later in a completely different set of clothes."[17] This was very odd behavior.

Nelson was intelligent. He was described as having, "cunning, intelligence and an abnormal sangfroid." In Winnipeg, Canada, Chief of Detectives George Smith told a news conference that the "Gorilla Killer" was "a clever man. He is different than any criminal with whom we have ever been called on to deal."[18]

"He often studied his worn Bible, using it to disarm his victims, who felt no danger from a man who carried a copy of the good book wherever he went," declared one recent analysis. Others believe that Nelson's faith was sincere. "He was obsessed with the Bible," Gribben suggested. According to another study, Nelson both read the Bible and used it to disarm unsuspecting potential victims.[19]

In one city, posing as Roger Wilson, Nelson made a good impression on a lucky landlady—lucky because she lived to tell her tale. She told the Winnipeg police that "her last lodger had been Roger Wilson, who had been carrying a Bible and was highly religious." Nelson tended to give unsolicited Bible lectures to others.[20]

Nelson had a drinking problem. He was most likely an alcoholic. At about the age of fifteen, "Earle Nelson began drinking heavily, often disappearing for days at a time on alcoholic binges," recalled Gribben.[21]

THE CRIMES

No one knows for sure precisely how many lives were taken by Earle Nelson. The estimates range between twenty-one and twenty-six. In this section, to familiarize ourselves with these crimes, we will examine six topics, including the number of murders, the modus operandi (MO), and murder locales. Mutilation, the frequency of murders, and public fear caused by the murders will also be discussed.

The Number of Murders

There is no consensus or agreement over the number of murders committed by Nelson. He killed at least twenty women, and an eight-month-old infant, according to one estimate.[22] That estimate is a bit below the norm.

Most authorities believe that Nelson claimed twenty-two lives. Schechter listed his twenty-two Nelson victims: Clara Newman, San Francisco, February 20, 1926; Lillian Beal, San Jose, March 2, 1926; Lillian St. Mary, San Francisco, June 10, 1926; Ollie Russell, Santa Barbara, June 24, 1926; Mary Nisbet, Oakland, August 16, 1926; Beata Withers, Portland, October 19, 1926; Virginia Grant, Portland, October 20, 1926; Mabel Fluke, Portland, October 21, 1926; Anna (William) Edmonds, San Francisco, November 18, 1926; Florence Monks, Seattle, November 23, 1926; Blanche Myers, Portland, November 29, 1926; Mrs. John Brerard, Council Bluffs, Iowa, December 2, 1926; Bonnie Pace, Kansas City, December 27, 1926; Germania Harpin, Kansas City, December 28, 1926; Robert Harpin, Kansas City, December 28, 1926; Mary McConnell, Philadelphia, April 27, 1927; Jennie Randolph, Buffalo, May 30, 1927; Fannie May, Detroit, June 1, 1927; Maureen Oswald Atorthy, Detroit, June 1, 1927; Mary Sietsma, Chicago, June 4, 1927; Lola Cowan, Winnipeg, June 9, 1927; and Emily Patterson, Winnipeg, June 10, 1927.[23]

Nelson killed twenty-two people in sixteen months, Everitt claimed. He murdered at least twenty-two women, according to Schechter and Everitt. According to one analysis, "Over a period of less than two years the bible-loving killer raped and strangled twenty-two landladies in the USA and Canada." Wilson and Seaman noted that Earle Nelson, also known as "The Gorilla Killer," slayed twenty-two people. Most of the victims were landladies.[24]

There is one more estimate to consider. Nelson was suspected in the murder of twenty-six women in approximately twenty months. However, the total could be higher, Burchill suggested.[25]

Modus Operandi

Most criminals have a certain way of doing things, called a modus operandi (MO). In the Nelson case, the killer's MO was obvious. The Winnipeg Police Department instantly recognized the MO of the Gorilla Murderer, one source noted. Scott explained the basics of Nelson's method: he would find a room that was for rent, and make inquiries. Once inside, he would attack the landlady at the first opportunity.[26]

"Nelson's victims were mostly landladies whom he would approach on the premise of renting a room and would quickly attack them, often leaving their corpses under the nearest bed. By using false names and moving on quickly after his kills Nelson easily avoided detection during his year-and-a-half long murder spree," according to one recent report.

Schechter and Everitt explained Nelson's MO in detail. Nelson could be charming when he felt the need. He would arrive at a home with rooms to rent and ask to see a room. Once he was alone with his victim, he would seemingly become a different person. He would usually strangle the woman to death, commit necrophilia with the corpse, and then hide the body in some secret hiding place. One victim was crammed into an attic trunk. Some others were secreted behind basement furnaces or other large objects. Burchill noted that "Nelson's MO led him to be labeled the 'Gorilla Strangler.'"[27]

Murder Locales

Nelson struck in many different places during his 1926–27 murder spree. Reading these murder locales allows one to appreciate the wide geographic area of Nelson's crimes. For instance, Wilson and Wilson referred to murders in San Francisco, San Jose, Portland, Oregon, Council Bluffs, Iowa, Philadelphia, Buffalo, Detroit, and Chicago.[28]

Scott referred to Nelson's crimes in Buffalo, New York, Detroit, Michigan, Council Bluffs, Iowa, and Kansas City, Missouri. Wilson and Seaman's description gives the reader a sense of the chase. Nelson was constantly moving, from northern California up to Oregon, then cross country to Iowa. He headed east to New York state, then doubled back and went to Illinois, and then north into Canada. "Nelson claimed victims in several West Coast cities, throughout the upper Midwest, and finally in Canada," according to one report. Murder locales included San Francisco and San Jose, California, Portland, Oregon, Council Bluffs, Iowa, Kansas City, Philadelphia, Buffalo, Detroit, Chicago, and Winnipeg, Manitoba, Canada, according to Everitt. A Canadian study noted that "His trail of dead bodies led from Philadelphia to Chicago, San Francisco, Baltimore, Oakland, Buffalo and ended in Winnipeg."[29]

Mutilation

There was at least one instance of mutilation in the Nelson murders. Wilson and Wilson observed that Nelson slept with the body of Lola Cowen under his bed for three nights. Lola Cowen's body was under Nelson's bed, mutilated in a manner reminiscent of Jack the Ripper, they added.[30]

Murder Frequency

It might be apparent already that if Nelson killed about twenty-two people in a year-and-a-half, the interval between murders must have been brief on many occasions. In fact, the relative frequency of the Nelson murders was quite rapid, at times.

"From San Francisco to Philadelphia he raped and strangled twenty women—at the peak of his activity, murdering once every three weeks," one recent study concluded. When Nelson killed Emily Patterson on June 9, 1927, "Patterson had been Nelson's fifth victim in just ten days."[31]

Public Fear

Considerable public fear was caused by Nelson's murders. The public reaction to one of Nelson's later depredations duplicated closely the reaction to the Beal murder a scant three weeks earlier. There was mass hysteria.[32]

The magnitude of the public fear can be determined, in part, by the ferocity of the police response to the danger. There were squads of uniformed and plainclothes officers, heavily armed with revolvers and sawed-off shotguns, patrolling the city and the suburbs. Other officers were mounted on motorcycles or packed into cars, racing through the streets in pursuit of the hundreds of leads that were pouring into the police stationhouse switchboards. In the rural districts, Canadian provincial police searched the countryside, using bloodhounds to track the elusive "Gorilla."[33]

THE INVESTIGATION

The investigation of Nelson's crimes was exceptionally difficult. He killed at a time when serial murder was relatively unknown as a type of crime. In addition, he literally killed coast-to-coast in the United States, and then ventured into Canada. An additional complication was the arrest of numerous innocent suspects, which repeatedly delayed the pursuit of the real culprit.

After the murder of Laura Beal in San Jose, California, on March 2, 1926, local police consulted with a mental health professional to better understand the criminal they sought. Dr. L. E. Stocking, administrator of a local mental hospital, offered an informal profile of the murderer. "A maniac possessing extreme criminal cunning," was Stocking's assessment.[34]

Police were inundated with false leads and misleading information. Schechter noted that "Most of the ostensible 'leads' that flooded police headquarters in the days following Laura Beal's murder were utterly useless, either facts that had no bearing on the case or sheer, overwrought fantasy."[35]

Then began a series of erroneous arrests. Four days after the Beal murder, police arrested Joe Kesesek, an Austrian national who was arrested for "acting suspiciously" on Market Street. He was dressed in clothes similar to those worn by the killer. It was quickly determined that Kesesek had been nowhere near San Jose on the day of the Beal murder.[36]

Mary Nisbet was another Nelson victim. The investigation into her murder led to the arrest of her husband, Stephen. Despite the complete lack of any evidence against him, he was arrested and held in jail for two days.[37] After releasing Nisbet, Oakland police "launched a massive search" aimed primarily at landlords and others who ran boardinghouses, to see if any had additional information.[38]

Isabel Gallegos was Nelson's next victim, on August 19, 1926. Two days later, a Russian émigré named John Slivkoff was arrested by John Greenhall, a Sacramento police detective. Mrs. Mary Kent of Sacramento and Mrs. H. Wallis of San Francisco identified Slivkoff as someone who asked to rent a room and acted suspiciously. When witnesses who had seen Nelson viewed Slivkoff in a line-up, none identified him.[39]

At this point in time, August 1926, the investigation was going nowhere. "Investigators were no closer to a solution than they had been in February," Schechter remarked. On August 28, Oakland police admitted to being "stumped," and "up a tree" in their efforts to apprehend the serial killer.[40]

J. E. Ross was the next suspect. He had talked his way into the residence of Mrs. DiFiori at 181 Fruitvale Avenue in San Jose, and raped her at gunpoint. This time the police were sure they had their man. The headlines in the *San Francisco Chronicle* declared that the suspect was positively identified by eye-witnesses as the strangler.[41]

The investigation continued after Nelson was in custody. His fingerprints and photograph were disseminated to police agencies throughout the United States. As a result, Nelson was positively identified by several witnesses. Margaret Currie, Rose Egler, and Sarah Butler had been neighbors of Nelson victim Mary McConnell in Philadelphia, and each identified Nelson as the killer. So did Fred Merritt, a boarder of Jennie Randolph, who was murdered by Nelson in Buffalo, New York.[42]

San Francisco police discovered Nelson's real name. They also located his police, military, and medical/psychiatric records.[43]

THE ARREST

Nelson was arrested twice, on consecutive days, in Wakopa, Manitoba, Canada. He was initially arrested by Constable Wilton Gray, and was incarcerated in the local jail on June 15, 1927, a little after 7:25 p.m. He gave his name as Virgil Wilson. He picked two locks and escaped that evening.[44]

Nelson was rearrested the next morning, a little after 8:00 by Constable W. A. Renton of the nearby Crystal City Police Department. Winnipeg Police Commissioner H. J. Martin personally handcuffed Nelson, and Nelson needed less than thirty seconds to slip out of them, remarking "These aren't much good." He was then manacled. He said he was Virgil Wilson, of Vancouver, before admitting his identity.[45]

THE TRIAL

Nelson's trial date was set for June 27, 1927, less than a month after his arrest. James H. Stitt and Chester Young were his court-appointed attorneys. Their first task was to request a postponement of the trial, to give them extra time to prepare. Mr. Justice McDonald consented, resetting the trial for early November.[46]

Nelson was also wanted for trial in the United States. As of June 1927, he had been indicted for murder in Buffalo, Detroit, Philadelphia, Portland, and San Francisco. Other indictments would follow.[47]

The trial began on November 1, 1927. It was conducted in Courtroom Number One of the Manitoba Law Courts Building, on Kennedy Street. The jury was comprised of seven farmers, a machinist, a warehouse superintendent, a chauffeur, a fireman, and a steel worker.[48]

Prosecutor R. B. Graham presented a low-key, persuasive case against Nelson. The defense strategy tried to poke holes in the prosecution's case, and portray Nelson as mentally ill and therefore not responsible for his crimes. The defense tactic failed; Stitt, with no evidence to present on behalf of his client, was clearly grasping at straws. The state's case fared much better. By Thursday afternoon, the prosecution rested what seemed to be an impregnable case.[49]

The insanity defense was not persuasive. Nelson's wife testified that he was out of his mind. Under cross-examination, prosecutor Graham suggested that Nelson was merely "eccentric." Mrs. Nelson disagreed vehemently, claiming, "He was absolutely insane." However, the prosecution countered with the testimony of Dr. Alvin T. Mathers, chief of the psychiatric ward at Winnipeg General Hospital. Mathers examined Nelson five times between July 27 and October 24, and testified that "I did not find any evidence that to me would constitute insanity."[50]

The trial concluded on November 5, 1927. The jury entered the deliberation room at 11:14 a.m., and reached a verdict within forty minutes. Jury Foreman William Weidman read the jury's guilty verdict, "Guilty, my lord." Nelson was hanged at 7:30 a.m. on January 13, 1928.[51]

PUBLIC INTEREST

There seems to be a life cycle of public reaction to serial murder. It may take a while for public interest to grow, but then it peaks and subsides. In this section, we will consider three facets of public interest in the Nelson crimes. There was great initial interest, but distractions and the passage of time led to waning interest.

When the courtroom used in Earle Nelson's trial opened on November 1, 1927, at 1:30 p.m., a loud spontaneous shout was heard, and the eagerly waiting crowd surged forward like a huge wave. It was like trying to stop the tide, and the policemen posted at the door had to use all their might to control the crowd and prevent injury to members of the mob. Within a few minutes, the courtroom was filled beyond capacity, noted a reporter from the *Winnipeg Tribune*. By noon, a crowd of two thousand was waiting in line, for seats in a facility designed for less than two hundred.[52]

Additional evidence of public interest in the case was suggested by Nelson himself. He bragged to a reporter that more than fifty thousand extra copies of the *Free Press* were sold on the day of his capture.[53]

Another factor to consider—the public can be easily distracted. For instance, Earle Nelson's murderous exploits were repeatedly driven off the front pages by other news. In the United States, the story of Nelson victim Newman's death made headlines like "Fiend Murder of Spinster" in the *San Francisco Chronicle*. It was a front-page story. But this was a time when virtually every day produced frightful news of yet another stabbing, shooting, bombing, poisoning, or other means of murder. The Nelson murders quickly faded from the papers.[54]

Earle benefited from competing news in Canada, as well. Schechter noted that reporting on the Nelson case faded away. The Canadian public, having been consumed with the story for weeks, turned its collective attention to other matters. For instance, there was an election campaign in Manitoba, a promising new gold strike in the far northeast corner of the Manitoba, up near Hudson Bay, and a visit from His Royal Majesty the Prince of Wales.[55]

Earle Nelson, who terrorized the western parts of both the United States and Canada, elicited substantial media coverage part of the time. However, by Thursday, June 17, 1926, the Nelson murders story vanished from the front pages. The only Nelson article to appear in the *Chronicle* that day was a brief, pessimistic article that reported that the police investigation had hit "a blank wall."[56]

POSITIVE MEDIA EFFECTS

Earle Nelson's serial murders elicited a series of official warnings throughout the United States and Western Canada. In their efforts to catch the killer, the police used the media. Two positive effects were realized. The media helped apprehend the suspect, and it helped disseminate public safety information.

A telegram was sent to all cities along the West Coast, warning local police to be on the watch for a person like the description provided of Nelson. The next morning, a similar report was run on the front page of the *Santa Barbara Daily News*.[57] In San Francisco, Detective Lieutenant Charles Dullea emphasized that "I personally advise elderly women who have furnished rooms to rent to take every precaution in admitting strangers to their homes and to telephone the police whenever they have something to be suspicious of."[58]

In Portland, Oregon, Chief of Detectives John T. Moore declared to all Portland landladies, "Do not show your houses or rooms for rent while alone. If necessary, call a policeman to accompany you. Crimes such as these should be prevented and could have been prevented if women would be more careful. I do not wish to unduly alarm the people of Portland. But there is no denying that the situation is grave."[59]

When Nelson hit Council Bluffs, Iowa, the local police chief, Sheriff P. A. Lainson, used extensive newspaper publicity in an attempt to promote public safety:

> Prominently featured on page one was a black-bordered box headlined WARNING! The text read as follows: "Saying it was possible that Mrs. John Brerard was killed by a 'strangler;' such as has killed women in California, Oregon and Washington during the last few months, Sheriff P. A. Lainson this afternoon asked *The Nonpareil* to warn housewives of this city against admitting to their homes a man of the description of the 'Mr. Williams' known to have called at the Brerard home shortly before Mrs. Brerard was found dead. The description is: *Height*—Five feet,

eight inches. *Weight*—180 pounds. *Complexion*—Dark. *Eyes*—Dark, piercing. *Clothing*—Pearl-colored hat, mouse-colored overcoat, over-shoes.[60]

NEGATIVE MEDIA EFFECTS

In light of the great public interest in the Nelson case, it should be no surprise that there was extensive media coverage. Unfortunately, there were negative consequences of this media involvement. In this section, we will examine four different types of media-caused problems. The media motivated Nelson. Media zones were created, and the media influenced trial outcome. There were numerous instances of media misbehavior.

Media Motivated Nelson

Earle Nelson was very interested in his press. According to Schechter, Nelson remained alone in his room, venturing outside only at night. Then he would briefly leave his room to purchase the daily *Oregonian*.[61] He also bragged to a reporter at his trial about his effect on newspaper sales.

The Nelson Media Zones

In this case, given the substantial public and media interest in Nelson, media zones were almost inevitable. We can examine four Nelson media zones: his arrest, his wife's testimony trip, the trial, and the funeral parlor after his death.

After his apprehension, Nelson was brought back to Winnipeg. His arrival created quite a media zone. According to a Canadian study, "Nelson's return to Winnipeg was met by a boisterous crowd of 400 people."[62]

Earle Nelson's wife traveled to Winnipeg, Canada, to testify on his behalf. Her arrival created a news zone in the Canadian city, despite attempts at keeping her presence secret. Before long the Winnipeg and Manitoba press learned of her arrival. Early Saturday morning, a *Free Press* reporter knocked on their hotel room door. After he identified himself, Mrs. Fabian became highly agitated. "We don't want to talk about it," she yelled at the reporter.[63]

A third Nelson media zone was the courtroom where his trial was held. Courtroom Number One of the Manitoba Law Courts Building held 175 spectators. The problem was the thousands of people desiring admission. In fact, approximately two thousand people showed up for the beginning of the trial.[64]

The last media zone in the Nelson case unfolded at the funeral parlor where his body was taken after his execution. Rumors quickly spread that public viewing of the body would be permitted. More than one thousand people showed up to view Nelson's body.[65]

Influencing Trial Outcome

In the Earle Nelson case, prejudicial newspaper reports influenced public opinion about Nelson's guilt. As Schechter reported, an even more significant

problem was the accusatory behavior of the local press, which had already virtually convicted Nelson in print before his trial.[66]

Nelson's trial in Winnipeg, Canada, was characterized by prejudicial pretrial
publicity. Chief Justice T. H. Mathers complained about the setting of an early
trial date. He contended that the press coverage had agitated the public mind
into a state of anger and vengeance that precluded a calm consideration of the
evidence against Nelson. The newspapers carried on a campaign during which
Nelson was condemned repeatedly.[67]

Media Misbehavior

The tendency to embellish the truth was noted in the Earle Nelson case.
Nelson appeared quite docile and innocent, and looked as frightening as a
baby. It became the task of reporters to improve their reports with invented or
exaggerated details. In one article by the *Tribune's* correspondent, Nelson's
slate-gray eyes suddenly acquired a "demonic yellowish hue."[68]

PUBLIC RELATIONS TACTICS

Public information efforts typically accompany serial murder investigations.
The Earle Nelson case was no exception. In fact, it can be argued that Nelson
was ultimately apprehended due to law enforcement public information.

There were five specific public relations tactics used in this case. They
included news conferences, radio, fliers, posters, and newspapers.

News Conferences

Most serial murder press conferences are probably conducted by law
enforcement agencies. In the Earle Nelson serial murder case, a series of news
conferences was held in various cities, as he moved on to new killing grounds.
With Nelson on the loose somewhere in the Bay Area, San Francisco Police
Chief O'Brien convened a news conference. He called the strangler (Nelson)
"the most dangerous criminal now at large." He urged women who owned
houses with rooms for rent to be extraordinarily careful in scrutinizing potential lodgers of the general description of the strangler.[69]

When Nelson moved to Buffalo, New York, his murderous onslaught precipitated a press conference. At a news conference, the Buffalo Chief of Police shared
his suspicion with the press. He announced that Jennie Randolph was probably
killed by the "long-sought Pacific Coast Bluebeard—perhaps the most brutal
killer, and certainly one of the most cunning, in the history of this country."[70]

Radio

Radio was repeatedly used as Earle Nelson moved from one place to
another. Announcers regularly interrupted the scheduled radio programs
with the latest description of the suspect.[71] It was too late to save two

women, as one radio broadcast informed listeners. The discovery of the second Nelson slaying victim confirmed the worst fears of Canadian police. Bulletins were quickly revised. At approximately 6:30 p.m., an announcer interrupted the weekly broadcast of the Sunday evening church service with the news that the two women had been strangled to death, possibly by the same notorious killer already being sought for about twenty similar murders in the United States.[72]

These radio broadcasts helped in the apprehension of Nelson. A farmer named Roy Armstrong recognized Nelson, then contacted the authorities. Like just about everyone else in southern Manitoba, Armstrong was keeping an eye out for the "Gorilla," informed and alerted by the police bulletins broadcast by the radio every hour or two. When Armstrong spotted Nelson, he put his foot to the accelerator and sped to his farmhouse, and ran inside to telephone the police.[73]

Fliers

Fliers are relatively inexpensive media. Also called circulars and flyers, they are a common serial murder public relations tactical choice. New circulars and fliers contained updated information about the "Gorilla Man's" latest clothing. They were printed and disseminated to local police departments in western Canada, and to departments in North and South Dakota, Montana, Idaho, and Oregon.[74]

Buffalo Police Chief Higgins was able to identify Earle Nelson as the offender in a local case thanks to fliers. According to Schechter, Higgins had recalled recently seeing a flier about the strangler, which had been posted by the Philadelphia Police Department.[75]

Canadian authorities similarly were alerted to Nelson's presence by circulars. According to the Winnipeg Police Department, "Chief of Detectives, George Smith, had recently received various circulars describing murders of a similar nature in the United States, and soon established that they were seeking the infamous 'Strangler'."[76]

Posters

Posters are typically used in serial murder public information campaigns. They are a cost-effective way of displaying a suspect's likeness and enlisting public support. In this case, because he was recognized from his poster in the local post office, Nelson was apprehended and incarcerated.[77]

Winnipeg Police Chief Christopher Newton created a reward bulletin. It was printed and sent to all police departments from western Ontario to Calgary, Alberta.[78] The key role of the poster in Nelson's arrest was provided by Everitt; after killing two women in Winnipeg, he was seen as he left town. His rather distinctive features were compared with the photograph on his wanted poster.[79]

Newspapers

The press is motivated by private commercial interest, but sometimes that private interest and the public interest coincide. That was true of the Nelson murder case. The newspapers benefited financially from their crime coverage, while disseminating public safety information to the public.

In Winnipeg, for example, both daily newspapers continually featured almost-regular articles on the Nelson case. The same thing had been true earlier, in the Bay Area. In the San Francisco Bay Area, news that the "Dark Strangler" had killed again outdid every other story, even the health problems of Rudolph Valentino.[80]

CONCLUSION

Earle Nelson began life under less than auspicious conditions. He was an orphan, and a severe childhood accident left him with possible brain damage. He had numerous childhood scrapes with the law, over burglary, shoplifting, and sexual misconduct charges. He never had a semblance of a normal family life.

Nelson was briefly married, while he was escaped from the mental institution where he had been institutionalized for diagnosis and treatment. His first wife suffered a nervous breakdown, and was hospitalized. While she was in the hospital, Nelson tried to rape her.

Media coverage of Nelson's crimes assisted law enforcement in apprehending him. Posters and radio, in particular, played a role in Nelson's capture. News conferences and newspaper coverage of the crimes promoted public safety. It would not be unfair to contend that Nelson was apprehended because of mass communication.

Unfortunately, the media had some negative impacts on the case, as well. It assisted Nelson in avoiding apprehension, and created media zones. It is believed that the publicity affected Nelson's right to a fair trial. The media also misbehaved.

4

---·•·---

THE MANSON FAMILY

THE 1968 ASSASSINATIONS of Robert F. Kennedy and Reverend Martin Luther King Jr., were two of the watershed events that established a demarcation line between the "Peace and Love Sixties" and the following eras. The Manson "Family" murders rank with those assassinations as culture-changing events. Many of us have vivid memories of Charles Manson's lunatic stare and the "X" on his forehead.

Manson and his followers were responsible for at least seven and as many as thirty-five murders, almost all in California. The victims were stabbed, shot, and bludgeoned to death. The apparent randomness of the crimes was truly frightening.

The murders attracted considerable attention, in part due to the accompanying communication. The Manson Family members wrote messages on the walls in their victims' blood, and carved a message into one victim's body.

There was substantial public and media interest. The media crossed the line into improper behavior in several ways. There were numerous types and instances of media misconduct and negative behavior. Public information played a prominent role.

Manson and his followers captivated America, first with the crimes and then with their trial behavior. To better understand these crimes, nine subjects will be considered. The criminals and their crimes will be described. We will examine the investigation, arrest, and trial. Relevant criminal communication will be considered, and media and public interest documented. The negative effects of media coverage will be explained, and public relations aspects discussed.

THE CRIMINALS

One factor complicating our understanding of the Manson murders is the number of individuals involved. Seldom do serial murders involve as many participants. Unfortunately, space limitations make it impossible to consider each of the Manson murderers individually. Sections on Charles "Tex" Watson,

Susan Atkins, Leslie Van Houten, Patricia Krenwinkle, Clem Grogan, Bobby Beausoliel, Bruce Davis, Mary Brunner, and others would be necessary. In this section, we will therefore reluctantly only consider Charles Manson.[1]

He was "Born no name Maddox in 1934 to a prostitute mother," contended one source. Another study agreed, noting that on November 12, 1934, "Charles Manson was born as 'No name Maddox,' in Cincinnati, Ohio." An encyclopedia gave his birth name as Charles Milles Manson. Norris indicated that the place of birth was Ashland, Kentucky.[2]

His was an unhappy childhood. "His father, who Manson never met, was a 'Colonel Scott' from Ashland, Kentucky." When he was five years old, "His mother, a heavy drinker, was sentenced to prison for armed robbery." According to another source, "Manson was born in Cincinnati, Ohio, to an absentee father and attended Walnut Hills High School. When he was thirteen, his mother put him in a foster home."[3]

Manson "had virtually no childhood bliss at all," according to Norris. He added that "An illegitimate child, he was passed like a football from relative to relative and finally to his mother, who brought him up in bars and on street corners where she hustled." Manson was largely raised by his grandparents; he "never saw any affectionate displays between his grandparents," and his grandfather became psychotic.

Kathleen Maddox was a 16-year-old when she gave birth to Manson. Norris noted, "The parent/child bond between Charles Manson and his mother was tenuous at best." Kathy Maddox frequently failed to come home in time to pick up the boy from a baby-sitter. Manson claimed that when he was a young child, "he was sold to a bar waitress for a pitcher of beer."[4]

Manson did several terms in reform schools. He initially was sent to the Gibault School for Boys, in Terre Haute, Indiana, in 1947. He escaped, and made it to California before being captured in 1951 and sent to the National Training School for Boys, in Washington, D.C. His institutionalization at the Gibault School for Boys was court-ordered. After committing two armed robberies in 1948, he was sent to the Indiana School for Boys. Manson said he didn't realize for two days that his mother was not coming back to get him when he was committed to the Terre Haute facility.[5]

In 1955, Manson married a waitress. A study conducted at a university in Missouri recalled that in 1955, "Manson marries Rosalie Willis, a waitress from Wheeling." In 1960, five years later, "In January, Manson marries again—this time, a nineteen-year-old." Rosalie Jean Willis was seventeen when she married Manson. The second Mrs. Manson was named Leona.[6]

Manson sired two children through his marriages. Charles Jr. was born to his first wife in 1955. Charles Luther Manson was born to his second wife in 1960. Charles Jr. committed suicide in 1993, at age thirty-eight.[7]

Manson had a lengthy prison history. One analyst reported, "Manson was arrested many times for theft, stealing cars and pimping. He spent half his childhood in prison or juvenile halls." He began his criminal career at age thirteen, robbing a grocery store and a casino. In 1948 he committed the grocery store heist, along with two other armed robberies in the same year. After escaping from an Indiana facility, he stole a car and headed West, burglarizing fifteen to twenty gas stations en route. In 1959 he received a ten-year suspended sentence for forging a treasury check. On June 1, 1960, he was arrested for soliciting prostitution. By the age of thirty-two, Manson had been in prison or reform school for twenty years of his life.[8]

At one point in his childhood, Manson was sent to live with an aunt and uncle in Maychem, Virginia. His uncle continually berated him for being a sissy. Finally, to make a point, "His uncle sent him to school the first day dressed in girl's clothing."[9]

Manson was probably mentally ill. Norris described Manson's "epileptoid symptoms or indicators of limbic psychosis," including wanderlust, hypersexuality, hypervigilance, obsession, and extreme interest in cults. When he was a 16-year-old, he was labeled as "aggressively antisocial." At eighteen, a prison psychiatrist diagnosed Manson as suffering from "psychic trauma." In 1961, prison psychiatrists perceived "deep-seated personality problems."[10]

It is interesting to note that Manson did not take anyone's life, according to the prosecutor. The state argued that Manson directed the killings. "Although Charles Manson never fired a pistol, or physically murdered the victims, he had power over his followers, who did his bidding," noted one source.[11]

"I have killed no one and I have ordered no one to be killed," Manson testified at his trial. Norris agreed, adding that Manson personally never directly acted in the Tate/LaBianca murders, but he motivated and managed them through information to and control over his followers. One recent study agreed, and concluded that Manson was convicted of planning and ordering murders, although he was not accused of actually committing them physically.[12]

THE CRIMES

The murders and related criminal activity by the Manson Family frightened and angered Americans. We will examine these murders, in some detail. Seven topics will advance our understanding of the crimes. The number of crimes will be explored, along with description of the Hinman, Tate, LaBianca, and Hughes murders. The motive will be explained, and the significance of the crimes shown.

The Number of Crimes

How many Manson murders were there? As in most serial murder cases, I have an equivocal answer to this question. At the least there were seven victims, five at the Tate residence and the LaBiancas. Many experts believe that Gary Hinman, Donald "Shorty" Shea, and Ronald Hughes were also Manson Family victims, which brings the total to ten. But the actual total might be substantially higher.

"As hair-raising as the Tate/LaBianca killings were, some believe that they constituted only a portion of the murders committed in the name of Manson's family," suggested serial killer expert David Everitt. He added that the Hinman, Shea, and Hughes homicides were most likely Manson Family activities.[13] Psychomedical expert Jennifer Furio agreed, adding that "While these cases resulted in sentencing against Manson and his followers, many unsolved murders are directly linked to the clan but conclusive evidence is lacking."[14]

Several studies suggest that the Manson murder victim total was thirty-five people. An encyclopedia recalled that "They claimed a total of some 35 killings." According to noted crime expert Joel Norris, "Manson and his family might be responsible for more than thirty-five murders throughout the northern part of the state." Brian Lane and Wilfred Gregg, authors of an encyclopedia of serial murder, referred to Manson's boast to have murdered thirty-five people.[15]

A relatively radical theory has been recently proposed, that the Zodiac murders were the work of the Manson Family. There is a website dedicated to this notion. The site notes "the strong possibility" that "Charles Manson was the mastermind of the Zodiac crime spree."[16]

The Hinman Murder

The Hinman murder was similar to the Tate and LaBianca murders and associated crime scenes which followed. Manson sent Bobby Beausoliel, Susan Atkins, and Mary Brunner to Hinman's house, to search for and steal $20,000 he was rumored to possess. They couldn't find the money, so they nearly severed his ear. They forced him to sign over title to his cars, and then killed him. According to one recent study, "The first murder by the family was of Gary Hinman, a Los Angeles drug dealer and musician. His body was discovered on 1969-JUL-31."[17]

Gary Hinman was a musician friend of Manson's. He supposedly recently had received an inheritance of $20,000, Lane and Gregg observed. They added that Manson sent Brunner, Beausoliel, and Atkins "to try to beat the money out of him." Another study added that, "Members of the Manson family had previously been responsible for the murder of Gary Hinman, a music teacher, in Topanga, and were suspected of other murders." Most authorities agree that the participants in the Hinman murder included Atkins, Beausoliel, and Brunner.[18]

The Tate Murders

"On August 8, 1969, . . . a pregnant Sharon Tate, Abigail Folger, Jay Sebring, Voytek Frykowski, and Steven Parent were brutally murdered," claimed a recent study. Sebring was beaten so badly, it was hard to identify him, the study added. Parent was shot four times in the head, and Sebring and Frykowski had been shot as well. The victims were each stabbed repeatedly in a homicidal frenzy, Everitt claimed, adding that Frykowski had been stabbed fifty-one times.[19]

"Now is the time for Helter Skelter," Manson told Krenwinkle, Atkins, Watson, and Kasabian, instructing them to get a change of clothes. Before they left, he said, "Leave a sign. Do something witchy." This report concluded that a total of 102 stab wounds were inflicted upon four victims; Parent was only shot.[20]

The type and number of wounds was quantified by Levin and Fox. Tate had been stabbed sixteen times, and Jay Sebring was shot once and stabbed seven times. There were five gunshot wounds in Frykowski, who had also been stabbed fifty-one times and "bludgeoned" thirteen times on the back of his head. Folger was stabbed twenty-eight times. Parent was shot four times and stabbed once.[21]

"You're all going to die," Watson told the Tate victims. He and the other family members made good on that promise One report noted that "The murders had taken a little over a half-hour," and the result was "a total of 7 gunshots and 104 stab wounds." The carnage at the crime scene was so bad that there was a surreal atmosphere. The police officers responding to the call noted what appeared to be "mannequins that had been dipped in red," and then "deposited haphazardly on the lawn."[22]

The details of the Tate murders were horrific. A recent study arrived at slightly different numbers than did Norris. It stated that Folger was stabbed twenty-one times, Frykowski was shot once and stabbed fifty-one times, Sebring was shot twice and stabbed six times, Parent was shot three times, and Tate was stabbed sixteen times.[23]

"All I want to do is have my baby," Tate reportedly told her assailants. Atkins held Tate's arms while first Watson then the others took turns stabbing her. Atkins's cellmate, Virginia Graham, told police that Atkins claimed she had personally killed Tate. Tate said, "Please, please don't kill me. I don't want to die. I just want to have my baby." Atkins answered, "Look, bitch, you might as well face it right now, you're going to die, and I don't feel a thing behind it." The perpetrators were Watson, Atkins, Krenwinkle, and Kasabian.[24]

The LaBianca Murders

Manson and his followers killed again the very next evening. Exactly which members participated is in some doubt, but the end result was the same as the night before. Here is a resume of the crime, part of the official LaBianca Homicide Report of the Los Angeles Police Department (LAPD):

On August 10, 1969, during the early morning hours, the victims, Rosemary LaBianca and Leno A. LaBianca, were stabbed to death at their residence located at 3301 Waverly Drive by suspect or suspects unknown. The weapons used were a kitchen steak knife and carving fork belonging to the victims. Both victims were repeatedly stabbed and were found with pillowcases over their heads. Leno LaBianca's hands were tied behind his back with leather thongs. There was no evidence of forced entry and no indication of a struggle. The residence was not ransacked, but Mrs. LaBianca's purse had the appearance of being rifled and the wallet and contents were missing.[25]

"The following evening, Leno and Rosemary LaBianca were murdered and mutilated. They were tied up, and Leno had a fork and knife stuck in his chest," a recent study reported. Scott stated that the LaBianca assault took place two days after the Tate murders. She also noted that Tex Watson stabbed Rosemary LaBianca about a dozen times. As Leslie Van Houten held Mrs. LaBianca, Krenwinkle severed her spine with a powerful slash of the blade.[26]

The attack on Leno LaBianca was described by Sanders, "Tex began stabbing him and Leno struggled and screamed and shrieked, his hands behind him." In a moment, "Tex had him down on his back and slashed him four times in the throat leaving the serrated knife buried deep within. He stabbed him four times in the abdomen into the colon, all fatal wounds." Similarly, "Rosemary LaBianca was stabbed 41 times. Leno LaBianca was also stabbed at least two dozen times, and then pierced with a knife and fork that were left protruding from his body," recalled Furio. According to Levin and Fox, he was stabbed twenty-seven times, and she received forty-one knife wounds.[27]

Some evidence was collected by LAPD at the crime scene. Left by the assailants were a cigarette butt, twenty brown hair particles, a pink stained towel, and two leather thongs. In addition, LAPD located and lifted five sets of palm or fingerprints.[28]

The dogs did not bark. The LaBiancas had three dogs, which typically barked at the arrival of strangers. The LAPD homicide report mentioned this curious fact. "The LaBianca's have three dogs, all of whom bark at strangers. Investigating officers have been unable to locate witnesses who heard the dogs barking or any other noises of distress."[29]

One final fact to consider about the LaBianca murder—he was heavily in debt, and had embezzled a large amount of money from his business. The LAPD considered these facts important, along with LaBianca's gambling addiction.

"A deficit of approximately $200,000" was discovered at the Gateway Foods store he owned in June, 1969. Shortly thereafter, it came to light that LaBianca owned nine thoroughbred race horses. He was called "a chronic gambler," who went to the horse track every day and typically wagered $500 at a time. "Their properties were extensively mortgaged and they had personal loans totaling $30,000."[30] Was money the motive?

It is difficult to say for sure who was involved in these killings. Four studies were consulted on this matter, and all four arrived at different lists.[31]

The Hughes Murder

Ronald Hughes was a defense attorney who had represented Leslie Van Houten. It is unknown who killed him, but there are some indications. The Manson Family was most likely involved.

Van Houten's court-appointed attorney Ronald Hughes disappeared on a camping trip, observed one source. It added that Hughes "was accompanied by two Manson followers." His decomposed remains were located and identified five months later.[32]

Hughes vanished while on a camping trip to Sespe Hot Springs at the end of November in 1970. A study by the University of Missouri, Kansas City, noted, "Although no one was ever charged with the murder of Hughes, at least two Family members have admitted that the killing of Hughes was a 'retaliation murder.'" The study added, "Defense attorney Ronald Hughes fails to show up in court. He is never seen again, leading to speculation he was murdered by the Family."[33]

The Shea Murder

A final murder should be included, the death of Donald "Shorty" Shea. He was a long-time ranch-hand at the Spahn Ranch, which was invaded by Manson and his followers. One recent analysis listed each of the Manson murders, and concluded, "Finally, Donald Shea was murdered. He was a former stuntman and hired hand at the Spahn Ranch."[34]

Ex-convict Danny DeCarlo implicated Manson in the murder of Shorty Shea at the Spahn ranch. However, he told the interviewing LAPD detectives that he would be afraid to testify. DeCarlo was a biker and not a person to be easily intimidated. The participants in the Shea murder were most likely Manson, Watson, Bruce Davis, and Clem Grogan.[35]

The Motive

"What was most shocking was that the victims were chosen virtually at random—there was no rational motive," Scott declared. She added that "The arrests added to the mystery in that no motive could be found for the crimes."[36] In this section, we will examine the self-professed Manson Family motive, Helter Skelter, and a quartet of proposed motives.

Manson believed that the Beatles song, "Helter Skelter," was an allegory about an impending race war in America. Blacks would win the war, but be unable to govern themselves, and they would turn to Manson as their leader. Everett explained "If Family members committed savage murders in such a way that Black militants would become the prime suspects, Manson believed, then the race war would be ignited."[37] Furio agreed, adding that "The era was proclaimed: 'Helter Skelter.' It was up to the Manson family to light the fuse that would set off this event. A statement had to be made that could not be ignored."[38]

When he dispatched the death team to the Tate home, he announced that Helter Skelter had arrived.[39] He desired that Blacks would be falsely accused of the Tate/LaBianca murders, thus expediting the race war he predicted, Levin and Fox added.[40]

A more comprehensive analysis of possible Manson murder motives is available to us. Four possible motives identified by a recent analysis included:

1.   Manson hated society and wanted revenge.
2.   He sought to retaliate against the music industry in particular.
3.   He enjoyed killing.
4.   He wished to instigate Helter Skelter.[41]

Significance of the Murders

"Charles Manson may not be the most vile criminal in U.S. history, but he is one of the most frightening, and as he'd hoped to be, the most famous," according to Furio.[42] Scott agreed, adding that probably no other single event of the 1960s made the world seem so irrational as the Manson Family's two nights of mindless slaughter.[43]

Serial murder authorities Levin and Fox noted that the stories and names of serial killers like David Berkowitz and Charles Manson are better known by many Americans than the names of recent American vice presidents.[44] Norris added that the Manson Family was clearly the most infamous and notorious of the serial murder cults in America.[45]

THE INVESTIGATIONS

At 9:14 a.m. on August 9, 1969, LAPD officers J. J. DeRosa in West Los Angeles unit 8L5 and W. T. Weisenhut in unit 8L68 received a radio call from Central Dispatch, "Code 2, possible homicide, 10050 Cielo Drive." Sanders added, "Their job was to protect the scene and to make note of the original physical characteristics of the area, leaving it undisturbed." Eventually forty LAPD officers, four coroner's staff, and an unknown number of ambulance crews were at the Tate crime scene.[46]

Bill Garretson was the caretaker of the Tate estate, and he lived in a small cottage at the back of the property. He was arrested by the police because he seemed unresponsive to their questions. After passing a polygraph test, he was released two days later.[47]

Approximately 12:00 noon that day, the murder investigation was reassigned from LAPD's West Los Angeles Division to the Robbery-Homicide Division of LAPD. Lieutenant R. J. Helder, supervisor of investigation, was placed in charge of the case. He assigned the case to five LAPD sergeants: Michael J. McGann, J. Buckles, E. Henderson, D. Varney, and Danny Galindo. Coroner Thomas Noguchi "took charge of the bodies," ordering that the bodies remain undisturbed until he and his staff arrived.[48]

This was an intense investigation. "Some policemen would not sleep for three or four days, so forceful was the investigation," Sanders recalled. He added that, "The investigation facing the police was extremely complex and, for the most part, a labyrinth of blind alleys and tedium. Everything at the Polanski residence, even the wastebaskets, had to be sifted for data. Address books, personal papers, house and grounds, everything sifted for clues. Police combed the brushy hill-sides of Benedict Canyon looking for murder weapons."[49]

A further complicating factor was a plethora of suspects. LAPD was con-fronted with an "overwhelming number of suspects." In fact, there were three different categories of suspects: drug dealers, "fame-porn," and the occult.[50]

The LaBianca homicide investigation began at about 10:45 p.m. on August 10, 1969. Susan Struthers, Rosemary LaBianca's daughter from a previous mar-riage, became concerned and discovered the bodies at 10:30. She then called the police.[51]

Investigators quickly arrived at an incorrect conclusion. They declared that the Tate and LaBianca murders were definitely unrelated crime events. One study noted that "By Tuesday, August 12, 1969, detectives officially ruled out any link between the Tate and LaBianca homicides."[52]

LAPD Captain Paul LePage was in charge of the LaBianca case. He was assisted by sergeants Phil Sartuche, Manuel Gutierrez, and Frank Patchett.[53]

Numerous misdirections hindered the investigation. Initially, "The LaBianca investigation centered on business dealings and gambling activities of Leno LaBianca." The LAPD investigated another misleading lead, which claimed that the LaBianca murders "were contracted" by "a wealthy man in Kansas City."[54]

Investigators made extensive use of polygraph tests. According to Sanders, "They gave lie detector tests to most major acquaintances of the decedents." They found six unidentified fingerprints. And they used "M.O. runs."[55]

MO runs used the California State Bureau of Criminal Investigation computer. It "has a huge amount of information stored regarding crimes and criminals. An M.O. run collects all crimes with the same manner of perpetration." This would identify criminals and crimes similar to the one under investigation.[56]

THE APPREHENSION

While in prison, Susan (Sadie) Atkins "talked to her cellmate about having been involved in the Tate murders," according to one recent analysis.[57] Another source added, "Susan Atkins was arrested for a different incident, and while in prison, she boasted about her crimes, and about Charles Manson." The report's authors concluded that "Atkins knew so much about the crimes, her fellow inmate believed her, and called the homicide detectives to tell them the story."[58]

Susan Atkins was arrested on a prostitution charge. While still in police cus-tody, she confessed her active role in the Tate and LaBianca murders to a cell-mate, Lane and Gregg recalled.[59] According to Furio, Atkins was high on a number of drugs, and she indiscreetly babbled to her cellmate about her recent murderous exploits.[60]

Virginia Graham was the cellmate in whom Atkins confided. She testified in the Manson Family trial. She stated:

Well, we started talking, we were talking about many things. . . . She wasn't wor-ried about it anyway. And that the police were on the wrong track about some murders. And I said, "What do you mean?" And she said to me, "The murders at Benedict Canyon." And just for a moment I didn't quite snap to what she meant, and I said, "Benedict Canyon?" And she said, "Yes, the Tate murders." And she said, "You know who did it, don't you?" And I said, "No, I don't," and she said, "Well, you are looking at her."[61]

The Atkins disclosures provided investigators with the information they needed. A number of law enforcement and other governmental agencies collaborated, including LAPD, the Inyo County Sheriff's Office, the California Highway Patrol, the National Park Rangers, and the Federal Fish and Game Commission, on plans to arrest Manson and his followers at their remote residence, the old Spahn Ranch. On October 12, 1970, the ranch was raided and Manson and others were arrested. Manson was found hiding inside a cabinet in a bathroom.[62]

THE TRIAL

The Manson Family trial was held in Department 104, on the eighth floor of the Hall of Justice in Judge Charles Older's courtroom. Older received numerous death threats before and during the trial. Security was markedly upgraded.[63]

It was decided before the trial that the jury should be sequestered, to avoid prejudicial media publicity. The jury consisted of seven men and five women. They ranged from twenty-five to seventy-three years of age. There was an electrical tester, a retired sheriff, a school secretary, a dictaphone and teletype operator, a chemical company worker, a clerical supervisor, a drama critic, an executive secretary, an electronics technician, a mortician, a retired industrial security guard, and a highway engineer.[64]

The trial started on July 29, 1970. On July 24, Manson appeared in court with a crude "X" carved into his forehead. The next weekend, Susan Atkins, Patricia Krenwinkle, and Leslie Van Houten burned and cut "X's" into their foreheads.[65]

Prosecutor Vincent Bugliosi methodically laid out a persuasive, rational case. On the other hand, the defense was characterized by extreme behavior. Defense counsel Irving Kanerak had a particularly irritating strategy—he would incessantly and continually object to prosecution statements and questions. By the third day of the trial, he had registered more than three hundred objections. Because of his mindless objections, and other unacceptable tactics, he was cited for contempt of court four times, spending a night in jail. So did his fellow defense counsels Ronald Hughes and Dayne Shin. Kanerak's cross-examination of key prosecution witness Linda Kasabian lasted seven days.[66]

The trial ended on January 15, 1971. The jury rendered guilty verdicts on January 25. Manson was sentenced to death on April 19, 1971, but now serves a life sentence.[67]

THE COMMUNICATION

Communication played a major role in the Manson murders. Writing on walls in blood tends to get people's attention, as does body carving. In this section, we will consider the two types of crime-related communication evident in these crimes. They included wall writing (in blood) and body carving.

The United States was terrorized in summer 1969 by the seemingly random murders of Sharon Tate and her guests, followed shortly by the equally vicious murder of Leno and Rosemary LaBianca. The Manson Family is believed to have engaged in four separate acts of writing in their victim's blood.

There may have been a precursor to the Tate/LaBianca murders, involving the murder of a young musician and music teacher named Gary Hinman. His death was attributed to Manson Family member Bobby Beausoliel. He was found driving Hinman's car while covered in blood, with a knife hidden in the vehicle.

Vince Bugliosi, who prosecuted the Manson Family killers, noted that, as in the Tate and LaBianca homicides, a message had been left not far from the body. On the wall in the living room in the victim's own blood, not far from Hinman's body, were the words "political piggy."[68] According to Publications International Ltd., Bobby Beausoliel was responsible. He also sketched a panther paw to misdirect the police and make them think the radical Black Panthers were behind the murder.[69]

On August 9, 1969, Tate and four friends were shot and stabbed in a frenzied attack. Then Atkins dipped a towel in Tate's blood and wrote the word "pig" on a door, a message that was intended to convince the police to suspect violent Black revolutionaries. The next evening, the LaBianca's blood was used to write "Death to Pigs," "Healter Skelter," and "Rise."[70] "On the front door of the house, the word 'pig' was painted in blood," according to Lane and Gregg.[71] Another source recalled, "The murderers had scrawled the words 'PIG' and 'HELTER SKELTER' on the door and walls."[72]

Watson reminded Atkins as they were about to leave that they were supposed to leave a "witchy" sign, so she "scrawled the word PIG."[73] Atkins "knelt down to print PIG in blood type O-M."[74] Interestingly, an early LAPD report on the murders identified the Beatles' song as the basis for the wall writing.[75]

There was wall writing in blood at the LaBianca crime scene, as well. Lane and Gregg referred to the writings "Death to the Pigs," "Rise," and "Healter [sic] Skelter" in blood on the walls.[76] The LAPD homicide report mentioned, "the words, 'DEATH TO PIGS,' printed in blood. On the south wall of the living room directly to the left of the front door, the word 'RISE' was printed in blood. On the kitchen refrigerator door were the printed words, 'HEALTER SKELTER,' with helter being misspelled."[77]

Krenwinkle is credited with being the author of the LaBianca blood writing. Scott suggested that on the refrigerator door, Katie wrote "Healter [sic] Skelter."[78] Sanders confirmed Scott's perception of the writing and the writer, as did Everett.[79]

At about the same time as the Tate/LaBianca crimes, an American named Joel Dean Pugh was found dead in his room at the Talgart Hotel in London. His throat had been slit, and there was something else. "There were some 'writings' in reverse on the mirror, along with some 'comic-book' type drawings. . . . No one thought the drawings or writings important enough to take down (the manager later recalled only the words 'Jack and Jill')."[80]

Pugh had been a Manson follower, but escaped. He was married to family member Sandra Good. A letter between Manson Family members was intercepted by police; it included the line, "I would not want what happened to Joel to happen to me."[81]

In addition to writing on the walls in the LaBianca's blood, the Manson Family members engaged in yet another act of sadistic, brutal communication. They carved a word into Leno LaBianca's body.

Lane explained that, as a last act of senseless violence, the word "war" was carved into Leno LaBianca's body. Another study found that, "war" was carved into LaBianca's stomach, according to Publications International Ltd., in a parting act of contempt and gratuitous violence. The LAPD homicide report noted, "Inscribed by slashes on the exposed stomach area were the letters 'WAR'."[82]

There is some disagreement over the authorship of the LaBianca body carving. "Katie, in a stroke of brilliance, carved the word 'WAR' on the stomach of the dead man with a fork," one analysis contended. "Krenwinkle stabbed Rosemary LaBianca and carved the word 'WAR' on Leno LaBianca's stomach." But another person makes the same claim. Watson is said to have made the carving, with "the bayonet or perhaps the metal prongs of the electrical plug."[83]

MEDIA AND PUBLIC INTEREST

Americans were genuinely frightened by the Manson crimes. The nature of the crimes, the seemingly random and motiveless murders, scared people all across the country. We will now consider both public and media interest in these crimes.

The members of the public were not just interested, they were in a state of panic. One study noted that, "The murders caused panic in Hollywood." According to Everitt, the ensuing panic lasted for more than two months.[84]

As the panic abated, and time passed, fear was replaced with interest. For instance, there have been more than one hundred books written about the Manson Family. Today, there is a website catering to Manson fans. It is located at http://www.charliemanson.com.[85]

The Tate/LaBianca murders, committed by the Manson Family, frightened not merely Californians, but people from coast to coast. According to Bugliosi and Gentry, headlines dominated the front pages of the newspapers, and the Manson story became the lead story on radio and TV. It was possibly the most heavily publicized serial murder case in American history.

Manson's murders were not merely front-page news in America. One recent analysis explained the global appeal of this story. "The murder case and subsequent trial were major news stories throughout the world."[86]

NEGATIVE EFFECTS OF MEDIA COVERAGE

The major media interest in the Manson murders has already been mentioned. Because of the competitive commercial media environment, this media interest led to media misbehavior. Seven specific negative effects of media coverage will be explained and documented. The media motivated Manson, and celebritized people. Media zones were created, and malicious stories printed. There was direct media involvement in the investigation. Checkbook journalism was noted, along with media interference with the investigation.

Media Motivated Manson

Jennifer Furio interviewed Charles Manson. Her recollection of the interview was that the maniacal little man seemed to appreciate her attention almost as much as the sound of his own voice.[87] Manson's interest in his "press" was typical of serial murderers.

The Creation of Celebrities

Charles Manson and his followers frightened an entire generation of Americans due to their 1969 murders in Los Angeles, and possibly elsewhere. Manson has attained celebrity status. The fact that a convicted serial killer could become a counterculture hero seems incongruous, but for some people, Charles Manson had become a celebrity, Bugliosi and Gentry suggested. Norris perceived the inconsistency in serial murder media coverage. He correlated it to the degree of celebrity status of the offender, believing that the media was generally not interested in the violent person but in the celebrity or "superstar killers" like Jean Harris, Charles Manson, and Ted Bundy. The media also favor murder cases with a hero who escapes from a captor or a detective or parental victim whose brave acts save the day.[88]

Creation of Media Zones

The murderous activity of the Manson Family created a huge media sensation. As a result, several media zones were created. For instance, the physician who performed the autopsy, Dr. Thomas Noguchi, was "besieged by reporters at the gate" to the Tate home. At a grand jury session, "There must have been a hundred newsmen in the narrow hallway outside the grand jury chambers; some were atop tables, so it looked as if they were stacked to the ceiling."[89]

When the bodies of Sharon Tate and her friends were discovered, four West Los Angeles detectives were immediately dispatched to the crime scene. By the time the final detective arrived, print and broadcast reporters had already gathered outside the Tate gate. Prosecutor Vince Bugliosi estimated that his office received at least a hundred calls a day. Their only response to these media inquiries was "no comment." The media was desperate for information on this sensational case.[90]

Malicious Stories

The LAPD kept a tight lid on disclosures. So, some stories were enhanced, others made up entirely. These tended to be malicious pieces.

"The publicity had been bad," and as Steven Rogers, the *New York Times* bureau chief in Los Angeles, noted, "All the stories had a common thread—that somehow the victims had brought the murders on themselves." Even staid *Time* magazine was guilty of "imaginative embellishments." Tate's husband, Roman Polanski, "angered by a multitude of slanders," called a news conference on August 19 to chastise the media for the malicious reporting and to defend his late wife.[91]

Direct Media Involvement

Sometimes the media becomes directly involved in a case. The killer may call or write newspapers or TV stations. Or, the media may just dig a little harder than the police sometimes. That happened in the Manson case.

Evidence was located by the media, after the police could not find it. One study concluded that the police completely bungled the task of evidence collection at the Tate crime scene. LAPD was unable to locate the clothing worn by the murderers and subsequently discarded, but a television news crew was able to find the clothes later.[92]

Checkbook Journalism

The transcripts of the Manson grand jury were of considerable commercial concern to the media. As a result, Bugliosi recalled the rumor that an English magazine had offered $10,000 just to look at a copy of court documents. Crime scene photographs similarly had great value—Bugliosi noted that a German magazine had offered $100,000 for them.[93]

Media Interference with the Investigation

Media presence in the Manson case resulted in interference with the police probe. Reporters followed authorities involved in the case. This resulted in at least one high-speed chase.

"We looked out the window, we saw we were being followed by a Channel 2 TV unit," Bugliosi recalled. This mattered, because Bugliosi was escorting Linda Kasabian, whose identity as an informant was being kept secret. To try and protect her, "Once on the freeway, we tried to outrun the media unit, but without success. They filmed us all the way. It was like a Mack Sennett comedy, only with the press in pursuit of the fuzz."[94]

PUBLIC RELATIONS ASPECTS

There were two public relations communication tactics used in the Manson murder case. They included news releases and news conferences. We will also consider two other topics: LAPD's determination to limit information dissemination and polygraph keys.

The Manson Family case necessitated an unusual type of news release. According to Bugliosi and Gentry, each week the Los Angeles Board of Supervisors issued and disseminated a news release itemizing and summarizing trial costs to date, due to public interest in the case.[95] Most such releases, however, are voluntary.

LAPD also conducted news conferences. For instance, in one case, "The press conference had been called in an attempt to relieve some of the pressure on LAPD. No solid information was released, but a number of current rumors were denied," according to Bugliosi and Gentry. They added that, within a week, "On October 23, LAPD very hastily called another press conference, to announce that they had a clue to the identity of the killer—singular—of the five Tate victims."[96]

Limited Information Release Policies

Reporters and other media personnel sometimes express frustration with members of law enforcement. Media discontent with the serial murder investigators was expressed during the Manson murders, "The amount of information unofficially released so bothered LAPD brass that a tight lid was clamped on further disclosures. This didn't please the reporters," recalled Vince Bugliosi.[97]

In the case of the murders of Sharon Tate and her friends, there was restricted media information. When it came to the people indicted in the murders, however, there was a virtually complete lack of information, Bugliosi and Gentry recalled. The media begged for more facts.[98]

Polygraph Keys

Police investigating serial murders typically withhold several facts from the media. These facts, known only to the killer and the police, are called polygraph keys, because they can be used to weed out suspects and false confessors.

At LAPD Lieutenant Robert J. Helder's suggestion, the coroner, Dr. Thomas Noguchi, held back case specifics at his press conference. He did not specify or discuss the number or the nature of wounds, or say anything about two of the victims' testing positive for recreational drugs. And, in the same case, although LAPD informed the media that there were "no new developments," there in fact were some that went unreported.[99]

CONCLUSION

The Manson Family murders were frightening and unique events at the time of their occurrence. There was significant public and media interest, and public panic at certain times. Manson remains infamous, a cult hero to some.

The Manson murder victims were stabbed, and sometimes shot. On one occasion the killers carved a word into a victim's body. The Manson Family repeatedly wrote on walls in their victims' blood.

The mass media played a prominent and largely negative role in this case. The media followed law enforcement vehicles on high-speed freeway chases, and produced an abundance of derogatory and malicious pieces about the Tate murder victims. Chaotic media zones were created, and individuals were turned into overnight celebrities. Checkbook journalism was practiced, and the media motivated Manson and his followers.

In a sense, the Manson murders, mutilations, and messages were acts of domestic terrorism. The bloody wall writing and body carving were intended to cause fear, which they did. The explicit and implicit communication of the Manson murders was broadcast through the mass media, which was Manson's intent.

5

------·•·------

IAN BRADY AND MYRA HINDLEY

IAN BRADY AND Myra Hindley were responsible for the "Moors Murders," the most shocking crimes against children in Great Britain in some time. Brady and Hindley became perhaps the most hated people in England. Their crimes were truly terrible.

Four children and a seventeen-year-old boy died at their hands. But they did not just die. They were raped and tortured, and sometimes audiotaped and photographed during their murder, an early version of "snuff films." These crime recordings would later prove to be quite incriminating at trial.

These crimes occurred in the early 1960s. Serial murder was not as widely publicized or well known at the time. Nevertheless, there was considerable public interest in these crimes, and the media was all over the story, too. The media became a little too interested in the case, engaging in multiple acts of misconduct and behavior inimical to the investigation. The media followed the police, on the ground and through the air. Despite the best efforts of the police to conceal their activity from the media, the intrusive presence of the press was a pervasive feature of this case.

On the other hand, the police tried to use the media to its advantage. A variety of public information channels was tapped in an attempt to publicize the disappearances. To better comprehend the crimes of Brady and Hindley, seven main topics will be addressed. The criminals and their crimes will be described. The investigation, arrest, and trial will be examined. Public and media interest will be documented, and the negative effects of media coverage explored.

THE CRIMINALS

Most serial murderers work alone, but about one-fourth kill in teams, usually pairs. To better understand this phenomenon, three topics will be considered: Brady, Hindley, and the pair together.

Convicted Moors Murderer Ian Brady concluded, "What the average (if one can use the term in this context) serial killer seeks above all is power and the will to power. In this psychic ambience, power and sex are often synonymous or complementary."[1] To better understand Brady, we will examine his early life, and the influences on him. His criminal history will be explored, along with his sadism and prison problems.

Brady was born on January 2, 1938, in Glasgow, Scotland. He was named Ian Stewart, and he was the illegitimate son of a waitress and never knew his father.[2] The author of a recent study added, "Brady's childhood was entirely dysfunctional and he came to Manchester as an adolescent, with a record for petty crime to his name and a developing obsession with being a loner." He was called "a typical social misfit."[3] Until Brady reached the age of eleven he seems to have been an attentive student. Then he was enrolled in a "posh" school, along with a number of other boys from slum families, and he started to resent the more affluent students.[4]

Nazis, Nietzsche, and de Sade were among his main influences. One study reported, "As a young boy, Brady developed a keen fascination with Nazi Germany. He also developed a keen interest in the writings of the Marquis de Sade and Friedrich Nietzsche, focusing particular attention on Nietzsche's theories of Ubermensch."[5]

Brady had an extensive criminal history. One author wrote, "At a young age Brady burgled houses which got him time in prison." As a youth, he received probation on two different occasions, once for theft and again for housebreaking. In 1954, the court sent him to live with his mother and stepfather in Manchester. He was sentenced to two years for theft a week after turning eighteen, and in 1958 he was charged with murder, but pled guilty to drunk and disorderly conduct instead.[6]

It should come as no surprise to discover sadism in Brady's character. After all, he read and admired de Sade's writing. As a youth, Brady had earned a reputation as a neophyte sadist, torturing children and animals "for fun," Newton noted. Wilson and Seaman agreed. They added, "It becomes clear in retrospect that Brady always had a streak of sadism."[7]

Brady had some difficulty in prison. He conducted hunger strikes on numerous occasions. He was transferred from prison to a mental institution.

"Since 1999 he has been force-fed after going on hunger strike," according to one report. Another writer concurred, adding that "Brady has sought permission in vain to be allowed to starve himself to death."[8] Behavior like that got him transferred to the Ashworth Specialty Hospital in Merseyside.[9]

Hindley remains a controversial participant in the Moors Murders. Was she a willing co-killer, or forced into helping a madman? We will examine four topics, including her childhood, her feelings for Brady, her involvement in the murders, and her death. Hindley was born in Crumpsall, a northern suburb of Manchester, on July 23, 1942.[10] Her childhood sounded idyllic, as described by one source, "Hindley grew up in the Gorton suburb of Manchester and came from a stable, loving, working class background." Later in life, when she was eighteen, Hindley seemed like a normal girl from an ordinary family background, a convert to Catholicism who loved animals and children.[11]

"Myra Hindley harboured a crush on Brady for a year until he finally responded," recalled the British Broadcasting Corporation (BBC). Newton agreed, adding that Hindley fell in love with Brady on sight, writing endless declarations of eternal love in her diary. However, she was too timid and afraid to approach him. According to Wilson and Seaman, "within weeks, Myra was in love."[12]

The big question centered on the nature of Hindley's involvement in the case. Some thought she was an innocent victim of a bullying boyfriend. Others believed her to be equally culpable with Brady.

"Hindley now claimed to be a reformed Catholic woman who had acted under the influence of Brady, and that she had only carried out murder because Brady had abused her and threatening [sic] to kill her family if she did not," one recent report stated. She also claimed that Brady blackmailed her into serving as his accomplice, by drugging her and taking compromising photographs.[13]

On the other hand, some doubt her protestations of innocence. BBC News correspondent Peter Gould noted, "It was Hindley who helped to entice the children into the car, and Hindley who drove the vehicle onto the Moors. . . . Brady could not drive." Brady sent a letter to the London press in January, 1990, alleging that Hindley injured Pauline Reade's nose and forehead and performed "some form of Lesbian assault."[14]

The end for Hindley came on November 15, 2002. She passed away in West Suffolk Hospital in Bury St. Edmonds. Hindley died from a chest infection she developed in the hospital after a heart attack.[15]

They met at the workplace. She fell in love instantly, but he didn't notice her for a year. We will examine how they met, how they were together, and their breakup.

"They had met whilst working at a chemical company in Manchester, Millwards, him a stock control clerk, she a shorthand typist," one source claimed. According to another, "Ian and Myra met while working for a chemical company in Hyde, Greater Manchester." According to an encyclopedia and the BBC, they met at Millwards Merchandising; another study called Millwards a chemical factory.[16]

"As their love blossomed they became more obsessed with Nazi paraphernalia, pornography and sadism," one report concluded. According to another source, Brady introduced Hindley to German white wine, and she rode behind him on his motorbike. He frequently talked about the Nazis, and he liked to call her Myra Hess. They attempted to commit armed robberies, but Brady lost his nerve. Myra took shooting lessons and acquired a driver's license for plans that never came to fruition.[17]

Their breakup, like that of many people, was not entirely amicable. At his trial, Brady "burst into obscenities" when Hindley testified against him. He has not been happy with her since that time.

Over the years they grew apart. Brady seemed to accept his guilt and his responsibility while Hindley never stopped protesting her innocence. She increasingly blamed Brady for corrupting and incriminating her. In 1970, she ended all contact.[18]

THE CRIMES

The murders and related acts of the Brady/Hindley crimes were shocking at the time, to Britons and people all over the world. In this section, we will examine the reasons why these crimes were considered so atrocious. The number of murders and the social significance of the crimes will be described. The victims will be mentioned. The motive will be examined, and mutilation and torture discussed. The criminal modus operandi and sexual molestation of victims will be considered.

The Number of Victims

It seems that there is always some doubt as to the precise number of victims attributable to any particular serial killer. That is true in the cases of Brady and Hindley, as well. Although he was convicted of three murders, and she of two and assisting with another, that is just the tip of the iceberg.

Brady was convicted of the Edward Evans, Lesley Ann Downey, and John Kilbride crimes. Only later did police link him to the deaths of Pauline Reade and Keith Bennett.[19] "Ian Brady was responsible for five murders during the 1960s," one report concluded.[20] Wilson and Seaman concurred, adding that between July of 1963 and October, 1965, Ian Brady and Myra Hindley together were responsible for five child murders.[21] Another study reported that two more victims, Reade and Bennett, were added to the list after Brady and Hindley confessed to those murders in 1986.[22]

"It was estimated that they killed six young people," according to another study.[23] This is the sole estimate of its kind, specifying six crimes.

Then, after they had been in prison for a couple of decades, Brady made new admissions. "Twenty years after their arrest, Ian confessed to four new murders the police had never linked them to," according to a website on British homicide studies.[24]

"In 1987, he claimed to police that he had carried out another five killings and even said where he had buried the bodies. But the police were never able to prove whether these claims were true."[25] Newton offered a similar set of information; in August of 1987, Brady contacted the BBC, and provided incomplete information about five additional murders. These new victims included a man killed in Manchester, a woman dumped in an English canal, two victims shot in Scotland, and a victim buried on the moor.[26]

Hindley disclosed the existence of a previously unknown victim, a hitchhiker killed by the murderous couple. Linda Calvey, a former cellmate of Hindley, disclosed in 2004 that she had been told about the death of the female hitchhiker by Hindley. When Calvey asked Hindley why she had not mentioned the murder before, Hindley reportedly said, "Would you declare somebody nobody had ever mentioned?"[27]

In addition to the deaths of Downey and Kilbride, Brady and Hindley were prime suspects in approximately eleven other murders, according to Publications International Ltd.[28] In a rather vague estimate, Brady and Hindley's brother-in-law David Smith recalled that Brady had said there were undiscovered bodies. "Smith also told police the couple had bragged about having killed others and buried them on the moors."[29]

Social Significance of the Crimes

These crimes stunned England. They were unusual acts of unspeakable horror, involving photographing and audiotaping the torture and murder of children. That is perhaps why these murders attained an unusual status as instant legendary events.

"One of the ghastliest series of child murders in England's history," was the term used by Publications International Ltd.[30] Another author agreed, calling the crimes "the most reviled crimes in Britain some four decades after they happened."[31] "The Moors Murders were perhaps the most shocking crimes of the 20th century in Britain," declared the BBC.[32]

BBC correspondent Gould put the Moors Murders case in perspective, "The Moors murders shocked the public like few other crimes of modern times. The case is fixed in the memory of anyone old enough to remember the terrible search on Saddleworth Moor, as police officers with spades looked for the graves of missing children. More than thirty years later, Ian Brady and Myra Hindley remain two of the most reviled people in Britain."[33]

The Victims

There were five known victims of Brady and Hindley. This section examines the Reade, Kilbride, Bennett, Downey, and Evans murders. Some information about the victims and the crimes will be shared.

The first Brady/Hindley murder was that of Pauline Reade. She was a sixteen-year-old on her way somewhere when she encountered her killers. There is disagreement about precisely where she was headed.

"Pauline Reade disappeared on her way to a disco," noted the respected British newspaper, *Guardian Unlimited*.[34] Another news service agreed, adding that Reade was sixteen when she vanished on her way to a disco near her home in Gorton, Manchester.[35]

Reade vanished on July 12, 1963, when Hindley asked her to help her find a missing glove. She drove them to Saddleworth Moor, where Brady "pounced upon Pauline and raped her. He then smashed her skull with a shovel and slashed her throat with a knife."[36] It is worth noting that Reade lived two doors down from David Smith, Brady and Hindley's brother-in-law.[37]

"Brady pounced upon Pauline and smashed her skull with a shovel. He then subjected her to a savage rape before slitting her throat with a knife, her spinal cord was nearly severed and she was almost decapitated," one study recalled.[38] According to the BBC, she was on her way to a dance at a railwaymen's club in Manchester, and she was promised a stack of records in return for her help.[39]

But Reade was the one who needed help. Seaman and Wilson recalled that Pauline Reade's body was found lying as though discarded, her clothes in disarray. She had been raped, and her throat had been slashed.[40]

Twelve-year-old John Kilbride disappeared on November 23, 1963.[41] He was tricked, then murdered, as one source recalled. After they lured Kilbride to the moor, Brady sexually assaulted him before killing him.[42]

Kilbride was helping a market stall vendor in Ashton-on-Lyne, after he and his friend John Ryan had watched a movie earlier in the town cinema, when he was enticed away by Hindley. Brady tried unsuccessfully to stab the boy to death, but the knife blade was too dull. So, he strangled him with a pair of shoelaces.[43]

A slightly different version of events was related by another source. It claimed that "On the moor, Brady subjected John to a sexual assault and attempted to strangle him with a length of string but it didn't work so he stabbed him to death."[44] According to the BBC, Kilbride was abducted from Ashton-under-Lyne.[45]

The missing glove story was also used on Kilbride, with success. According to Seaman and Wilson, "In fact, Myra said, she was fairly certain that he had raped John Kilbride. He had explained that he had strangled him because the knife he had was too blunt to cut his throat."[46] Newton added that Kilbride was another victim of Brady and Hindley.[47] Kilbride's disappearance occurred about four months after the Reade crime.[48]

The third victim was Keith Bennett. The twelve-year-old was last seen on June 16, 1964.[49] Bennett simply seemed to vanish after leaving his home in Chorlton-on-Medlock in Manchester.[50]

"The third Moors Murder victim was another 12-year-old, Keith Bennett from Chorlton. He was walking to his grandmother's house on the evening of 16 June 1964 when Hindley enticed him into her minivan," declared a report. It added that Brady strangled the boy with a belt.[51] Hindley stated that she lured the lad by asking him to help her move some heavy cartons. Brady admitted raping the boy before strangling him.[52] Kilbride was last seen in the vicinity of the home where Brady's mother resided.[53]

Lesley Ann Downey was ten years old, and was "lured away from a funfair to her fate."[54] Her fate would not be fun, unfortunately. The child had been at a fair at Ancoats, along with her two younger brothers, when Brady and Hindley successfully used the box-moving ploy again.[55] Newton added that Downey just seemed to vanish, when she turned up missing without any clues on December 26, 1964.[56]

Edward Evans was the oldest victim, and he fought ferociously for his life. Seventeen at his death, he "died in a hail of axe blows."[57] Evans had been struck with an axe fourteen times, according to the autopsy, and the victim had also been strangled.[58] A similar version was rendered by another study, which suggested that Evans "was lured to Brady and Hindley's house and hacked to death on October 6, 1965."[59]

The Evans murder "was more bloody than the others, due to the victim's age," declared another source. It added that, "Brady had sprained his ankle in the struggle."[60] Another source observed, "Brady picked up 17-year-old homosexual Edward Evans, on 6 October 1965. Brady tied up Evans in his home and invited Smith over. Brady then smashed Evans [sic] skull in with an axe in front of Smith, who was horrified."[61]

Evans had been located in and enticed from Manchester Central Station by Brady and Hindley. According to the BBC, Smith walked in "and was confronted by Brady axing to death 17-year-old Edward Evans, a stranger who he had met earlier that evening in a local pub."[62]

Brady and Hindley were low on cash. "We'll have to roll a queer," Brady reportedly told Hindley. Brady indeed killed Evans with a combination of strangulation and fourteen hatchet blows, Newton claimed.[63]

Motive

The issue of motive was never directly addressed in their trials. We do not know for certain why Brady and Hindley decided to commit their crimes. Some motives have been suggested, and we will consider a few. "No motive, really, except perhaps sex, the desire to dominate and fun," speculated one source.[64]

Pleasure is another possible motive. The BBC reported, "Each time they elaborated on the process, taking more time over it, drawing out the agony for their victims and maximizing their own perverted pleasure." Hindley claimed that Brady considered power to be a motive. According to Myra, Brady informed her that killing a victim gave him a unique sense of personal power.[65]

Pride and power are a lethal combination. Brady was proud of his crimes because of the sense of power. Newton noted that Brady bragged about his murders in prison, telling other inmates that he had "three or four" victims planted on the moors. There is some feeling that power was behind these crimes. For instance, Wilson and Seaman observed that the Moors Murder case was all about power, not sex.[66]

Mutilation and Torture

There is some evidence of victims being tortured prior to death, and mutilated afterward. The photographic and aural records created and maintained by the killers revealed their treatment of their victims. It also incriminated the killers.

"The photographs and tape recording of Leslie's [sic] torture," were mentioned by a recent study. A different source recalled, "Sometimes the victim was subjected to rape and mutilation then killed and buried." A British homicide study group referred to "the screams of one girl's torturous end."[67]

Modus Operandi

There was considerable variation in aspects of the Brady/Hindley murders. For example, the murder methods used varied from strangling to stabbing to the use of both. Nevertheless, it is possible to offer some generalizations about the modus operandi (MO).

UKOnline.com offered a nice summary: "Brady and Hindley would cruise around Manchester, looking for a victim. They would then bribe them into their vehicle, and drive out to moors, using various excuses. Brady would then sexually assault the victims, and kill them. This was done in a variety of ways—slashing of the throat, strangulation, and with Evans, Brady hit him repeatedly over the head with an axe, and finished it by strangling him with some electric flex."[68]

Sexual Molestation

Sexual violation of the victims was a signature aspect of these crimes, present in almost every case. "Brady would sexually assault their victim," recalled one source. "Most of their victims were children whom they would sexually molest before killing," a recent analysis noted.[69] Newton recalled Brady's rape of his victims.[70]

THE INVESTIGATION

The Brady/Hindley investigation began the day after the assassination of American President John F. Kennedy. Searchers looking for John Kilbride used "tracker dogs" and soldiers from the Ladysmith Barracks, as well as cadets from the Police Training School at Preston. Chief Inspector Stebbing called a news conference to appeal for assistance.

"I am appealing for volunteers for a search that will continue till dawn if necessary," Stebbing pleaded. An estimated two thousand citizens responded to the request, and "They scoured derelict houses, canals, reservoirs, parks, woods, and every square foot of wasteland." Because of the police preoccupation with the Kilbride search, the Ashton newspaper *The Reporter* informed readers that, "Ashton police announce that owing to pressure of work the Police Dance in the Mecca Ballroom is cancelled."[71]

Newly appointed Detective Chief Inspector Joseph Mounsey interviewed the Kilbride family in an attempt to gather some previously overlooked valuable clues or information. Mrs. Kilbride offered what little she knew. She told Mounsey, "Things have to go on, don't they, we hardly ever mention John's name now." She added that she still hoped police would locate her son's body; "People should have a Christian burial, shouldn't they?"[72]

Thirteen months after the Kilbride disappearance, British police were again searching for a vanished child, Leslie Ann Downey. Williams recalled the intensity of the police search, "This time the police gritted their teeth. God, we'll find this one or else." She had disappeared at the fair.

After the fair closed for the evening, every piece of fair equipment was taken apart and searched, as the upset and distraught mother watched. And the next day and evening, the police photographers worked overtime to create photographs of the missing girl, and policemen went door-to-door showing the residents the pictures and asking for help, Williams recalled. He added that police cadets and fire-brigade trainees were enlisted in the search efforts to supplement regular police officers. Philips Park Cemetery was thoroughly searched, the Ashton canal was dragged and emptied of years of rubbish, and virtually every inch of territory was carefully examined.[73]

The murders occurred in different local police jurisdictions. The Ashton police headquarters was the site for a meeting of the five police forces involved. The Cheshire, Manchester City, Yorkshire, Lancashire, and Derbyshire police were represented. Chief Superintendent Arthur Benfield was placed in overall charge of the investigation.[74]

The single most important break in the investigation was David Smith's telephone call to the police. This call will be described later in this chapter. After Smith told the police his story, Police Superintendent Robert Talbot was called. "Sorry, boss, looks like a murder, and a sticky one," Talbot was told.[75]

THE ARREST

Brady and Hindley were caught as the result of their actions. They sought to include their brother-in-law, David Smith, in their homicidal activity. They thought he would be interested, but they were decidedly wrong.

Brady and Hindley decided to include Smith. So, they brought their victim Evans home, and were assaulting him when Smith walked in their home. "Smith was tough but what he witnessed horrified him and in the early hours of the next morning he made an emergency call to police which resulted in Brady and Hindley's arrest and the recovery of Evans' body," according to one analysis.[76]

Smith helped them clean up the murder scene, and move the body upstairs. He "convinced them that he would keep his mouth shut," and went home to his wife Maureen, who was Myra's sister. According to Wilson and Seaman, Smith convinced Brady that he would return the next day to help him dispose of the body. Instead, when he got home he became violently sick, and told his wife the whole story. The next morning they called the police. Newton concurred with these accounts of Smith's role in the apprehension of Brady and Hindley.[77]

At 6:07 in the morning on October 7, 1965, Smith called the Hyde Park Police Station from a roadside phone booth. He dialed the police emergency number, 999. He told the police that he was David Smith, and asked if he was speaking to the Hyde Police Station. When told that he was, he declared that he speaking from Attersley, and informed police of the murder.[78]

Smith's call sparked an immediate and serious police response. The police picked him and his wife up, and took them to the police station. There, Smith's tale motivated immediate police activity.[79]

As Talbot was about to leave the station to arrest Brady, Smith warned him that Brady was armed. Talbot then picked up the phone, and requested two dozen policemen and about a half dozen plainclothes men in a dozen patrol cars. He also brought along Policewoman Mary Slater, to deal with Myra.[80]

The police arrived at Brady and Hindley's flat at 8:19 a.m. By 8:35, Talbot decided that instead of waiting for Brady to come out, the police needed to enter the premises. He noticed Craig's Pantry Van parked on a nearby street, and he commandeered the deliveryman's long white coat to wear over his police uniform. Then, carrying a basket of loaves of bread and pastries, he walked up to the back door at 8:40. Myra answered the door, and Talbot talked his way inside, then identified himself as a policeman. After discovering Evans's body in a trunk in a locked bedroom, Talbot told the two, "I'm afraid there's a body. I shall have to ask you to come along to Hyde Station and answer a few questions."[81]

Detective Jock Carr, Talbot's sergeant and like Brady a Scotsman, accompanied Brady to the police station in one car, and Policewoman Slater escorted Myra in another. Upon arrival at the police station, at 9:33 Carr told Brady, "If ye'll step in here, ye are free to make any statement to me, which I will take down in front of Constable Fairly." Brady claimed Evans had attacked him, so he had killed Evans in self defense.[82]

Initially police only suspected Brady of complicity in the Evans murder. He was charged with that crime on October 8 at the Hyde Police Court. The hearing lasted three minutes. After it became clear that Hindley was actively involved in murders, she too was placed in police custody. Both Brady and Hindley were charged with the murders of Edward Evans and Leslie Ann Downey at Hyde Police Court on October 21.[83]

THE TRIAL

The two accused serial killers were tried at Chester Assizes, in proceedings beginning on April 19, 1966, and ending on May 6. Both defendants seemed oblivious to their surroundings, and the implications and potential consequences of their situation. Myra affected a disinterested, scornful expression that she saw in film posters and television dramas. She had an empty look. As for Brady, he sat and sketched a series of aboriginal profiles, frightening-looking men with heavy beards and eyebrows in their eyes. He kept one hand on his knee, while the other held his chin. He had a contemplative countenance, an intellectual onlooker who had lost interest in the proceedings.

Together, she appeared to be moody, whereas he was resigned to his fate. During the trial their look never changed. They resembled a young couple sitting in a register office seeking to be married, but who are subjected to delay after delay, yet keep their composure with dignity.[84]

Both pleaded not guilty to the three murder charges. Brady was convicted on all three murder counts. Hindley was convicted of the Evans and Downey crimes. She was found not guilty in the Kilbride case, but was convicted of being an accessory after the fact. Both were sentenced to life in prison.[85]

PUBLIC AND MEDIA INTEREST

Convicted British serial killer Ian Brady asked, "Why are the mass media and the public so fascinated by serial killers, yet show not the least interest in, and quite frankly, absolute boredom with, far more prolific legalized killers?" Brady offered his own, speculative answer, "It becomes transparent that the reason why the media and public are so fascinated by serial killers is that these people kill at will, requiring no legislation, without asking for or needing permission, the very concept never entering their mind."[86]

"The murder of Lesley Ann Downey created a particularly strong reaction from the public. The reason for this is that Brady took pornographic photos of her before her death. He also tape-recorded her last fifteen minutes of life, as she pleaded for him to stop," one recent source claimed. The BBC agreed, noting that Home Secretary David Burkett opposed Brady or Hindley's release from prison, "Public opinion is almost certainly behind him on this issue, such is the hatred which Brady and Hindley engendered for their crimes and their behavior during the trial and subsequently."[87]

In the Moors Murders case the press displayed considerable interest. "The media took hold of the case, dubbing it the 'Moors Murders,' comparing it to Jack the Ripper in England's history of grisly murders. The trial became known as the 'trial of the century.'"[88]

Ernie Lewis, then a correspondent with the *Sunday Mirror,* managed to reach a British government official at home by telephone during the Moors Murders investigation. He was permitted to ask two questions. The next day, stories ran based on this telephone interview on BCC television and in the *Mirror.*[89]

In Great Britain, however, coverage of the Moors Murders case was inconsistent. As Williams recalled, "On January 8, the very next week, the case was ousted from the front page by CIRCUS DOG SAVES CHILD and CONSTABLE GOT HIS MAN AT LAUNDERETTE. . . . The following week: WATER IN BEER RUMOR SCOTCHED."[90]

NEGATIVE EFFECTS OF THE MEDIA

Convicted Moors Murderer Ian Brady has written a book about serial murder. In it, he contends that "The media's vested interest is to deliberately inflate, out of greed to sell newspapers and boost TV ratings, an immense and often dangerous public hysteria and panic regarding the serial killer."[91] Two negative consequences of the media will be examined, following the police and the creation of media zones.

Following the Police

Williams noted that as Detective Constable Gelder took photographs of a crime scene, "Circling up in the sky, a *Daily Express* plane [was] taking photographs." He also described a car chase scene, where the press scrambled to follow investigators. "It was like a film chase, only this was the police being chased, by the press. Back through Glossop, then Stalybridge (What is this, a mystery tour?), then to the right. And up."[92]

Media Zones

The media created a zone of its own during the investigation into the Moors Murders case. Williams noted the effect of initial police reports of progress in the case; immediately, the police were swamped with newspapermen from everywhere. Later, when Brady and Hindley stood trial, the same phenomenon was noted, "And press press press. *Life, Time, Paris-Match, Der Stern, Quick,* eighty-flippin' five of them."[93]

In the case of Brady and Hindley, the press jumped the gun. Williams recalled that the press had somehow deciphered the police telegram about the discovery of bodies. The Manchester *Evening News* headlines dominated the front page: POLICE IN MYSTERY DIG ON MOORS. A scrap of paper reportedly containing the name of a person who vanished two years ago had been discovered by the police. At this time, the name Brady had not been mentioned in the papers, not even in connection with the Evans case.[94]

PUBLIC RELATIONS ASPECTS

There was a concerted public information effort in this case. While not a truly organized campaign, there was considerable activity. We will examine tactical communication use of television, outdoor advertising, posters, and news conferences.

Television

Williams added a description of an important use of television in this case; the appearance of a murdered child's sister on local television. On Wednesday the thirtieth, there was an event previously unheard-of in British television. Little Linda Downey appeared on a Grenada television program, with Lesley's mother watching at home, and made a public appeal for information about her missing sister.[95]

Outdoor Advertising

Extensive use of outdoors was also manifested in the Moors Murders case. Williams added a brief description of both billboards and transit ads used in this case. Everywhere could be seen the candid little face looking out from billboard, bus front, and station platform.[96]

Posters

Posters were also used widely in this case. According to Williams, "207 fairground visitors interviewed, 6,000 others, 500 handbills, 6,000 posters." After another murder in the series, "Meanwhile, a poster had been circulated of the same snap blown up to monster size: HAVE YOU SEEN THIS BOY? Where was he?"[97]

News Conferences

During this investigation, there were periods of time where the police held two news conferences daily.[98] This is not typical. But some cases have seen more.

CONCLUSION

The Moors Murders were landmark events in the United Kingdom. Since that day, there has been an increasing incidence of serial murder, there and in the United States as well. Today serial murder is not uncommon in either country.

The five murders committed by Brady and Hindley were cruel and sadistic acts. So was the accompanying behavior, like audiotaping the murders and taking photographs of murders and grave sites. Ironically, these communication records meant to gratify the killers resulted in their conviction and incarceration.

There was additional communication activity by the killers, equally incriminating. Police found incriminating written crime records and a notebook. These rhetorical artifacts were used against the pair at their trials.

Mass communication played a major role in this case. There was considerable public and media interest. This led to a variety of media transgressions, from following the police to the creation of chaotic media zones. Public relations efforts took a variety of forms.

6

ANGELO BUONO JR. AND KENNETH BIANCHI

ANGELO BUONO JR. and Kenneth Bianchi collectively were the Hillside Strangler. A journalist who was unaware that there were two killers apparently bestowed the nickname. But they acted in concert, like the adoptive cousins they in fact were.

Their 1977–78 killing rampage terrified Los Angeles. They raped, tortured, and murdered their victims, before depositing them at dumpsites in suggestive and posed positions. They degraded and demeaned their victims before death.

The mass media played a major role in this case. On a positive note the media provided public safety information, motivated the police, and assisted in the apprehension of the killers. But the media also seriously interfered with the investigation, created media zones, and invented celebrities. There were instances of checkbook journalism, and the media coverage motivated the murderers. In addition, much of the media coverage was sensationalized.

The Hillside Strangler crimes deserve our enhanced understanding. To assist in this task, this chapter presents nine main sections. The criminals and the crimes will be described. The investigation, arrests, and trials will be considered. Media and public interest will be examined, as will the positive and negative consequences of the media, and the public relations aspects.

THE CRIMINALS

Angelo Buono and Kenneth Bianchi are better known as the Hillside Strangler.[1] But there were two individuals at work, not one as the nickname implied. Therefore, we will examine both Kenneth Bianchi and Angelo Buono in this section.

Kenneth Alessio Bianchi was born May 22, 1951, in Rochester, New York.[2] One source claimed that "His biological mother was an alcoholic prostitute and she gave him up for adoption at birth." An Internet site devoted to this case also observed that Bianchi was "the son of an alcoholic prostitute."[3]

"He was adopted at age three by Frances Bianchi and her husband," one source noted. His adoptive father died when Bianchi was thirteen. As a youth, Bianchi was troublesome. "Early on, there were strong indications that there would be problems later on in Kenny's life. He was a compulsive liar, threw violent tantrums, and although he showed signs of artistic talent and above average intelligence, he was an underachiever in school."[4] Another source added, "By 11 he was behind in his schoolwork and had tantrums." O'Brien added that by the time Kenny was eleven, his disinterest in school and his violently angry "acting out" outbursts at home were of considerable concern to his adoptive mother. He had an I.Q. of 116, which is considered to be "bright/normal," and his teachers unanimously noted that he was performing "well below his capacity."[5]

His employment record was dismal. He lurched from dead-end job to job. For a time he was employed at the California Land Title Company, and later at a similar firm, Stewart West Coast Title. He also worked at Cal Land.[6]

His psychological health was assessed by numerous mental health professionals, both in his childhood and as an adult. Frances Bianchi took Kenneth to a child psychologist who prescribed "an extensive course of therapy" for Bianchi, who was described as "a hostile child." Schwartz suggested that "Ken may have been emotionally damaged before adoption."

"It is my opinion that Kenneth Bianchi is suffering from a Dissociative Reaction, extremely severe, bordering on psychosis. This condition has been present since at least age nine," declared serial murder expert and psychologist Donald Lunde. Another mental health professional, Dr. John G. Watkins, interviewed Bianchi. He concluded that Bianchi was "a very pure psychopath."[7]

Bianchi always wanted to be a cop. "There was only one career which strongly interested Bianchi—police work," Schwartz noted. He added that Bianchi had admired policemen and women since he was a child, and he tried to join LAPD. Dr. Saul Faerstein interviewed Bianchi, and recalled that Bianchi mentioned being rejected for law enforcement jobs in New York, California, and Washington. "All these rejections by law enforcement agencies made him bitter," Faerstein concluded.

"One of Kenny's big obsessions in life was to become a police officer," one source recently observed. The British Broadcasting Corporation (BBC) added, "Bianchi, who had ironically been rejected in applications for jobs with the police departments of LA and Glendale, was bitter and very easily led." According to the History Channel, "Bianchi was bitter and impressionable after repeatedly facing rejection in his attempts to join a police force."[8]

Bianchi operated a phony psychiatry practice. According to one report "He was still a con man and a liar, going so far as renting an office so he could set up a psychiatry practice." He had a bogus master of arts diploma from Columbia University, and certificates for sex therapy as well as general psychiatric credentials.[9]

Bianchi liked sex and violence. Typically together. One source referred to his "anger and objectification of women," which presumably derived from his childhood experience. "He also had a violent temper," recalled the BBC.[10]

There is some scholarly disagreement over Bianchi's marriages. O'Brien stated that Bianchi married Brenda Beck, a childhood friend, but the marriage only lasted for a couple of months. According to Schwartz, Bianchi married Laura (last name unknown) in 1971, and she left him eight months later.[11]

Bianchi had a minor criminal history. "Bianchi was a small-time con artist," suggested one study. According to another source, "Kenny was quite the con man."[12]

Finally, he and Angelo were pimps. The *New Criminologist* reported, "Eventually, at Buono's suggestion, the two became pimps." Bianchi needed money, so when Buono suggested operating a prostitution business, he agreed. Brady asserted, "Buono and Bianchi had terrorized a number of girls into working as prostitutes on their behalf." Another source added that "The pair were well on their way to setting up their own harem of prostitutes."[13]

Buono was born October 5, 1942, in Rochester, New York.[14] His parents were Angelo Buono Sr. and Jenny Sciolino. After his parents divorced, he and his sister Cecilia moved to Glendale, California, with their mother. "Buono was often in trouble during his teenage years and spent time in at least one reformatory," the *New Criminologist* noted.[15]

Buono attended Marshall High School. Nevertheless, he was not educated. The Crime Library noted, "Neither his religion nor public education had much impact on him. He remained uneducated throughout his life, spiritually, morally and academically."[16]

"Angelo Buono was an ugly man physically, emotionally, and intellectually. He was coarse, vulgar, selfish, ignorant and sadistic," one source stated. A website on the case agreed, "As opposed to his cousin Kenny, Angelo lacked good looks, brains and manners." O'Brien wrote, "Angelo Buono, inaptly named, looked like a gargoyle."[17]

Buono ran a car upholstery business. The Crime Library recalled that "by 1975, Buono had built himself a reasonable reputation as an auto upholsterer." Another study added that Buono "had established himself in business as a repairer of car bodies and a fine upholsterer, numbering Frank Sinatra among his clients."[18]

"A brutish sociopath" is how Buono was described by one study. Another source added that, "the overall developing portrait of Buono was that of a violent paranoid-psychopath with satyric sexual appetites."[19] He was very sick and very dangerous.

Of the two, Buono was the dominant personality. According to the History Channel, "Buono was the more dominant of the pair." The BBC added, "Seventeen years older than his cousin, Buono was definitely the dominant of the pair."[20]

His sexual appetite was enormous and perverted. His first wife divorced him because she did not enjoy being sodomized regularly. He seduced his fourteen-year-old stepdaughter and his own teenage son. According to one study, "Buono did not see sex as an act of love between two people, he saw it as an act of dominance and aggression." Along the same line, the Crime Library added, "Despite his need for sex and the practicality of occasionally being decent to a woman in order to get as much sex as he needed, he had a deep loathing for women and a desire to humiliate and injure them." The History Channel and the BBC noted Buono's "insatiable sexual appetite."[21]

Buono was married five times and produced eight children. The *New Criminologist* referred to four marital efforts, "all of them unsuccessful." Another source noted that Buono was married on several occasions. O'Brien placed his initial marriage to Geraldine Yvonne Vinal in June of 1955. He married Mary Catherine Castillo on April 15, 1957, and he wed Deborah Taylor in 1969. Tai-Fun Fanny Leung became his bride on March 29, 1978, and he married Christine Kizuka in 1986 while in jail.[22]

According to the BBC, Buono "was supplementing his living by working as a pimp with very brutal tendencies." Another source described him as "a sadistic pimp."[23]

Buono had an extensive crime history. "Angelo Buono did indeed have a criminal record," Brady noted. He added, "He had been in and out of police custody frequently, culminating in a term at a reformatory." He "stole cars for joyrides, and did all the things delinquents do," another source noted. According to one study, "It's not surprising that Angelo got in trouble with the law. He was sent to the Paso Robles School for Boys after he was convicted of Grand Theft Auto. His proclaimed hero and role model was the notorious rapist, Caryl Chesssman." He faced an auto theft rap in 1968.[24]

Buono was a sadist. Another study referred to him as "sexually insatiable and violently sadistic," with "a tendency towards sadism."[25]

Despite his sadistic nature and ugliness, girls flocked to him. He was "a big hit with the ladies," nicknamed the Italian Stallion. O'Brien recalled that lots of women were attracted to Buono. The *New Criminologist* concurred, adding "Bianchi was impressed by Buono's ability to attract women, especially younger girls."[26]

Buono died at age sixty-seven, on September 21, 2002. He was alone in his cell at Calipatria State Prison, in Imperial County, California. There were signs of coronary artery disease. He died in his sleep, probably after suffering a heart attack.[27]

THE CRIMES

These murders took place in a relatively limited period of time. In other respects, however, these were typical serial murders. We will examine seven dimensions of these crimes. The murders and victims will be considered, along with the number of murders. The age span of the victims, their torture, and the pace of the killings will be analyzed, along with the modus operandi and motive.

Murders and Victims

Yolanda Washington was the first known Hillside Strangler victim. She was killed on October 16, 1977, according to the History Channel. Caputi claimed that the killing took place on October 17.[28]

"Their first victim was Yolanda Washington, a leggy black prostitute," the BBC reported. The body was intentionally dumped where it would be found, at the Forest Lawn Cemetery.[29]

Police records identified the remains as those of Washington. She had an arrest record for prostitution. She worked the Hollywood Boulevard and was a part-time waitress.[30] A final note about the Washington murder. It is believed that she and Buono were acquainted. Brady asserted that Buono had known Yolanda Washington.[31]

The next victim was Judith (AKA Julie) Miller. She was found on Alta Terrace Drive, in Glendale. According to Brady, she was found on Alta Terrace Drive in La Crescenta on the morning of November 1, 1977.[32]

"The nude body of 15-year-old runaway Judy Miller is found in a garden in La Crescenta, a suburb near Glendale, California," a Hillside Strangler website claimed. It had been deposited on an anthill. The Crime Library explained that the tarp covering her body had been placed there by a neighbor.[33]

Lissa Kastin was found a week after the discovery of Miller. According to one source, a jogger found Kastin's body on the grounds of the Chevy Chase Country Club. The twenty-year-old worked as a dancer and as a part-time waitress. Another source suggested that Kastin was found near the Glendale Country Club, and that Kastin was a twenty-one year old waitress.[34]

Kastin was found on Chevy Chase Drive, according to a Hillside Strangler website, and her first name was Elissa. The Crime Library said that Kastin was twenty-one, and worked at the Healthfaire restaurant near the intersection of Hollywood and Vine. And, "She had made a comment to her mother that she was thinking of turning to prostitution to earn some extra money." As they murdered her, Buono shouted, "Die, cunt, die!"[35]

Jill Barcomb may have been the next Hillside Strangler victim. The eighteen-year-old was last seen at the intersection of Sunset Boulevard and Poinsettia, before the discovery of her nude body on November 10 at Mulholland Drive and Franklyn Cyn Drive. She had been arrested for prostitution in New York. "The nude body of 18-year-old prostitute Jill Barcomb is discovered in Franklin Canyon north of Beverly Hills."[36]

A seventeen-year-old high school student may have been murdered by Buono and Bianchi. Kathleen Robinson was found on November 18, 1977, at Pico Boulevard in Wilshire. Her body showed no evidence of sexual abuse. She was found clothed, on November 17.[37] Investigators nevertheless linked her to the Hillside Strangler.

The murders of Dolores Cepeda and Sonja Johnson will be considered together. After all, the girls were good friends. And they had been kidnapped, raped, and killed together, and their bodies dumped together. "The fifth and sixth victims were schoolgirls, Dolores Cepeda, 12, and Sonja Johnson, 14," Caputi noted. The History Channel recalled that on the morning of November 20, two young bodies were found in a garbage dump.[38]

Both girls attended St. Ignatius School and had been missing for about a week. They were last seen getting off a bus, and talking with someone in a two-tone sedan. One report spelled one girl's name Capeda. So did a different report, which added that the girls were last seen getting on a bus on November 13. The girls' bodies were found in Elysian Hills.[39]

Kristina Weckler was a twenty-year-old honors student at the Pasadena Art Center of Design. She lived at 809 East Garland Avenue in Glendale. The BBC report noted that Weckler was not a prostitute.[40]

"Hours after the bodies of Dolores and Sonja had been found, a third body was found in the hills overlooking Glendale. It was 20-year-old student Kristina Weckler," one report indicated. Another source noted that hikers discovered Weckler's body on a hillside near Glendale.[41]

One report placed the Weckler dump site in Highland Park. She had "mysterious puncture marks on her arms," where, it was determined, Buono and Bianchi had injected cleaning fluid.[42] Bianchi had once lived on the same street as Weckler.[43]

A couple of days later, police discovered the next Hillside Strangler victim. She was Jane King, whose body was found on November 23 near the Los Feliz off-ramp from the Golden State Freeway. Another source agreed, adding that King was twenty-eight, and her body was badly decomposed when found.[44]

King was a believer in Scientology, and an actress and model. She was last seen near Franklin and Tamarind avenues. According to O'Brien, her body was sexually violated during and after her death.[45]

Lauren Wagner was an eighteen-year-old business student. She lived with her parents in the San Fernando Valley. She was abducted from the street in front of her house.[46] Her body was found on a hill near Mount Washington on November 29. There were ligature marks, and her hands had been burned prior to her death. She was last seen in the 9500 block of Lemona, and her body was found at 1200 Cliff Drive.[47]

The next Hillside Strangler victim was Kimberly Diane Martin. She was a tall blonde prostitute who worked for the Climax Modeling Agency. She was called to Apartment 114 at 1950 Tamarind Avenue; it turned out to be vacant.[48] The seventeen-year-old Martin's body was discovered on December 13, 1977. Brady recalled that her naked body was found on December 14, "discarded in a disused lot near the City Hall."[49] The body appeared to be posed.

The final Hillside Strangler victim was Cindy Hudspeth. She was strangled and placed in her car, which was pushed off of a cliff on Angeles Crest on

February 16, 1978. The twenty-year-old lived across the street from Kristina Weckler, and was a clerk at Glendale Community College. Later police would connect her and Weckler's residence on East Garfield with the fact that Bianchi lived nearby at the same time. Her car was spotted by a helicopter, and Hudspeth's body was found in the trunk.[50]

The Number of Murders

How many victims did Buono and Bianchi account for? There is a lack of agreement on this matter. We will consider a variety of relatively similar estimates.

They killed nine young women, noted one study. Another source claimed that Buono was convicted of "killing 9 young women and dumping their nude bodies on Los Angeles area hillsides."[51] Bianchi was officially linked to fewer murders, "Kenneth Bianchi pleaded guilty to five of the murders and testified against Buono."[52]

There were nine victims, several sources say. The New Criminologist claimed that Buono and Bianchi "murdered nine California women during the 1970s." Confirming the New Criminologist, another study noted that "The bodies of strangled and brutalized women were found in and around the L. A. area. Nine in total were found."[53]

Perhaps there were ten victims. That was the conclusion of Darcy O'Brien, the author of a respected book on these crimes. Between October, 1977, and February of 1978, Bianchi and Buono raped, tortured, and strangled at least ten female victims.[54]

Approximately a dozen young women were murdered, Ted Schwartz recalled. He authored another important book on this case. In agreement with Schwartz was another source, "The murderer killed 12 young women over 4 months."[55]

We might consider a final estimate. The BBC believed that Buono and Bianchi killed more than commonly thought. They were "responsible for 14 murders across the West coast of America in the late 1970s."[56]

Victim Age Span

There is virtual consensus on one Hillside Strangler case fact. The victims were between the ages of twelve and twenty-eight. Four studies all agreed on this fact.[57]

Torture

Bianchi and Buono tortured their victims. Some were strangled to the point of death, revived, and then strangled again, and again. One had chemical substances injected into her body. Another was slowly asphyxiated using a gas stove.

"These women had all been abducted, tortured, raped by two men, and strangled to death," Fuhrman recalled. Bardsley added that "Newspapers and television stations talked of rape, abduction, torture and murder." Caputi claimed, "Their bodies showed evidence of lengthy tortures." According to another source, Buono and Bianchi's victims were young girls and women who were raped, tortured, and killed. Other authorities agree that torture was a central aspect of the Hillside Strangler crimes. Strange marks on Lauren Wagner's body "looked as though the killers were experimenting—possibly with methods of torture," according to Bardsley.[58]

Bianchi described the torture of Kristina Weckler, who was severely treated prior to her murder. They laid her on the kitchen floor with a bag over her head, connected by a hose to the gas stove. Bianchi recalled that she twisted and turned in terror before she died of suffocation. In the Wagner case, "There were also burn marks on her hands indicating that she was also tortured." And, "The two egged each other on, raping, torturing and murdering women without remorse," an Internet site dedicated to this case claimed. The *New Criminologist* also recognized the significance of torture to the crimes.[59]

The Pace of Killings

The pace of the crimes was variable. At times, the pace was very rapid. Then, it slowed down. As the Crime Library noted, eight victims were discovered in two months' time. Then the police investigation intensified, and the killers were inactive for awhile. "Everything changed Thanksgiving week when five young women and girls were found on hillsides in the Glendale-Highland Park area," Bardsley commented. During Thanksgiving week, five more bodies were discovered, O'Brien recalled. Fuhrman added that in October and November of 1977, there were six victims. According to the BBC, "Over the next eight weeks Bianchi and Buono claimed the lives of another nine women in the hills around the City of Angels."[60]

But then, the pace of the murders slowed considerably. The History Channel noted that "After November, the pace of the killings slowed down. There was a murder in December, and then one in February, but the close intensity of the investigation was not lost on Bianchi and Buono." In very similar terms, the BBC agreed, "After November's killing spree, the pace dropped off. There was another murder in December, and then another in February. But the heat was on and both cousins were becoming nervous."[61]

Modus Operandi

Modus operandi (MO) refers to the methods habitually used by criminals in their crimes. Certain characteristics typified the Hillside Strangler murders. This section will consider the Hillside Strangler MO.

"Buono and Bianchi would pose as police officers while driving at night, pull over unsuspecting women drivers, abduct them and take them to Buono's suburban home. There, they would rape, sodomize, strangle and dump their nude bodies," one study reported. Bianchi told investigators in his confession that he and Buono used fake badges to abduct prostitutes, telling them they were being taken "downtown" for booking. Nonprostitutes "were harder to manipulate," but they used ploys such as asking for directions or pretending to have car trouble to lure these victims.[62]

The similarities uniting the cases represented the MO. These included the fact that all the victims had been abducted, raped, sodomized, and strangled. All had ligature marks, and they had each been washed prior to being dumped on hillsides.[63]

Motive

What was the reason behind the Hillside Strangler crimes? Was there a specific purpose being achieved by the murders? Interpersonal competition may have been a factor. A recent analysis claimed that Buono and Bianchi "egged each other on," competing to be the "baddest" during their crimes.[64]

LAPD Detective Bob Grogan questioned Bianchi. When asked about the motive, Bianchi replied, "I'm not going to sit here and say that there perhaps wasn't something in the back of my mind as a fantasy sort of thing. It may have been just the chemistry between two people."[65]

THE INVESTIGATIONS

There were actually two investigations in this case. The first was in Los Angeles, where the police searched for the Hillside Strangler. The other was conducted in Bellingham, Washington, where Bianchi killed two women after leaving Los Angeles.

The Los Angeles probe was a difficult investigation. The police seemed almost as close to panic as the general public, because they were keenly aware of how inept and ineffective they appeared, Schwartz suggested. He added that the more bad leads and dead ends they pursued, the more bodies were discovered, and the killers were apparently beyond the ability of the police to apprehend.

"We had reached a dead end. None of our leads had proven conclusive," stated Lieutenant Phil Bullington of the Los Angeles Sheriff's Office Homicide Squad. "We had checked everything that could be checked," he concluded. "There were too many good suspects," Schwartz observed, referring to "several thousand leads."[66]

Another problem plagued the investigation—false arrests and bogus confessions. In November of 1977, the Glendale Police Department arrested Bennett Merett, who was a clerk in a clothing store. Actor Ned York confessed to being the killer, and was arrested and interrogated by LAPD.[67]

Law enforcement suspected that the killers were either policemen or journalists. At first police feared that they were looking for offenders from a law enforcement background, because the victims seemed to willingly accompany their abductors. Schwartz referred to "the possibility that a law enforcement officer might be the Strangler." And members of the media were also under suspicion; "Newspaper, radio and television reporters were checked."[68]

By the end of November 1977, the need for a more effective investigation was apparent. A task force was created, combining the efforts of LAPD, the Los Angeles Sheriff's Office, and the Glendale police. It was headed by LAPD Lieutenant Ed Henderson.[69]

The investigation used grid searches at the location where the bodies were discovered. This systematic search system failed to uncover any clues, because the murders were not committed there. To keep track of pertinent case facts, the task force created a visual chart in the task force room, which nearly covered all of the walls.[70]

Bianchi moved to Bellingham, Washington, where he killed Diane Wilder and Karen Mandic on January 11, 1979. The probe into these murders was an exemplary one. "The Bellingham Police conducted what is now considered to be a perfect crime-scene investigation. Every fact-gathering method was used."[71]

After Bianchi's arrest for these murders, later that day Bellingham Police officer Dan Fitzgerald called police departments in Los Angeles and Glendale to inform them of Bianchi's arrest. As a result of this new development in the case, the task force "was reconvened to open an intense investigation of Buono, including surveillance of his activities." Within four months of Bianchi's arrest, the task forced searched Buono's home, on April 21, 1979.[72]

Bianchi acted strangely in police custody after his arrest. He feigned insanity, as a number of alternate personalities emerged in interviews. He confessed to the Hillside Strangler crimes, but claimed that it was the fault of one of the other personalities residing in his body.[73] His behavior convinced both Dr. John G. Watkins, a professor of psychology at the University of Montana, and Dr. Charles Moffatt, a psychologist in Bellingham. However, not taken in by Bianchi were Dr. Martin Orne, from the Department of Psychiatry at Pennsylvania State University, and Dr. Saul Faerstein, a Beverly Hills psychiatrist.[74]

THE ARRESTS

Bianchi was arrested on January 13, 1979. Although he carried a weapon, since he was a security guard, he made no effort to resist. In the records of the Bellingham Police Department, it was designated Event No. 79B-00770.[75]

Buono was apprehended on October 22, 1979. This was four months after he was implicated by Bianchi.[76]

THE TRIALS

Bianchi pled guilty in Bellingham, in a plea-bargained agreement that spared him the death penalty in exchange for his guilty plea and testimony against Buono. Then he was returned to Los Angeles to testify against his cousin. The preliminary hearing in Case No. A 354231, which lasted for ten months, decided that Buono should be tried.[77]

During this hearing, Bianchi reneged on his plea deal. He recanted his testimony against Buono on June 6, 1981, in a morning court session, then in the afternoon he again confessed and implicated Buono once more, only to later recant again. Because the case against Buono depended almost entirely on Bianchi's testimony, Los Angeles County Deputy District Attorney Roger Kelly moved for dismissal of the charges against Buono.[78]

However, in a bold and unexpected move, Superior Court Judge Ronald M. George refused to accept Kelly's motion, giving a rationale explained during remarks lasting an hour and five minutes. The California Attorney General, George Beukmejian, contended that there was sufficient evidence for the trial to continue. The District Attorney's Office withdrew from the case, which was then prosecuted by the State of California.[79]

Jury selection began on November 16, 1981. The process consumed fifty-four days of court time, spread out over three and a half months. A jury of seven women and five men was selected.[80]

In Bellingham, Bianchi had been represented by Dean Brett. In L.A., Buono was represented by court-appointed attorney Gerald Chaleff, assisted by Katherine Mader. Michael Nash and Roger Boren served as prosecutors.[81]

Jury deliberations began on October 21, 1983. The verdict was decided nine days later, on Halloween. Buono was convicted on nine of ten murder charges.[82]

Buono spoke at the penalty phase of his trial. On November 16, 1983, Chaleff asked him what he thought his punishment should be. "My morals and constitutional rights has been broken," he replied. When Judge George asked him to speak louder, he repeated the same sentence, and added that "I ain't taking any procedure in this trial." Chaleff began another question, but Buono cut him off, declaring "I stand mute. I am standing mute to anything further."[83]

Sentencing took place on January 9, 1984. Buono received five life sentences. Bianchi, whose plea bargain called for him to spend thirty-five years in California prisons before being returned to Washington, was instead immediately sent back to serve two life terms in Walla Walla State Prison in Washington.[84]

MEDIA AND PUBLIC INTEREST

There was great contemporary concern over the Hillside Strangler case. Initially, this concern was manifested as fear and panic. The media was fascinated by the case.

The Hillside Strangler case terrified those in Los Angeles at the time. The mindless and spreading public terror in Los Angeles was noted by O'Brien. "The police were facing panic within the city," added Schwartz. He also noted, "Area citizens continued to live in constant fear."[85]

"People do what they always do in a panic," the Crime Library added, specifying remedies such as warning children, purchasing large dogs, carrying weapons for self-protection, and installing new locks and security systems.

Fuhrman added, "Soon the city was terrified." According to Bardsley, "The city went into a panic."[86]

"Nowhere was safe," noted one study. The Hillside Strangler case was "causing panic across the city and its suburbs," the BBC reported. Brady added that "Fear and panic were by now spreading throughout Los Angeles." In addition, "During the 1970s L.A. was terrorized by a sex killer called 'The Hillside Strangler,'" one recent analysis recalled. At the end of November 1977, "Panic ensued," one source noted.[87] Clearly, these crimes elicited a strong and fearful public reaction.

The Hillside Strangler case received enormous publicity. O'Brien reminisced about this unpleasant memory. Every morning and evening the residents of L.A. were confronted through newspapers, the radio and television with graphic, detailed and frightening news stories about the murders. There was a general public fear, approaching a certainty, that the Hillside Strangler would begin to kill again in the near future. On the day the verdict was announced, media interest was off the scale. O'Brien recalled that L.A. radio and television stations broadcasted all developments about the impending verdict at half-hour intervals.[88]

"The story of the Hillside Strangler became important news throughout the world," Schwartz observed, citing news coverage in Australia, England, France, Italy, Germany, Japan, and "countless other countries." The BBC agreed, adding that "Suddenly the Hillside Strangler was making front-page news." O'Brien recalled sensational headlines and scary stories proliferating throughout every media mode. These stories, ironically, increased the very fear they were reporting on, but they also accurately depicted reality.[89]

Yolanda Washington was the first Hillside Strangler victim. Before her death was connected to the other Hillside Strangler victims, it received relatively little media attention. The moral and journalistic calculations involved in allocating media attention in serial murder cases were explained by Schwartz, "The Los Angeles news media analyzed Yolanda Washington's death the same way as the police. The value and moral judgment may be unfair but it resulted in the news media's almost ignoring the story."[90] In the Hillside Strangler case, O'Brien explained what happened to media interest over time. On October 17, 1978, it was a year to the day after Yolanda Washington's murder. The investigation was going nowhere. The Los Angeles media had lost interest in covering the case.[91]

Coverage of serial murders varies. For instance, the death of the first victim, Washington, received minimal interest. According to the History Channel, "Her death attracted little press attention." The media did not become actively involved in covering the story until two of the victims were schoolgirls, not prostitutes, Caputi claimed. "At this juncture, media coverage exploded and public panic along with it."[92]

Not just the public panicked. So did the media. "A media panic ensued and the Hillside Strangler was front page news," the History Channel contended.[93]

POSITIVE EFFECTS OF THE MEDIA

In this case, media coverage of the crimes was beneficial in three respects. In this section, we will consider the dissemination of public safety information, motivation for law enforcement, and assistance in the apprehension of the killers.

Dissemination of Public Safety Information

There was "strong public awareness during the early discoveries of bodies." Schwartz recalled the difficult decision facing investigators, "The only action they could take would be to release the information that Buono was a suspect, hoping that people would be wary in his presence."[94]

Motivation for Law Enforcement

In the Hillside Strangler investigation, the media motivated the police. This is not uncommon in serial murder cases. "Spurred on by public criticism of their efforts, the police labored long and hard to break the case."[95]

Used to Apprehend Killers

After Judy Miller's death, there was little media coverage. So, "Salerno persuaded the newspapers to run a small story on her, along with a sketch and a request to contact the police if anyone recognized her."[96] Sadly, no one did.

NEGATIVE EFFECTS OF THE MEDIA

There were numerous negative consequences of media coverage of the Hillside Strangler case. These included interference with the investigation, checkbook journalism, the creation of media zones, celebrization, motivation for killers, and sensationalism.

Interference in the Investigation

"Blown" Stakeouts. During the Hillside Strangler investigation, "Some 'media asshole,' as Grogan phrased it, broke the LAPD code, and the undercover operation was thwarted by the presence of reporters, including TV cameras and lights. Grogan, called 'walrus' after his mustache and immensity, had to get a new code name."[97]

Following the Police. The media spent so much time following Hillside Strangler detectives working on the case, the police devised a plan to give them some space. Schwartz noted that, "As often as possible, the searches were timed to coincide with routine press conferences. . . . By sending out the men during the time the press conferences were being held, the police continued searching without interference."[98]

Tampering with Witnesses.   O'Brien criticized interfering reporters in this case. He concluded that newspapers and television stations were more interested in selling newspapers and drawing high viewership ratings than whether or not the murderers were captured or more victims killed. The reason? He contended that the relations between the LAPD and local media were at their lowest point. Reporters were interviewing witnesses, sometimes before the police found them, influencing and sometimes altering their perceptions and recollections, putting them in potential danger, and occasionally falsely claiming to be the police to obtain interviews.[99]

Checkbook Journalism

In the Hillside Strangler case, at least one person tried to make money from the crimes. George Shamshak was a twenty-seven-year-old inmate in a Massachusetts prison. He claimed to have valuable information about the Hillside Strangler case.

"He telephoned the Los Angeles *Herald Examiner,* offering to provide the paper with the exclusive right to tape recordings of at least one of the killings. The cost for this privilege would be $10,000, a discount price compared with the up to $50,000 he had already been offered by other media," Schwartz recalled.[100] There were no takers.

Creation of Media Zones

The arrest of Angelo Buono led to a media zone. O'Brien recalled that on October 22, the police finally arrested Buono, swooping down on Colorado Street trailed by the media—press and television reporters and their lights and cameras. The next July, Buono appeared in "a courtroom packed with newspeople."[101]

The Creation of Celebrities

Serial murder cases result in people being made into celebrities. Buono believed he was a celebrity. At his arrest, Angelo acted like his usual arrogant, cocky self, behaving like a celebrity, which he thought he was.[102]

Motivation for Murderers

Some murderers are motivated by the media. They relish coverage of their crimes. After their first murder, Bianchi remarked, "We really did it this time. Wait till they find her. It'll make the papers. It'll be on every channel." However, they were disappointed by the media coverage. Bianchi proclaimed, "It finally made the papers. Little dipshit story way back where nobody will read it."

O'Brien explained the role of publicity in the killer's motivation; "For nearly two weeks after Lauren Wagner, publicity and the still-warm memories of their most recent killings were enough to buoy the cousins." After another murder, "They took pleasure from the front-page photograph of Kimberly Diane

Martin." O'Brien added, "The more the news reports increased, the more pleased with themselves they became."[103]

Sensationalism

Sensationalized stories were noted in this case. Fuhrman observed cynically that "The Los Angeles media wanted its own serial killer and welcomed the opportunity, responding with graphic and sensational coverage." Brady agreed, adding that "media sensationalism" had caused public panic in this case.[104]

PUBLIC RELATIONS ASPECTS

This section presents discussion of the Hillside Strangler public information efforts. Five main types of communication tactics will be examined; radio, television, telephone hotlines, news conferences, and media kits. The LAPD media relations practices will be considered, along with Hillside Strangler case polygraph keys.

Radio

Fame came to at least one radio journalist covering the Hillside Strangler case, Jim Mitchell at KFWB. Schwartz noted that it was during the Hillside Strangler case that Mitchell attained both his greatest notoriety and created intense public awareness of the murders. His reporting elicited both the praise and the criticism of police officers working the case.

The Hillside Stranglers investigators used radio. There was "a news broadcast on *KFWB* indicating that an unknown body had been found in Glendale." The victim's father heard the broadcast, and identified his daughter's body.[105]

Television

Local Los Angeles television was used in the hunt for the Hillside Stranglers. Lieutenant Dan Cook of LAPD's public information staff was on television, discussing the murders and what police were doing. Photographs of the crime scenes were shown. A Strangler hotline number was provided, and numerous calls were received.

Television coverage of these crimes may have assisted in the identification of a victim. According to TrueCrime.com, "Police attempted to identify the body by broadcasting an artist's sketch on a local TV programme. Within minutes a man called to say that he believed the girl to be his daughter Lissa Kastin, who had been missing from her home for three days."[106]

Telephone Hotlines

The Hillside Strangler investigation also used a phone tip hotline. LAPD officer Cook mentioned the phone line during his local television appearances.

Dedicated case telephone numbers were provided, and numerous callers responded.[107]

News Conferences

There were several news conferences during the Hillside Strangler case. Some were LAPD sessions, and others were politically predicated conferences convened by the mayor of Los Angeles. Most serial murder stakeholders participated in such meetings.

Because of a lack of investigative progress, news conferences were held to mollify the media and public. One source recalled that the LAPD was reduced to holding news conferences to apologize for police inability to make any investigative progress in the case. At one such session, LAPD Chief Daryl Gates remarked, "I come to you with empty hands."

Sometimes good news was the reason for news conferences. For instance, LAPD Chief Gates conducted one news conference to announce that LAPD finally had a Hillside Strangler suspect in custody. He then released a photograph of Bianchi to the media.[108]

Media Kits

A media or press kit is an efficient way to compile a great deal of information into an organized, easily understood package. It is not a common part of serial murder cases, although this instance was not unprecedented. O'Brien referred to the "police press information kits" prepared by LAPD during this case.[109]

Police Media Relations

The Hillside Strangler case posed important tactical informational decisions. Detective Ralph Salerno asked himself, how much information about the case should he and the Glendale police disclose to the media? The more that the killers knew about what the police knew, and how police deductions were arrived at, the greater the likelihood that they would alter their methods to confuse the police and throw the investigators off their track. The killer's MO was the best lead Salerno had. And so the police departments involved decided to reveal a little case information but not much. Salerno would prefer that not even that much be released, but they always had to give the media some case facts. Otherwise, they would be forced to work harder to discover something.[110]

Polygraph Keys

Information restriction tendencies were noted in the Hillside Strangler investigation. The media publicized only a few details about the strangulation of Kimberly Diane Martin. Law enforcement agencies involved in the investigation were withholding as much information as possible.[111]

CONCLUSION

The Hillside Strangler case had a major impact on Los Angeles. The city was in a state of panic. The media did its share to cause that panic.

Media misbehavior was rife in this case. There were, however, some benefits of the intense media coverage. But, on balance, the considerable number of acts of media misbehavior outweighed the good. Public relations played a major role in this case.

The murders were horrible, sadistic events. The women were violently raped, and in many cases tortured. Buono and Bianchi were dysfunctional and merciless individuals.

7

---·•·---

JEFFREY DAHMER

JEFFREY DAHMER DID not have the happiest childhood in the world. In fact it was quite sad. His parents were temperamentally unsuited to each other. The friction resulting from the Dahmer marital strife spilled over on the rest of the family. Jeffrey seemed particularly affected. Then when he was eight, he was sexually molested by a neighborhood boy.

Before long, he began to display some of the classic early signs of a serial killer. He was cruel to children. Death fascinated him, and he experimented with animals.

His murders spanned three decades, the 1970s, 1980s, and 1990s. He also had earlier convictions for indecent exposure, sexual misconduct, and other similar offenses. Every time he was caught and convicted the sentence was light, he was given probation, or he only served a small portion of his sentence.

Seventeen murders were officially attributed to him, although the actual number may be a bit higher. But he did not just murder his victims. He decapitated and dismembered them. He dried and painted some of his victims' skulls. He cut off and saved body parts as souvenirs—genitalia, hands, and other sections. He ate some parts.

And neither the police nor the media knew a thing about it until after Dahmer's arrest. At least seventeen people died before Dahmer's murderous escapades eventually ended. And a virtual media circus appeared virtually overnight. In this chapter we will explore the Dahmer crimes, and the media interactions involved in this case.

To best understand Dahmer's crimes, and the media interaction with other serial murder stakeholders, we will consider eight main topics in this chapter. The criminal and the crimes will be profiled. The arrest, trial and conviction will be examined. Media interest will be considered, along with negative effects of media coverage, Milwaukee Police Department media relations, and public relations tactics.

THE CRIMINAL

Prior to his murder sprees, Dahmer had been convicted of indecent exposure and sexual misconduct. He was given lenient sentences, and continued in his criminal progression. How did this happen? He knew how to "play the system."

Jeffrey Dahmer had been convicted and sentenced for crimes similar to those that resulted in his eventual incarceration, but he was never severely punished. Dahmer's attorney, Gerald Boyle, defended those previous sentences at a press conference. "He had no bad marks, he was doing everything his probation officer and everyone else told him to do. I don't think anybody in the world would have thought this young man capable of doing what he is accused of doing."[1]

Jeffrey Dahmer was considered to be manipulative. Schwartz noted that the police depicted Dahmer as a master manipulator who completely persuaded them that Konerak Sinthasomphone was his lover.[2] Serial killers are frequently described as master manipulators.

He was born on May 21, 1960, at Evangelical Deaconess Hospital in Milwaukee, Wisconsin. His proud parents were Lionel and Joyce Dahmer. They named their first child Jeffrey Lionel Dahmer.[3]

His father earned an undergraduate and a graduate degree at Marquette University, majoring in electrical engineering. He earned a Ph.D. at Iowa State University.[4] Unfortunately, Jeffrey Dahmer did not find school that interesting.

Adults liked Dahmer as a child. He was obedient, respectful, and friendly. Davis recalled that most adults liked young Jeffrey. He acted polite, was very clean and neat, and seemed ready and anxious to please.[5]

It was a different story with his peers, unfortunately. "Jeffrey Dahmer had a hard time keeping friends," Davis noted. He added that by the time Dahmer began junior high school, the isolating loneliness that haunted his life was already beginning to show.[6] Perhaps this led to the initiation of his drinking.

As an adolescent, Dahmer experimented with dead animals. When Dahmer was about ten years old, it was common for people taking walks to discover animal bones in the leaves in yards and fields off West Bath Road.[7] Everitt agreed, adding that "one of Dahmer's favorite pastimes growing up was the butchering of animals. Many ended up in the pet cemetery he kept alongside his house. Others were staked to trees in the woods behind the Dahmer property."[8]

One of the formative events of Dahmer's life may have occurred when he was eight years old. His father claims that Jeffrey was sexually molested by a neighborhood boy when he was that age.[9] Newton concurred, and suggested that the 1968 sexual molestation, which went unreported at the time, may have played a significant role in Dahmer's subsequent crimes.[10] Another critical factor in Dahmer's childhood was his parent's marital problems. According to Everitt, Dahmer was raised in a home rocked by severe and unrelenting marital strife. While his parents fought each other, they paid little or no attention to Jeffrey, which meant they neglected him most of the time.[11] His parents fought over custody of Jeffrey's younger brother David, but no one seemed to particularly want him. Davis recalled Dahmer alone on the sidelines during the family dissolution, feeling left out as his home was destroyed. He no doubt felt forsaken as his parents contested custody over David, while neither parent requested him.[12]

Despite these issues, Dahmer was considered relatively bright for his age, an intelligent boy. Dahmer had a relatively high I.Q., Davis recalled.[13] Nevertheless, he only lasted one semester at Ohio State University. Too much partying, liquor in particular was a weakness.[14]

Dahmer was gay. In interviews with a probation officer, he admitted to having known as far back as high school that he was not a heterosexual. However, he adamantly refused to publicly admit his sexual preference until 1991.[15]

A psychiatrist who interviewed Dahmer concluded that he was suffering from paraphilia. This is a mental illness characterized by sexual arousal by inanimate objects, such as corpses. Dr. Frederick Berlin of Johns Hopkins University claimed that Dahmer's paraphilia made him unaware that his actions were wrong.[16]

Dahmer may have been a racist. Many of his victims were black, Hispanic, or Asian. That fact did not escape people's attention in Milwaukee. Dahmer once told a prison cellmate that he hated blacks and wanted to kill as many as he could, thousands if possible.[17]

One very important thing should be mentioned. Dahmer was an alcoholic. He drank heavily, beginning before high school. His alcohol addiction led to his dismissal from the military.[18] His drinking in public led to disorderly conduct convictions.[19]

What Dahmer did to animals as a youth both presaged his later crimes and mimicked them, but with animals instead of humans as victims. We have already learned about the boneyard near Dahmer's Ohio home. Davis observed that at about age ten, Dahmer was experimenting with living animals, bleaching bones of dead animals, killing insects by inserting them into formaldehyde, and decapitating rodents. He considered this an interesting hobby and an endeavor that satisfied him, and he would continue to pursue it in adulthood.[20] Newton concurred with Davis.[21]

Here is an important informed assessment of what set Dahmer off:

Silent rage built to white heat within him. It appeared to Jeffrey that, once again, nobody wanted him. His father had moved out and both of his parents seemed to want only David, because that was whom they were fighting over. The court wasn't the least bit interested in him; in the stack of court documents surrounding the divorce, Jeffrey was hardly mentioned at all . . . A sense of impending loneliness settled on him like a dark shroud.

Years later, police and psychiatrists would say that the paramount thing that triggered Dahmer's towering, murderous rage was simply not wanting people to leave him. If you tried to leave, you died.[22]

THE CRIMES

It is for his crimes that Dahmer will be remembered. He killed a relatively large number of victims over three decades. But he did not just kill—he kept body parts as souvenirs, and he ate parts of his victims.

To understand Dahmer's crimes, one has to examine his full repertoire of criminal activity. The murders will be considered. The souvenirs in Dahmer's apartment will be described, along with brain surgery, cannibalism, and necrophilia. These topics collectively reveal the depth and diversity of Dahmer's deviance.

The Murders

The first acknowledged victim was Steven Hicks. Hicks was hitchhiking and Dahmer gave him a ride, and after some partying at Dahmer's home he killed Hicks. This occurred on June 18, 1978.[23]

Norris suggested that the incident took place a week later, on June 25, 1978, when Dahmer encountered Hicks hitchhiking along Cleveland-Masillon Road in Bath Township, Ohio. Hicks grew up in Coventry, about fifteen miles from Dahmer's home in Bath. Dahmer told police that he and Hicks were engaged in consensual homosexual acts when Hicks tried to leave. The result was "a physical fight," Dahmer told interrogators.[24]

The next Dahmer murder victim was Steven Tuomi, twenty-eight, who was from Michigan. He disappeared about a decade later, on September 15, 1987. He was not reported as missing until 1989. Dahmer claimed credit for the murder.[25]

Tuomi was twenty-five years old, according to Norris. Dahmer said that he picked Tuomi up in Club 219 and took him to the Hotel Ambassador, where he was killed, sexually violated, dismembered, and stuffed into a suitcase. Dahmer claimed no memory of the killing, suggesting that Tuomi killed himself.[26]

James E. Doxator became another Dahmer victim in January 1988. He was a fourteen-year-old Native American boy.[27] Doxator agreed to accompany Dahmer back to his apartment, where he was drugged and killed. His mother, Debra Vega, reported him missing on January 18, 1988.[28] The interval before the next murder would be brief.

Two months after Doxator's disappearance, Dahmer committed another serious crime. Richard Guerrero met Dahmer, and was killed at Dahmer's West Allis, Wisconsin, residence. This was March of 1988.[29] Dahmer encountered Guerrero at the Phoenix Club. He took him to the basement apartment at his grandmother's house in West Allis on March 18.[30]

Anthony Sears met Dahmer at LaCage Bar. Dahmer again killed his victim in the basement at his grandmother's house. Sears died sometime on March 25, 1989.[31] Dahmer and Sears had met the day before, on Easter Sunday. Sears was dismembered and disposed of, except for his head, which Dahmer admired and kept.[32]

A little more than a year later, in June 1990, Dahmer killed again. This time the victim was Edward W. Smith. Dahmer took Smith back to Dahmer's apartment, where he first drugged him and then murdered him.[33] According to Norris, Smith was nicknamed "the Sheik," and was murdered on June 14, 1990.[34]

Club 219 in Milwaukee was where Dahmer met his next victim, a month after the Edward Smith murder. Raymond Smith, who went by the street name Ricky Beeks, was killed in July 1990.[35] Another source suggested that Beeks/Smith was killed on May 29, prior to Eddie Smith's demise. Dahmer boiled the skin off from the skull and kept the cranium.[36]

Two months later, Dahmer killed again. Ernest Miller was murdered on September 3, 1990. Miller left his aunt's house and seemed to vanish. According to Dahmer, he picked Miller up outside of a bookstore on North Twenty-seventh Street in Milwaukee, then took him home and killed him.[37] Miller lived in Chicago, and the last his family saw of him was at the Golden Rule Church of God and Christ on September 2, 1990. He seemingly vanished after his late-afternoon stroll.[38]

Dahmer killed about three weeks later. David C. Thomas was reported missing by his girlfriend. He died on September 24, 1990, in Dahmer's apartment.[39] Another source suggested that Thomas disappeared on September 10, 1990. According to Dahmer he met Thomas near the Grand Avenue Mall, lured Thomas to his apartment, and the result was another grisly death.[40]

Curtis Straughter became Dahmer's tenth murder victim on February 18, 1991. He was last seen by his grandmother. He encountered Dahmer near Marquette University, and the two wound up at Dahmer's apartment, where Straughter was killed.[41] Straughter, an eighteen-year-old, called himself Demetra. He had dropped out of high school, and belonged to Gay Youth Milwaukee. Dahmer strangled Straughter, and once more kept the skull after boiling the skin away.[42]

On April 7, 1991, about two months later, Errol Lindsey was killed. He was last seen by his sister, as he left to go to the store. Dahmer said that he met Lindsey at the corner of Twenty-seventh and Kilbourn. Dahmer then took Lindsey to his apartment, where he was killed.[43] Lindsay sang in the Greater Spring Hill Missionary Baptist Church choir. After Dahmer killed him, he was dismembered and decapitated, and the skull was retained as a souvenir.[44]

Dahmer met his next victim a month and a half later. Anthony Hughes was a deaf-mute. He met Dahmer at Club 219 on May 24, 1991, and died later that day.[45]

Dahmer said that he wrote Hughes a note on that evening, inviting him to Dahmer's apartment to watch some videos. Dahmer made a bizarre organic statue from Hughes's remains. His decapitated head was cupped in his dismembered hands.[46]

On May 26, 1991, Konerak Sinthasomphone disappeared. The next day, police investigated a call and found a drugged and incoherent Konerak in the street. It seems that Konerak, although drugged and probably shackled, managed to escape from Dahmer's apartment. When Dahmer arrived on the scene, he convinced the police that the two of them were lovers and that Konerak was drunk, so the police let them go. Dahmer immediately took Konerak back to his apartment and killed him.[47] Their decisions that evening would have profound and long-lasting consequences for police officers John A. Balckerak, Joseph Babrish, and Richard Porubcan.[48]

A month later, Dahmer killed his next victim. He met Matt Turner at a bus station in Chicago, after a Gay Pride Parade. He murdered and dismembered Turner, parts of whom were later secured by the police in Dahmer's apartment.[49] Turner was twenty years old at the time of his death. His head wound up in Dahmer's freezer, while the torso went into the fifty-seven gallon drum to decompose with other parts.[50]

Within five days Dahmer killed again. This victim, on July 5, 1991, was Jeremiah Weinberger, a twenty-three-year-old who met Dahmer in Carol's Speakeasy, a bar on Wells Street. Dahmer took him home, killed, and dismembered him.[51] Weinberger stayed two days with Dahmer, then was killed as he attempted to depart.[52]

Oliver Lacy became Dahmer's next victim. He was killed on July 15, 1991.[53] Dahmer claimed to have met Lacy on Twenty-seventh Street and Kilbourn. Lacy had a two-year-old son, and a fiancée named Rose Colon. Lacy's head was discovered on the bottom shelf of Dahmer's refrigerator.[54]

The last known Dahmer victim was Joseph Bradehoft. The twenty-five-year-old Bradehoft met Dahmer at a bus stop. Dahmer took him to his apartment and killed him.[55] This final victim was the married father of three children. He had journeyed to Milwaukee in search of employment. His head was recovered from Dahmer's freezer.[56]

Dahmer met Tracy Edwards on July 22, 1991, three days after the Bradehoft murder. But unlike previous Dahmer "visitors," this one escaped and flagged down a police car. Dahmer was arrested.[57]

Souvenirs

But Dahmer did not just kill his victims. He played with their corpses, kept parts as souvenirs, and ate other parts. Wilson and Wilson described what police found in Dahmer's apartment:

> The freezer compartment of the refrigerator contained meat in plastic bags, one of which ominously looked like a human heart. Another freezer contained three plastic bags, each one with a severed head inside. A filing cabinet contained three skulls—some painted gray—and some bones; a box contained two more skulls, and an album full of gruesome photographs. Two more skulls were found in a kettle, while another contained some severed hands and a male genital organ. The blue plastic barrel proved to contain three male torsos.[58]

A slightly different inventory of the refrigerator contents was provided by Everitt. He noticed the presence of human heads, intestines, kidneys, lungs, livers, and a heart in the freezer and refrigerator. Scattered and strewn around the rest of Dahmer's apartment were numerous other horrible momentos, including rotting hands and genitalia, and bones, with skulls, complete skeletons, and small, broken bits.[59]

The initial official skull tally was conducted at Dahmer's apartment the night of his apprehension. It was conducted by Medical Examiner Jeffrey Jentzen. He counted seven skulls, and four heads that still contained some flesh. There was evidence of eleven different bodies.[60]

Another slightly different quantification of Dahmer's human souvenirs was provided by Lane and Gregg. They noted that a total of nine severed heads was discovered. Two were in the refrigerator, and seven others were in various stages of having the flesh stripped from the skull. Four male torsos were wedged into a barrel, and numerous pieces of male genitalia were stored in a pot. Dahmer's apartment was littered with pieces of human bodies and limbs, and the overpowering smell was unbearable.[61]

Brain Surgery

This is one of the strangest aspects of this case, but also a somewhat logical one. Dahmer experimented with amateur brain surgery, in an attempt to create compliant, submissive sex partners he could keep in his apartment. This fact was disclosed at Dahmer's trial.

"Subject used to perform rudimentary brain surgery on his live but drugged victims via holes bored through their skull with an electric drill," declared Dr. Frederick Fosdal after examining and interviewing Dahmer. Fosdal further explained that Dahmer sought to create "Zombie-like creatures," who would be "subject to Dahmer's will."[62]

Cannibalism

Perhaps the most revolting of Dahmer's criminal activity was his cannibalism. He claimed that he had used salt, pepper, and steak sauce to season the bicep of a victim, which he consumed.[63] Dahmer was definitely a cannibal, according to Wilson and Wilson.[64]

Necrophilia

Dahmer was getting further out of control much of the time. Killing was no longer enough. In 1991 he initiated some awful new crimes. These included necrophilia, which is having sexual acts with the body of a deceased person, Davis recalled.[65] According to Norris, "The experts also pointed to Dahmer's necrophilia, his need to have sex repeatedly with the corpses of his victims."[66]

THE ARREST

In the Dahmer case there was no prearrest investigation, because law enforcement was completely unaware of these serial murders. It was not until Edwards escaped and flagged down a police car that Dahmer faced any threat from the police. Dahmer's arrest was not a peaceful event, as we shall learn.

Milwaukee Police Department officers Robert Rauth and Rolf Mueller were patrolling their District Three beat in the vicinity of Twenty-fifth Street and Kilbourn on July 22, 1991, at approximately 11:35 p.m., when they observed a black male with handcuffs dangling from his left wrist running in what seemed to be a state of panic. The two officers were only a half-hour away from the normal end of their four-to-midnight shift. Another account noted that it was nearly 11:30 when Squad 31 officers Rauth and Mueller spotted a terrified Edwards.[67]

After Edwards began to describe his encounter with Dahmer to the policemen, they returned with him to Dahmer's apartment.[68] Dahmer answered their knock on the door to Apartment 213 at the Oxford Apartments. When asked by the police for his version of events, Dahmer explained, "We were just drinking some beer. I lost my job."[69]

The trouble began when the police asked Dahmer to unlock the handcuff on Edwards's wrist.[70] He refused, and a struggle broke out between Dahmer and the policemen, "a wrestling match that spilled them into the living room." Another source referred to the altercation in this way, "Suddenly the three of them began spilling and tumbling into the living room, crashing across the floor, and yelling as they fought for control." Perhaps the most dramatic aspect of the fight was Dahmer's primal scream. "Then there was a sudden, long ear-splitting scream that seemed to penetrate through the walls and out into the street. It was a scream so profound in its misery that the people who heard it were frightened, and saddened at the same time. This was Dahmer's scream of acquiescence, a primal scream, a death scream."[71]

Dahmer was initially detained and placed under arrest by Rauth and Mueller. He was subsequently transferred to the custody of detectives Patrick Kennedy and Michael Dubis of the Wisconsin Criminal Investigation Bureau.[72] Dahmer was definitely cooperative with the authorities after his arrest.

"They found a suspect willing to talk to them," Norris noted. He added, "He was ready to talk . . . Dahmer was anxious to release himself from the secrets he had been carrying since his first homicide back in Ohio in 1978."[73]

THE TRIAL

Dahmer was initially charged with four murders, on July 25, 1991. Bond was set at $1 million. Eight more murders were added to the indictment on August 6, and Dahmer's bail was raised to $5 million. Dahmer was charged with an additional three killings on August 22, bringing the total of Wisconsin murder charges to fifteen.[74]

Judge Laurence C. Gram presided over the trial.[75] This trial differed from many in that there was only one legal issue being contested—Dahmer's ability to stand trial and assist in his defense. According to Norris, "Both the defense and prosecution agreed that Dahmer exhibited abnormal behavior. The question they debated was whether that behavior was abnormal enough to be considered the result of a mental disease; one which diminished Dahmer's capacity to form judgments so that he was unable to conform his actions to the law."[76]

The Dahmer crimes touched off vehement reactions and strong opinions. One source asserted that the court made a sincere attempt to accommodate the exceptionally substantial levels of public dismay, post-traumatic disorder, anguish, anger, and grief.[77]

Dahmer's trial began on January 22, 1992. He pled guilty but insane, but on February 15, the jury declared him fit to stand trial. He was given fifteen consecutive life sentences, requiring him to serve 936 years before being eligible for parole.[78]

MEDIA INTEREST

Jeffrey Dahmer elicited major media interest. Cannibalism stories appeal to the media, and this story was a major news event. After it became known that a possible serial murderer had been arrested in Milwaukee, the media jumped all over the story. Not only was Dahmer a serial killer, but there were additional factors involved, possibly cannibalism, Davis observed.[79] Schwartz added that in the period of time immediately after the discovery of Dahmer's crimes, the case was extensively publicized in newspapers. From coast to coast the public was inundated with television coverage of the police searching the Oxford Apartments for clues. As the body count grew higher, so did the media interest.[80]

Referring to the Jeffrey Dahmer serial crimes, Davis recalled that this story was one that would not go away. The media relish such continuing sagas, because it allows reporters to explore the story from several vantage points and find new, relevant, and interesting facts and story angles.[81]

When Jeffrey Dahmer's serial murder escapades ended, the media had benefited. Schwartz declared that the Dahmer serial murders were tragic and sad, but they also created a financial windfall for the *Milwaukee Journal/Sentinel*. Circulation and sales figures for the week ending July 28, 1991, hit record highs.[82]

According to Anne Schwartz, who broke the story of the Dahmer killings as a reporter for the *Milwaukee Journal/Sentinel*, media interest was intense. She noted that at 3:30 p.m. on the day the story broke, a Milwaukee television station broadcast a thirty-minute special on the killings called "Murder Factory." Another station devoted the entire newscast to the case, which the news director said was unprecedented except for the Persian Gulf war.

The murders also were the lead story on the *CBS Evening News* that day.[83] Chicago's WLS radio station broadcast its morning show from the apartment of Vernell and Pamela Bass in the same building as Dahmer's former abode.[84] Norris added that "The news media was fascinated by Dahmer's appearances in court."[85]

Typically, however, serial murder stories tend to wane after a while. That happened with respect to the Jeffrey Dahmer case. Public interest in the Dahmer serial murder story was greatly reduced by the middle of September.[86] The media simply moved on to other stories.

NEGATIVE EFFECTS OF MEDIA COVERAGE

There were five main negative consequences of media coverage of the Dahmer case. These included media interference with the investigation, checkbook journalism, the creation of celebrities, the creation of media zones, and sensationalism.

Media Interference in the Investigation

Media interference in the Dahmer case was repeated and potentially contrary to the law. We can consider four different types of media interference in this investigation: witness tampering, crime scene contamination, illegal conduct, and the insensitive treatment of others.

Schwartz recalled how defense attorneys used the inconsistency between witnesses' original statements to police and their later, "enhanced" versions. Tracy Edwards said on the *Geraldo Rivera Show* that eight locks were on Dahmer's door and he "luckily" opened the correct ones. Rivera then produced a photograph of Dahmer's apartment door taken the night of his arrest. It showed only one deadbolt lock, and a small push-in-type lock on the doorknob.[87]

The problem was his changing story. Edwards appeared on numerous national talk shows. During each interview his story inexplicably became more detailed and outlandish. What he told rapt national television audiences was extremely different than his sworn statement to the police.[88]

Witnesses to the Dahmer serial killings were similarly pursued and influenced by reporters. According to Fisher, the process of reporting news can influence it. Witnesses in the Dahmer case changed and embellished their stories in repeated media interviews.[89]

There have been other cases of reporters tampering with crime scenes, but few confessions as explicit as that of former *Milwaukee Journal/Sentinel* reporter Schwartz, who covered the Dahmer case. "I approached the open door of apartment 213 and stepped cautiously inside. Because most officers know me from three years of covering crime scenes they have often beckoned me inside when other reporters were kept away by the yellow tape that reads, 'POLICE LINE. DO NOT CROSS'."[90]

The *New York Times* played an ignoble role in media coverage of the Jeffrey Dahmer case. Schwartz recalled that privileged court information was divulged in a report stolen by a janitor. The documents were purloined from the District Attorney's office and sold to a reporter from the *New York Times*.[91]

Stephen Sessions was a twenty-nine-year-old janitor for the Milwaukee County District Attorney's office. He admitted to making photocopies of confidential Dahmer case material, and arranging to meet a reporter from the *Times* at a Milwaukee tavern. He was subsequently fired by the county personnel review board.[92]

The day after the Dahmer story broke, Jeffrey's father Lionel Dahmer placed a note on his mother's front door. The note read: "Please do not ring the doorbell or phone. A Milwaukee reporter woke us up at 7:30 a.m. after a very hard night of stress and crank calls. Catherine Dahmer cannot endure more harassment. She is 87 years old, just recovering from pneumonia, and had her car damaged in a very recent accident. She really cannot put up with the stress of media people such as yesterday and this morning." Schwartz reported, "True to form, a reporter called and asked her to comment on the note."[93]

Other instances of boorish media behavior in the Dahmer case can be easily cited. One victim's mother, Catherine Lacy, tried to be nice to the media. But when she welcomed members of the media into her living room, reporters and careless cameramen reciprocated by stepping on her furniture and breaking her framed photos.[94] Schwartz concluded that the media concern for the victim families did not prevent editors from sending reporters to camp out at their homes until someone came out and consented to be interviewed.[95]

In the Jeffrey Dahmer case, reporters interviewed Dahmer's grandmother, Catherine Dahmer. They did not tell her of the reason for the interview. Schwartz recalled that reporters made many judgment calls covering the Dahmer story, like Mendoza's decision to conceal from Catherine Dahmer knowledge of her grandson Jeffrey's crimes.[96]

Checkbook Journalism

In the Dahmer case, everyone seemingly wanted to profit from the crimes. There were the two Bath, Ohio, girls with their concession stand selling coffee, lemonade, and cookies to the numerous reporters working on the road near Dahmer's boyhood home. Some of Dahmer's neighbors discovered that they could charge the media for their interview time.[97]

Schwartz noted the advantage enjoyed by relatively deep-pocket media companies, "The job of the local journalists was made especially difficult when the national media showed up and checkbook journalism ran rampant. Television shows like *Inside Edition* and newspapers like the *National Enquirer* had bulging wallets tailor-made for events like this one. I watched as residents were offered free rides in limousines: one received five hundred dollars from a supermarket tabloid for his story."[98] Schwartz added an example. Tracy

Edwards was on national talk shows, and he told his story to the tabloids for a considerable sum, usually in the thousands of dollars.[99]

Creating Celebrities

As the Dahmer news broke, reporters for the hometown *Milwaukee Journal/Sentinel* found themselves at the center of a media hurricane. Reporters were celebrities. They were overcome with it all, recalled the reporter who broke the story, Anne Schwartz.[100]

There was plenty of media fame to pass around. Schwartz noted that as the news of the murders spread, the newspaper received calls from around the country and the world. Their bylines appeared in French, Spanish, and German. When reporters from out-of-town papers called the newspaper's newsroom and spoke to whoever answered the phone, it was as if all *Journal/Sentinel* employees were experts on the case. The assumption was, if you worked for the *Journal/Sentinel* you must know all about Dahmer.[101]

Schwartz of the *Milwaukee Journal/Sentinel* and fellow reporters became celebrities because other reporters came to them as sources. It should be noted that Dahmer, as well, achieved a semblance of celebrity. "Dahmer's serial killings achieved mass-media and tabloid celebrity," Seltzer suggested.[102]

Creation of Media Zones

The media interest in this case led to creation of at least one media zone. Norris referred to "the growing media frenzy in the alley and on North Twenty-fifth Street."[103]

Sensationalism

Serial murders are frequently gruesome and terrible events. Nevertheless, the media often sensationalizes its reporting of such crimes. In the Dahmer case, "I both observed and participated in the sensationalism while attending the Dahmer case," confessed Schwartz.[104]

MILWAUKEE POLICE DEPARTMENT MEDIA RELATIONS

Schwartz noted the adversarial Milwaukee police/press relationship. "I couldn't see the day when I would have a warm conversation with Philip Arreola [Milwaukee's police chief]. True, cops and reporters were natural enemies, but this adversarial relationship the Milwaukee media had with Arreola severely hampered our news-gathering efforts."[105] A reporter with the *Milwaukee Journal/Sentinel* received a tip of a gruesome crime scene the night of Jeffrey Dahmer's arrest, and she called the designated Milwaukee Police Department contact person to inquire further. "How the hell do you know about that? Jesus Christ, you reporters! Do you guys mind if we get there first and find out what's happening before you tell the whole world?" he replied.[106]

PUBLIC RELATIONS TACTICS

There were four communication tactics used during the investigation into the Dahmer murders and related crimes. We will consider media centers, public statements, news conferences, and posters.

Media Centers

"The media center for the Dahmer trial could be compared to the Rashid Hotel in Saudi Arabia for reporters covering the Gulf War. It was the nerve center," Schwartz suggested.[107] Schwartz described this media room in greater detail:

The media center was set up in two rooms on the second floor of the building; the trial was in room 578, three floors above. The media center became our home and we began to interact as a family. The small yellow room had long tables with chairs crowded behind them along each wall and one down the center of the room. A separate room housed wire-service reporters and print reporters from *Newsweek* and the Associated Press to people from England and Australia. In addition to Milwaukee's four local television stations, one [of] which carried the trial live, there was a barrage of Chicago television and radio stations crowded into the yellow room. Editing machines were stacked three high, and hot lights burned constantly.[108]

Public Statements

Through his attorneys, Jeffrey Dahmer made this statement: "I have told the police everything I have done relative to these homicides. I have not committed any such crimes anywhere in the world other than this state, except I have admitted an incident in Ohio. I have not committed any homicide in any foreign country or in any other state. I have been totally cooperative and would have admitted other crimes if I did them. I did not. Hopefully this will serve to put rumors to rest.[109]

News Conferences

Both Milwaukee Mayor John O. Norquist and State Representative Gwen Moore held press conferences. Norquist announced the formation of a blue ribbon citizen's commission to thoroughly evaluate police community relations. Moore held her conference in front of Dahmer's former apartment building.[110]

There were other notable news conferences. Schwartz noted the story of Father Peter Burns, who appointed himself spokesman for the family of Konerak Sinthasomphone. He conducted several press conferences.[111]

Posters

Several poster campaigns were motivated by Jeffrey Dahmer's serial murders. Schwartz recalled that after Weinberger's disappearance, his family and friends distributed posters with photographs of him in all of the gay bars, requesting any information on Weinberger's whereabouts. One poster was posted in Milwaukee's Club 219.[112] In the aftermath of another Dahmer murder, Walter Tuomi, the father of Steven Tuomi, searched Milwaukee for clues to his son's disappearance, questioning Steven's friends and associates and disseminating posters with his son's photograph.[113]

CONCLUSION

Jeffrey Dahmer did not enjoy a pleasant home life as a child. Lacking in the social graces and self-confidence necessary to be popular with his peers, he was lonely and drank heavily. He was basically unhappy.

The Dahmer legal proceedings were the costliest in Milwaukee court history, with the total amount exceeding $120,000.[114] The grim fiscal reality of the trial to Milwaukee city officials mirrored the entire proceedings. The Dahmer crimes were truly horrible ones, and they shocked and horrified residents of Milwaukee. The ironic thing is that no one realized that there was a serial murderer at work until Dahmer's apprehension and confession. Strangely, no one in Milwaukee knew that a serial murderer was at large in the community.[115]

The mass media played a major and negative role in the Dahmer investigation. There was repeated and serious media interference with the investigation. Witnesses were tampered with, and privileged court documents were stolen. The media made numerous people connected with the case into celebrities, especially Dahmer himself and some members of the Milwaukee media. The Dahmer case became a media circus.

His was the first televised trial of a major serial killer.[116] Different stakeholders interpreted the crimes differently. Gays and lesbians perceived the murders as anti-gay crimes, while blacks considered them as racial hate crimes.[117]

But is there a simpler explanation? Norris contended, "Dahmer was so emotionally starved that he was unable to interrelate socially with another person." Near-victim Edwards recalled, "One minute he's nice and he's saying how he doesn't want people to leave him or abandon him."[118]

Dahmer died in prison on November 28, 1991. Christopher Scarver, a fellow inmate, killed Dahmer and another inmate, Jesse Anderson. It was called a racial killing.[119]

8

———•—

DOROTHEA PUENTE

DOROTHEA PUENTE IS a member of the minority in serial murder circles, in a couple of ways. She is a woman, as are about 20 percent of serial killers. And she killed for financial gain, which is a distinct rarity.

The media played a two-toned, major role in this case. It led directly to Puente's arrest. But it also was guilty of numerous acts of serious media misconduct. Puente was returned to Los Angeles (after fleeing from Sacramento) in an airplane chartered by a Sacramento newspaper and a television station. She talked with reporters throughout the flight.

Her childhood was not wonderful. Her father died when she was four, followed by her mother within two years. She went to live with an aunt and uncle. She received five years' probation for a Treasury check forgery incident. A few years later, she was convicted of drugging elderly men she met in bars, and then robbing them. She is alleged to have "wiped out" a couple of her victims, financially. Puente spent two-and-a-half years in prison.

In 1986 she opened a lodging house. It was marketed to California state social service clientele. She poisoned between seven and twenty-five of her tenants. Seven were decapitated and buried on Puente's property. Another victim was found in a specially constructed wooden box on the banks of the Sacramento River. It was rumored that she poisoned two of her husbands.

THE CRIMINAL

Dorothea Puente was a complex individual, like all human beings. Where she differed from others, however, was her willingness to hurt others to get what she wanted. Even if that involved the murder of helpless elderly tenants entrusted to her care.

Dorothea Helen Gray was born on January 9, 1929, in the town of Redlands, in California's San Bernardino County, to Jesse Gray and Trudy Yates.[1] A very different set of facts was alleged by Kelleher and Kelleher. They wrote that "Puente was born in Mexico in 1929, to an early life of poverty and abandonment. She was given up to an orphanage while still an infant and had no family to whom she could turn."[2]

What could explain this factual discrepancy? She wasn't born twice in two different places, after all. Blackburn cleared up this confusion. He claims that for twenty years, Dorothea had misinformed people of her true origin, claiming instead to have been born in Mexico as the youngest of eighteen children.[3]

Sadly, Puente's father passed away when Dorothea was only four years old. Her mother died the next year. Dorothea went to live with an aunt and uncle in Fresno.[4]

Puente was married four times. "Over the next forty years, Puente married four times but had only a single child."[5] Her first husband was allegedly Joe McFall, but some doubt exists that they were ever legally married. Public records document her next three marriages, however, beginning with Axel Johanson, a Swede, in 1952. She also married Roberto Puente in 1966, and Pedro Montalvo in 1976.[6] Despite four marriages, there is evidence of only two divorces.[7]

As was mentioned previously, Puente had only one child—a daughter. According to Newton, "Her only child, a daughter, was put up for adoption at birth." When she met Dorothea years later, her daughter described her as having "no real personality."[8] Kelleher and Kelleher confirmed Newton's contention about a sole daughter.[9]

Puente was not mentally healthy. One study concluded, "Puente had been diagnosed as suffering from 'chronic undifferentiated schizophrenia,' a condition that sometimes produces delusions."[10] She claimed to be an indigenous "holistic healer."[11]

"She spent hours working in the garden," Newton recalled. He added, "neighbors described her as 'very protective of her lawn.'" One neighbor told reporters, "If somebody walked on her lawn, she'd cuss at them in language that would make a sailor blush."[12] Lane and Gregg referred to her "immaculately tended garden."[13]

Her residence was a two-story gingerbread Victorian house. It was located in the 1200 block of F Street.[14] It soon became a tourist attraction.

Surprisingly, this sweet little old lady could be mean, vicious, and even violent at times. Blackburn explained, "The dark side of Dorothea always lurked near the surface, however. She had a reputation for being physically tough. She would get howling drunk and have knock-down, drag-out fights with her upstairs roommates, including Mervyn John McCauley."[15]

Another important aspect of Puente to consider was her previous crimes and convictions. She spent two-and-a-half years in prison after her 1982 conviction for robbery. Her crime involved meeting elderly men in bars, drugging them, and robbing them.[16] Newton agreed, adding that Puente was convicted and imprisoned for drugging and robbing elderly men she met in various taverns.[17]

Forgery was another Puente crime. In 1978, as Dorothea Puente Montalvo, she was convicted of forging a U.S. Treasury check. Her punishment was five years' probation, which was revoked by her state felony conviction in the bar scam cases.[18]

Puente actually had a rather extensive criminal history, all things considered. In 1948, after the death of her first husband, "For money she tried to forge checks but was eventually caught and sentenced to a year in jail: she was paroled after six months."[19]

Diversity characterized her criminal career. One recent study recalled, "In 1960 she was arrested in a brothel and was sentenced to 90 days in Sacramento County Jail. After her release she was arrested again, this time for vagrancy, and sentenced to another 90 days in jail. Following that, she started to get involved in miscellaneous illegal acts that over time became more serious."[20]

NNDB summarized Puente's criminal career. It missed her sex trade bust, but it uncovered the rest. These crimes included, "Forgery, fraud, murder, theft and vagrancy."[21]

One last thing about Puente was her claims to have friends in very high places. According to Blackburn, Puente bragged to several friends that she was personally connected to the Shah of Iran, the King of Jordan, and the Pope.[22]

THE CRIMES

Puente's crimes were not discovered in time to prevent decomposition of some of her victim's bodies, rendering them unidentifiable. Other bodies have never been found. In this section, we will examine her crimes through consideration of eight subjects, including the number of murders, how she obtained victims, and her motive. Discovery of the bodies will be described, with seven bodies found. The victims will be noted, and three additional deaths will be explored, along with the question of accomplices.

The Number of Murders

No one knows exactly how many people were murdered by Dorothea Puente. There is a wide variance in the estimates of the total number of murders she committed, compared to the crimes with which she was charged. She was only convicted of three murders.

We will never know exactly how many elderly persons were victimized by Dorothea Puente's growing greed and cold-blooded methods. It is believed that approximately two dozen elderly citizens were taken in by her lethal plans, Kelleher and Kelleher noted.[23] Another estimate asserted that there were at least nine and perhaps as many as twenty-five victims.[24] Police estimated that between 1986 and 1988, approximately twenty-five of her tenants had disappeared.[25]

A police spokesman stated, "We are getting a large volume of calls from people with relatives who stayed there. There are a lot more than seven names." He added that, in fact, as many as twenty-five former tenants were missing.[26] Another source recalled that, although Puente was charged with nine murders, she was a solid suspect in twelve homicidal deaths.[27]

Her manner of procuring victims was especially painful when disclosed at trial. She offered room and board to mentally-challenged, alcoholic, and elderly residents of Sacramento, in return for payment from California social services agencies and the tenant's government checks. She abused the trust placed in her, and she abused her tenants, killing several of them but continuing to pocket their checks.

"Both Dorothea and her gardens were sources of inspiration to her Sacramento neighbors, and to the local welfare department which boarded elderly and alcoholic mental patients with her in the sure confidence that they would enjoy the very best of care," according to one source.[28] In 1986, Puente solicited Sacramento-area social worker administrators, offering high-quality lodgings for elderly persons on fixed incomes. Peggy Nickerson referred to Puente as "the best the system has to offer." Nickerson herself referred nineteen clients to Puente's institution over the next two years.[29] The Kellehers agreed, noting that in 1986, Puente persuaded Sacramento, California, social workers that she could provide care for a good number of elderly and frail persons by boarding them at her F Street home.[30]

In this case, the motive was plain and rather ordinary. Puente was motivated by greed. She killed her lodgers, notified no one, and kept cashing the victim's monthly government checks.

Lane and Gregg noted cynically that, while Puente killed and disposed of her boarders, "only their pension cheques remained to keep the old lady company."[31] Another report concluded, "Puente had apparently attacked her victims in order to divert their Social Security payments or other personal income to her own uses."[32]

Discovery of the Bodies

The initial body was found at Puente's residence on November 11, 1988. The next day, two more bodies were found. By November 14, a total of seven decapitated corpses had been discovered in her yard.[33] Puente was also linked to a body discovered on January 1, 1986, in a wooden box next to the Sacramento River.[34]

After the neighbors complained about the smell emanating from the Puente residence, and after receiving missing persons complaints about her residents, the police finally decided to investigate. They went to the Puente home, talked to Dorothy, then began to dig. The results were horrifying.

The initial corpse was dug up on November 11, and two more were found the next day. By November 14, police had recovered seven bodies, Newton noted.[35] Lane and Gregg referred to the badly decomposed remnants of seven victims.[36] Kelleher and Kelleher confirmed the discovery of seven headless bodies.[37]

Several of the bodies located on Puente's property were so badly decomposed that they could not be identified. There were two unidentified female bodies, and the remains of one unidentified male, unearthed in her yard.

Ben Fink was a fifty-five-year-old tenant of Puente, and was found buried in her yard. Alvaro Montoya, another Puente renter, was fifty-two when last seen alive. Dorothy Miller and Vera Martin were both relatively healthy sixty-five-year-olds when they disappeared, only to be found by the police in their search of the Puente property.[38] The body found near the Sacramento River was initially a mystery. He was later identified as Everson Gillmouth, Puente's ex-boyfriend.[39]

A footnote to the Puente case involves allegations that she had murdered two of her husbands. When suspicions about Puente were aroused, this claim was made. "Dorothea Montalvo, Puente, or whatever name she now used, had either attempted or had succeeded in poisoning two of her previous husbands," Blackburn noted.[40]

Was there another Puente murder? Some suspect so. For instance, one study noted, "Ruth Monroe, age 61, dies of a drug overdose in Puente's boarding-house." A more detailed description of Monroe's death was provided by another study, "In April 1982 sixty-one year old Ruth Monroe arrived in Puente's room-inghouse but soon died from an overdose of Codeine and Tylenol. Puente told police that the woman was very depressed because her husband was terminally ill. They believed her and judged the incident a suicide."[41]

Two other individuals were implicated in the Puente murders. One, John McCauley, was a Puente tenant, and the other was Ismael Carrasco Florez. He was accused of being an accomplice in the Sacramento River body case.

McCauley was arrested on November 14, 1988, while Puente was hiding in Los Angeles. Newton recalled that John McCauley, age sixty-nine, was arrested and charged with being an accomplice in the Puente murders. He was later freed, for lack of evidence.[42] McCauley was not suspected of complicity in the murders themselves, police admitted, but "he was accused of lying to police on two occasions during the excavation of the bodies."[43]

Florez was accused of being an accessory in the 1986 case. He was charged with building the box that contained the body, and with helping Puente dispose of the body.[44]

THE INVESTIGATION

The investigation into Puente's serial murders began with the concerns of one woman, Judy Moise. She was an administrator in the California state social services system, and she had been attempting to contact Bert Montoya, a client she had referred to Puente's lodging house. When Puente offered excuse after excuse about Montoya's whereabouts, she contacted Sacramento homicide detective John Cabrera. A meeting was held with Moise, Cabrera, and several other detectives working the case on November 11, 1988, to consider the evidence and make investigative decisions.[45]

Cabrera also interviewed Puente on November 11. However, "his interrogation had failed to secure the slightest self-incriminating statement from her." Police decided to dig in her yard.[46]

The next day, November 12, the police began excavating her back yard at about 7:00 a.m. Just before 9:00, Puente asked Cabrera if she could walk to the nearby Clarion Hotel, to have a cup of coffee with her nephew. Instead, she and McCauley took a taxi to Tiny's Lounge in nearby Broderick, where she drank four vodka and grapefruit juices. By 2:00 p.m. she was on a Greyhound Bus to Los Angeles, which arrived at the destination about 10:00 p.m. She then took a cab to Third and Alvarado Streets, where she checked into the Royal Viking Motel as Dorothy Johansen.[47]

Sacramento police immediately discovered that their prey had fled. They issued bulletins nationwide. They also arrested McCauley.[48]

The next day, Dorothea ventured out for some entertainment. She found the Monte Carlo I, a seedy bar, and struck up an intimate conversation with Charles Willgues. She offered to visit his apartment that night, but he demurred, saying he'd call her instead and they could get together the next day. He was bothered by her questions about his finances, and she looked familiar to him. He later saw television coverage of the crimes, and contacted the television station, which in turn informed LAPD.[49]

The Sacramento chief of police was out-of-town during the initial stages of this case. He criticized his own police later at a news conference. "She should have been followed, she should have been tailed very closely. She was a prime suspect in a homicide case and there isn't any excuse, as far as I'm concerned, why the suspect wasn't kept under surveillance. It was a judgment call gone awry. The Sacramento Police Department made an error and as a result of that, we lost the suspect."[50]

Evidence collection and preservation were important investigative tasks. Police were "faced with the chore of preserving, to the highest degree possible, the integrity of every piece of evidence that might exist at the scene."[51] The remains were examined and identified by San Francisco forensic anthropologist Chick Cecil and Rodger Heglar of San Diego.[52] That was an important task, but not as exciting as the "seven day nationwide hunt" resulting in Puente's arrest.[53]

THE ARREST

Puente was arrested in Los Angeles on November 15, 1988. She was on the telephone with Willgues when LAPD Sergeant Paul Von Lutzlow and fellow officers knocked on her door and asked for her identification. Her driver's license identified her as Dorothy Johanson, but when police searched her purse they found another driver's license, in the name of Dorothea Puente. She was placed under arrest on the spot.[54]

She was cuffed, and taken to the Ramparts precinct police station. There she was booked, and fingerprinted. It was a little after 11:00 at night.[55]

The LAPD had a problem. They could not hold Dorothea for more than five hours without her being arraigned.[56] There were no commercial flights available at that time, but the Sacramento NBC affiliate, KCRA-TV, and the *Sacramento Bee* newspaper offered to charter a jet and get her, bringing along the Sacramento Police Department officers working her case.[57]

Officials took no chances on Dorothea vanishing again. LAPD had her wear shackles on her wrists, connected to her waist. The Sacramento police secured her with handcuffs.[58]

It took Sacramento police nearly an hour to process Puente into their system. She was arraigned the next morning at 9:20. Sacramento Municipal Judge John V. Stroud conducted the hearing. Dorothea appeared "drawn and haggard."[59]

THE TRIAL

Puente was initially charged with one count of murder, in the Bert Montoya case. That was on November 17. According to Blackburn, she was charged with eight additional counts of murder on March 31, 1989.[60]

"She was finally tried in Monterey on a change of venue," recalled former Sacramento television newsman Mike Boyd.[61] Another source recalled the lengthy pretrial delays, "Two years later, in November of 1992, Puente's trial finally began after incessant legal wrangling and a change of venue to Monterey, California."[62]

The trial was a study in contradictions. "The prosecution portrayed Puente as an evil-hearted woman bent upon obtaining profit at the expense of her elderly, often frail, tenants." The defense provided an alternate perspective, "The defense countered by developing an image of Puente as kind, caring and misunderstood."[63]

It was a lengthy trial. Even the jury deliberation took quite some time. One source noted, "The Puente trial was a marathon affair that went on for nearly six months." The jury began its deliberations on July 16, 1993, and reached a verdict on August 27.[64]

Puente was convicted on three counts of murder, with the other charges dismissed for lack of evidence.[65] "Seven bodies were eventually found and Puente was convicted of three murders and sentenced to life in prison."[66]

The penalty phase of the trial began on September 21. "Finally, on October 14, 1993, at the age of sixty-four, Puente was sentenced to life imprisonment without the possibility of parole."[67]

PUBLIC AND MEDIA INTEREST

All sensational crimes attract public and media attention, and the Puente case was no exception. There was a considerable media contingent on scene at the Puente house, and at other locations. Public interest was substantial when roominghouse landlady Dorothea Puente was charged with murdering her elderly tenants: "For the first week or two after Dorothea's arrest and arraignment, the fever of interest that had accompanied the gruesome discovery was sustained."[68]

Dorothea Puente's serial tenant murders elicited substantial media interest. "The gathering of media personnel was expanding tremendously, now featuring representatives of the national television networks, the wire services, and major newspaper chains."[69]

POSITIVE MEDIA EFFECTS

The Puente murder case witnessed major negative media consequences; however, the media also had a positive effect in two ways in this case. Media coverage and criticism motivated law enforcement, and it facilitated the apprehension of the fleeing killer.

When Sacramento police allowed serial murder suspect Dorothea Puente to walk away from them, the public reaction was understandable. "The murmur of public criticism had grown to a roar."[70] A *Sacramento Bee* editorial was taken very seriously: "The *Sacramento Bee*'s critical editorial questioning certain police decisions made during the heat of the F Street discoveries stung Kearns."[71]

Puente fled to Los Angeles when police began excavating her yard. She hid out in a cheap hotel, trying to escape attention or notice. She was turned in by a man she tried to pick up in a bar, who recognized her from the television news broadcasts on Channel 2 about the case.[72]

NEGATIVE MEDIA EFFECTS

It is difficult to imagine a serial murder case with more negative media consequences than the Puente case. There were at least six serious negative effects of media coverage. They included the creation of media zones, interference with the investigation, direct media involvement, checkbook journalism, the creation of celebrities, and the revelation of the investigative details to the killer by the media.

There were several media zones during the unfolding of the Dorothea Puente case. A body was found buried on her property on November 11. That night, "The glaring lights of television cameras dispatched from several local TV stations illuminated the street like a large movie set." On November 12, 1988, the day after the initial body was discovered, "Newspaper, radio and television reporters from all over the state were beginning to arrive, drawn by the increasingly ghoulish tales that a larger cache of bodies might be buried in Dorothea's backyard." By the next day, "The streets were blocked off on every intersection, creating a large area for people to gather. . . . The square block was packed with an estimated crowd of more than six hundred gawkers and reporters. The air throbbed with the sound of cranked-up generators powering the lights and cameras of the media horde. . . . Neighbors were recalling Dorothea-related incidents as fast as the television camera operators could focus on their faces."[73]

After her capture in Los Angeles, Puente faced a media zone there. As Blackburn recalled, Dorothea was transferred from Ramparts to the Parker

Center, the downtown Los Angeles police headquarters complex. There the media once again caught up to her.[74]

The dramatic scene in store for Dorothea when she returned to the Sacramento Executive Airport was one that neither she nor law enforcement agencies could have predicted. There were constant very bright lights, television video cameras, newspaper photographers, reporters, and local TV anchors, Blackburn recalled. Then, the informal caravan of police, media, and photographers departed on the fifteen-minute drive downtown to police headquarters, where there was a second set of newspeople waiting.[75]

The media was intensely interested in the Puente case. This led to aggressive tactics. The media, as a result of these tactics, interfered with the police in two ways. They followed the police, and they interfered with witnesses.

Media "shadowing" of police was noted in the Dorothea Puente serial murders investigation. Blackburn described the chaotic situation. The field officers were required to work the crime scene of a newly discovered murder, while keeping an eye on several people who might be suspects. This all transpired under the critical gaze of newspaper photographers and television cameras.[76]

The aggressive media presence caused problems for investigators probing Puente's serial murders. The media was now moving ahead of the police in the information-gathering process, discovering the identities of Dorothea's tenants and heralding her criminal history. As a result, reporters were providing to the police virtually all of the important information about the circumstances involved in the disappearance of Bert Montoya.[77]

There was an act of direct media involvement in the Dorothea Puente case. Shortly after the beginning of the nightly newscast on November 15, officials at KCRA-TV, Channel 3, the Sacramento NBC affiliate, made the police an offer. The police could share space on the Lear jet that the station, along with the *Sacramento Bee,* had just chartered. The Sacramento police agreed instantly, and they quickly departed for Los Angeles.[78] They picked Puente up, then flew back to Sacramento.

Puente's media-enhanced plane ride was not appreciated by her attorney, Kevin D. Clymo. He told a news conference throng of reporters, "It's unheard of to have a suspect transported with reporters before she's talked to an attorney. I can give you all my feelings in one word—unfair."[79]

In the Dorothea Puente case, television and movie producers, checkbook in hand, crowded on Hollywood/Burbank-to-Sacramento commuter flights. They hoped to buy story rights to the Dorothea Puente drama from anyone and everyone who had ever crossed paths with her. In fact, "Many media and entertainment companies have tried to reach Dorothea, all making generous cash offers."[80]

Others tried to cash in as well. Blackburn claimed that "Entrepreneurs pocketed unexpected but welcome profits from the brisk sale of Dorothea-related memorabilia."[81]

Sacramento boardinghouse landlady Dorothea Puente was convicted of killing several of her tenants. She became infamous as a result. In a short time,

Dorothea achieved international notoriety and recognition. Even Dorothea, with her aggressive style and self-confidence, could not have predicted how rapidly her celebrity would spread.[82]

Others were celebrated, besides the killer. Take the man who turned her in, for example, Charles Willgues. In Los Angeles, tipster Willgues became a celebrity. Television camera crews, print reporters, and photographers trooped through his small apartment that Dorothea saw as a refuge.[83]

In the case of Sacramento serial killer Dorothea Puente, she monitored what was happening back in Sacramento from Los Angeles. She accomplished this by watching television and reading the paper. Dorothea's diligent reading of the Los Angeles newspapers and constant monitoring of the color television in her motel room kept her informed about the law enforcement progress and the drama unfolding in Sacramento.[84]

PUBLIC RELATIONS ASPECTS

Public relations was instrumental in the Puente case. Puente's public relations and publicity tactics secured her the victims she preyed upon. On the other hand, public information tactics were useful in her apprehension.

Dorothea Puente catered to social service organizations to obtain referrals. Blackburn described how Puente used her promotional skills to facilitate her financially-motivated serial murders, "Dorothea was perfecting the fine art of public relations. Discovering that the free-dinner concept worked so well, she began to sponsor occasional drop-in buffet dinners for no particular reason and with the social workers as primary invitees."[85]

Posters, also known as bulletins and broadsheets, are common communication tactics used in serial murder public information campaigns. They are relatively inexpensive, but they convey both visual and verbal information. They were used in the Puente case.

The Sacramento police were in a full-blown panic. They had disseminated so many messages and bulletins for the missing landlady that other police departments began to resent the continual communication, Blackburn recalled.[86]

It was through the medium of television that Puente was caught. The citizen who informed the police of her whereabouts knew who she was and that she was wanted by watching television news. Not only did Willgues receive his crime-related information through television, he called the assignment editor at Channel 2, Gene Silver, to report his suspicion that he had met Puente.[87]

News conferences were used by both parties in this case. Puente's defense used one to blast the police for sending her on an airplane flight with reporters. There were numerous law enforcement conferences.

Clymo's partner on the defense team, Peter Vlautin, addressed a conference. "The only thing we can tell you now is that our client denied killing anybody and the true facts will come out in the courtroom, not in the hallways of the courthouse."[88]

There were numerous law enforcement and prosecution news conferences. For instance, one such conference featured comments by Sacramento Police Chief Kearns and District Attorney John Dougherty about the identification of bodies and dropping of charges against McCauley.[89] These conferences were mainly held in self-defense.

CONCLUSION

Puente's crimes were pretty simple, in motive and execution. She poisoned her victims, then buried them in her back yard. She continued to cash their Social Security and other government checks. She accounted for between nine and twenty-five deaths.

Mass communication played a significant role in this case. There was substantial public and media interest, which resulted in a very competitive media environment. Media coverage of the Puente case accomplished two beneficial outcomes; it motivated the police, and it facilitated apprehension of the killer.

However, the competitive nature of the intense media coverage led to many negative consequences, ranging from interference with the investigation to tampering with witnesses. The net impact of the media on the investigation was decidedly negative.

Puente was a controversial and complex person. Her nicknames attest to that. Some called her "The Black Widow of Sacramento."[90] Her other nickname was "The Grandma Serial Killer."[91]

9

---•·•---

GARY RIDGWAY

THE GREEN RIVER murders are much better known than the person who admitted being the killer, Gary Ridgway. The crimes themselves are notorious, and are proclaimed to be the most numerous of any serial murder episode in American history. The investigation into the Green River case was the longest to date, according to experts.

Prostitutes were Ridgway's target, along Seattle's vice area known as the Sea-Tac Highway, between Seattle and Tacoma, Washington. At his trial he stated that he hated prostitutes, and sought to kill as many as he could. He became a suspect relatively early in the investigation, in 1984, but he passed a polygraph test. Again, in 1987 his house was searched, but nothing incriminating could be found.

He used dumpsites to dispose of his victims. He deposited the bodies in "clusters," so he could visit them all relatively easily. He had sex with at least ten of his victims' dead bodies.

This is a classic case of media interference in a serial murder case. There were numerous instances of negative media behavior. The police and press were protagonists.

THE CRIMINAL

The Green River murders baffled investigators for more than twenty years. During that time, there was much speculation about the criminal. Convicted British serial killer and author Ian Brady was certain, for instance, that there were two or more individuals involved in the Green River killings.[1]

Gary Leon Ridgway was born in Salt Lake City on February 19, 1949. His proud parents were Tom and Mary Ridgway. He had two brothers, Greg and Ed.[2]

Ridgway attended Tyee High School, in Sea-Tac, Washington. He was not a particularly good student. He graduated in 1969 with a "D" average.[3]

He was married three times. Ridgway was known for reading the Bible at work. At the same time, he was regularly patronizing prostitutes.[4]

There was a good deal of conceit in Ridgway. Dave Reichert was on the Green River case from the beginning. He recalled, "The last time I talked to Gary Ridgway, he said that he had killed 71 and that I was too stupid to find the other bodies."[5]

One ironic fact about this serial murderer—the perpetrator, Gary Ridgway, was a suspect since at least 1984, if not earlier. According to Preusch, "Mr. Ridgway, 54, a truck painter from Auburn, had been a suspect since the early 1980s, after one of the victims was seen getting into his truck. But when investigators confronted him about it at the time, he passed a polygraph test."[6] Ridgway attracted the attention of authorities after his initial 1984 brush with the law. Smolowe observed that "detectives continued to harbor suspicions about Ridgway." She added, "Armed with a search warrant, they seized carpet fibers, ropes and plastic tarps from his home and cars in 1987. But none of the samples could be matched with evidence found on the victims."[7]

Investigators familiar with Ridgway were unimpressed with his character. One report noted, "Court documents summarizing the interviews conducted by detectives and the sheriff with Mr. Ridgway described him as a pathological liar who, at times, tries to portray himself in 'the best possible light' because he believed a true crime author would write a book about him."[8]

Necrophilia was included among Ridgway's criminal behaviors associated with the serial murders. The New York Times recorded the fact that "Mr. Ridgway told detectives that he had sex with ten of his victims after they were dead." Dave Reichert, who worked the case from the initial stages, asked him why he had sex with the corpses. Ridgway answered, "Well, for one thing you'd have to pay for it and she was already dead."[9]

Ridgway habitually used prostitutes. Nevertheless, he was married three times.[10] His was a distinctive, dangerous, and diverse sexual libido.

THE CRIMES

Perhaps America's most productive serial killer, in terms of numbers of victims, the Green River killer was arrested in 2001. In this section, we will attain an enhanced understanding of the Ridgway crimes through consideration of five topics. The unknown number of murders will be noted, along with estimates of the highest known victim total. The victims will be named. Recent findings and victims will be described.

Unknown Number of Victims

There is no definite, reliable, and precise victim count in the Green River serial murder case. There is a range of estimates, from the low forties to seventy-one. The most frequent estimate is forty-nine murders.

"Two decades ago, 49 women were killed and their bodies found in the Green River and wooded areas around Seattle," reported The New York Times recently.[11] Crime historian Gini Scott agreed, adding that "The number of victims reached at least forty-nine."[12] Kershaw recently reported that "Green River ranked as one of the nation's deadliest serial murder cases, with 49 identified victims."[13]

According to Mendoza, there were forty-nine victims. He noted that "Using a library of missing persons' dental charts, the King County Police Department was able to identify 40 of the 49 sets of remains they recovered."[14] However, Mendoza suggested that the actual Green River slaying total might be substantially higher, "The task force, at its investigative peak, reviewed 38 other unsolved homicides from between 1973 and 1982 in King, Pierce and Snohomish Counties with identical traits to the Green River killings."[15]

Brady provided a lower estimate. "The sum total of murders the Green River Killer is said to have been responsible for—over forty in number by the last body count."[16] Smith and Guillen reported a total of forty-one certain and eight possible victims, for a total of either forty-one or forty-nine.[17] In court, Ridgway pled guilty to forty-eight murders.[18] Hickey referred to "nearly fifty murders."[19]

A study by Crockett identified fifty Green River victims.[20] Somehow, Ridgway's personal estimate—sixty victims—has escaped public and media attention. Kershaw reported, "Prosecutors said that Mr. Ridgway, who will not be sentenced for six months, had told them he had killed 60 women."[21]

On November 5, 2003, Ridgway "pleaded guilty to more murders than any other serial killer in U.S. history." Another *New York Times* story referred to "his 48 victims—the most of any killer in U. S. history." Newman noted, "He admitted to killing more people than any other serial killer in United States history."[22] Or was his boast to Reichert of seventy-one victims the truth?

The Victims

In a very real sense, the victims are the story in serial murder cases. They suffer at the hands of their killer, and their lives are ended prematurely. Then, they are forgotten by the media, public, and law enforcement, it seems. Serial murder victims deserve recognition and respect.

Listed here are the fifty names associated with the Green River murders, their age and the date of their disappearance, when known: Wendy Lee Coffield, 16, July 15, 1982; Deborah Lee Bonner, 23, August 12, 1982; Cynthia Jean Hinds, 17, August 15, 1982; Marcia Faye Chapman, 31, August 15, 1982; Opal Charmaine Mills, 16, August 15, 1982; Patrisia Jo Crossman, 16, June 13, 1982; Leann Virginia Wilcox, 16, January 22, 1982; Angelita Bell Atkinson, 25, June 19, 1981; Virginia King Taylor, 19, January 29, 1982; Theresa Kline, 27, August 27, 1982; Gisele Lovvorn, 17, September 25, 1982; Trina Deanne Hunter, 17, December 29, 1982; Mary Bridgit Meehan, 19, September 15, 1982; Shawndra Lee Summers, 17, October 7, 1982; Kimi Kai Pisor, 16, April 28, 1983; Carol Ann Christensen, 21, May 8, 1983; Kimberly Ann Reames, 27, June 13, 1983; Constance Elizabeth Naon, 21, June 8, 1983; Yvonne S. Antosh, 19, May 30, 1983; Patricia Lee Osborn, 19, January 24, 1984; Martina T. Authorlee, 18, May 15, 1983; Debra Lorraine Estes (AKA Debra Jones), 16, July 1982; Rebecca

Fashaw, December 2, 1982 (age unknown); Joanne Michelle Hovland (AKA Harbard), 16, March 16, 1983; April Dawn Buttram, 17, August 4, 1983; Mary Exzette West, 16, February 6, 1984; Amina Agisheff, 26, July 7, 1982; Tonja Harry, 20, July 9, 1983; Angela Anderson, 16, December 2, 1983; Vickie L. Williams, 19, April 23, 1984; Alma Anne Smith, April 2, 1984 (age unknown); and Marie M. Malvar, 18, April 30, 1983.

Here are the names and ages of victims in whose cases it was not possible to ascertain their likely date of disappearance: Joan Lucinda Reed Connor, 16; Terri Renee Milligan, 16; Kase Ann Lee, 16; Denise Darcel Bush, 24; Shirley Mae Sherrill, 19; Sandra K. Gabbert, 17; Keli (or Kelli) K. McGuinness, 18; Debbie Mae Abernathy, 26; Tina Lee Tomson (AKA Linda Lee Barkey), 26; Tracy Winston (AKA Tracy Gordon), 20; Carrie Rois, 16; Mary Bellow; Becky Marraro (AKA Rebecca Murrero), 20; Vicky Johnson; Cheryl Lee Wyms, 18; Colleen Renee Brockman, 15; and Essie Jackson, 24.[23]

It was generally believed that the Green River murders occurred between 1982 and 1984. However, Ridgway pled guilty to more recent murders. We will briefly consider these cases.

In September 2003, authorities positively identified bones discovered about twenty-six miles east of Seattle as those of April Dawn Buttram. The remains were reportedly located in August in Snoqualmie, Washington.[24]

"Most of the slayings were in the mid-1980s, but one of the slayings to which Ridgway will plead guilty was in 1998," reported the Associated Press in 2003.[25] A week later, the same reporter added that "But one killing Ridgway admitted to was in 1990 and another was in 1998."[26]

THE INVESTIGATION AND APPREHENSION

"The Green River case has been the longest, costliest, and most frustrating investigation in American history," Mendoza contended. He noted the fifteen-year duration of the investigation, how it grew to two lieutenants, four ser-geants, a dozen detectives and nearly two dozen plainclothes officers then peaked at fifty-six police personnel assigned full time to the task force. By 1989, the cost to law enforcement had reached approximately $15 million.[27] In 1997, Hickey estimated that more than $20 million had been invested in the case by the authorities.[28]

The case has been called "one of the longest cold cases in American history." Kershaw added that "It is still perhaps the longest homicide investigation ever undertaken, crime experts say, as well as one of the most expensive: In 2003 alone, the investigation has cost $9.3 million, officials say."[29] In similar terms, Newman offered her recollection for the *New York Times*, "The Green River case was one of the longest cases in American history, and one that went cold several times. It is also one of the most expensive, costing the government more than $9 million in 2003."[30] When the pre-2003 total of $20 million is added to the nearly $10 million spent on the case in 2003, the Green River case can be said conservatively to have cost in excess of $30 million.

One problem with the probe was the plethora of potential suspects. Hickey cited a study quantifying more than 20,000 Green River case suspects.[31] Smolowe reported "leads pointing to more than 12,000 suspects."[32]

The size of the investigative staff fluctuated over time. It began small, then grew to the previously mentioned totals of forty and finally fifty-six officers. In 1992 the task force was reduced to a one-person operational staff, detective Tom Jensen.[33]

Advances in scientific evidence analysis led to the breakthrough in the case after so many years of fruitless effort. A *New York Times* report observed that "It was not until 2001, after DNA technology linked Mr. Ridgway to seven of the killings through semen and traces of paint found on the bodies, that he was arrested."[34]

An Associated Press account differed in some respects. It asserted that "In 1987, the Malvar connection prompted the police to take a saliva sample from Mr. Ridgway. He was arrested in 2001 when technology advanced enough to allow a DNA match from the saliva sample to trace evidence from three early victims."[35] Another study agreed, and disagreed, with the other accounts reported here, as studies tend to do. According to Johnson, "Advances in DNA technology had finally allowed detectives to link Ridgway's 14-year-old saliva sample to semen found on three of the earliest victims."[36]

THE TRIAL

Ridgway cooperated with authorities, in a plea-bargained deal. In return for a life sentence, Ridgway led investigators to undiscovered bodies and pled guilty to forty-eight murders. One recent account stated, "Ridgway agreed to cooperate with investigators in a deal to avoid the death penalty."[37] There were added details to this seemingly simple decision. An Associated Press account reported, "Prosecutors agreed to spare Ridgway the death penalty in exchange for his helping investigators find four previously undiscovered sets of remains and confessing to the murders."[38]

Michele Shaw, one of Ridgway's attorneys, is credited with securing the plea bargain. The *New York Times* reported that "One of his lawyers, Michele Shaw persuaded Mr. Ridgway to cooperate with prosecutors last April, after telling him that his two brothers, Greg and Ed Ridgway, and his only son, Matt, wanted him to live." Shaw had reportedly visited Ridgway every week for a year and a half. When she informed him of his family's concern, Ridgway "just broke down and sobbed profusely," Shaw said.[39]

Ridgway's appearance and demeanor at his court hearings was described by an Associated Press account. It referred to "Ridgway, a short figure with glasses, thinning hair and a sandy moustache." He spoke with "chilling calm," as he admitted and described the murders.[40] He pled guilty on November 5, 2003.

Ridgway made a few public statements during court appearances. Prosecutor Jeffrey B. Baird read a statement from the serial killer. Each set of statements reveals something about Ridgway.

"Choking is what I did, and I was pretty good at it," he said in court documents. He added that he had murdered "so many women I have a hard time keeping them straight."[41] He sounded quite different in court, speaking to the judge and victim's families. In that public venue, he declared, "I have tried for a long time to keep from killing any ladies. I'm very sorry for the ladies that were not found. May they rest in peace. They need a better place than where I gave them. I'm sorry for killing those ladies. They had their whole lives ahead of them. I'm sorry for causing so much pain to so many families."[42]

Here is how Ridgway explained his motive in the murders. "I hate most prostitutes and I did not want to pay them for sex. I also picked prostitutes as victims because they were easy to pick up without being noticed. I knew they would not be reported missing right away and might never be reported missing. I picked prostitutes because I thought I could kill as many of them as I wanted without getting caught."[43]

Bodies of his victims were dumped in "clusters," according to Ridgway. He explained how this furthered his psychological and sexual desires, "I placed most of the bodies in groups which I called clusters. I did this because I wanted to keep track of all the women I killed. I liked to drive by the clusters around the county and think about the women I placed there."[44]

MEDIA COVERAGE

Media interest in and coverage of the Green River slayings typified the behavior in these cases. There was substantial interest at times, which tended to wane after awhile. The profit motive was evident in media coverage of these crimes.

By the fall, the Green River murder investigation was a matter of intense publicity. Each of the Seattle-area news media had invested the time to learn about these crimes. They had all covered them closely.[45]

Occasionally, a serial murder case regains "newsworthiness," as a result of new developments in the case. That happened in the Green River case. Kershaw reported in 2003, "Now, with the local television news and newspapers regularly reporting on the intensified search for victims, a gruesome, almost unfathomable, crime story has come to the fore once again."[46]

"It was almost as if the media had a vested interest in the investigation continuing, certainly, reporting on the task force sold newspapers and filled the airwaves. It was a topic that the news media had taken a proprietary interest in," Smith and Guillen noted of media interest in the Green River investigation.[47] "If it bleeds, it leads," proclaims an axiom of professional journalism. The contemporary expression is, "Cha-ching."

Brady criticized the Seattle public. It had become complacent about the serial murders, he declared. He suggested that in the Green River case, in the remaining half of 1982, another six victims were discovered, bringing the total to sixteen. But by then the public had already actually become bored with the murders.[48] This phenomenon tends to baffle and upset the victims' survivors.

According to Publications International Ltd., there have been no Green River murders since 1984. The size of the police task force was reduced by 75 percent, and most residents in the Seattle-Tacoma area lost interest in the case long ago. The prostitutes have returned to work on the Sea-Tac Highway.[49]

POLICE/MEDIA RELATIONSHIP

Law enforcement and the media are two of the central stakeholders in serial murder cases. Unfortunately, sometimes they work at cross purposes, as their stakes differ. As a result, neither party expresses much respect for the other.

Many police express disregard for the media during serial killer investigations. A Green River Task Force member, who criticized media serial murder coverage, declared emphatically that "Some dickhead media person who had too little to do that day would capitalize on that aspect of it, and I think unfairly."[50] This degree of intensity of police dislike for the media is not uncommon.

Professional friction was evident during the long investigation into the Green River slayings. The Seattle newspapers and television stations were increasingly incensed about the murders. The police explained how and why they had withheld notification to the news media about the discovery of the initial victims' bodies.[51] After almost a year of escalating tension between the Green River Task Force and the Seattle media, a crisis point was reached. The police media relations problems that increased throughout the summer and in the early fall eventually reached a climax in November. In the previous months, the news agencies inundated Frank Adamson, Vern Thomas, and County Executive Randy Revelle with criticism about inadequate media access to the Green River case detectives.[52]

POSITIVE EFFECTS OF THE MEDIA

Given the complexity of stakeholder interactions and relationships in serial murder cases, there is bound to be conflict at times. There are also instances of mutual benefit. In the Green River case, the media coverage resulted in two positive effects, dissemination of public safety information and motivation for law enforcement.

Dissemination of Public Safety Information

There was repeated media coverage of the crimes, and the investigation to find the killer. This promoted the public safety.

Massive publicity was afforded these serial murder cases. The Seattle morning newspapers featured the Green River murders story at the top of their front pages. "Three More Young Women Found Slain," headlined the *Seattle Times.* Kraske's recorded announcement Sunday night via the message telephone motivated the news organizations to rush and race for facts.[53]

Motivation for Law Enforcement

The Green River serial murder investigation was one of the longest in American history. This was due to the large number of victims, and the difficulty in locating many of the victims' remains. During most of that time, the media was a factor.

Toward the end of 1985, investigators were considering scaling back the probe, as no new bodies were being found, and there was virtually no progress in identifying the assailant. A meeting was held to discuss this possibility, but women's groups and the media had politicized these crimes. The need for their solution was elevated to the status of a political icon. Hill could not just declare that the investigation had ended: "Sorry folks, we couldn't do it."[54]

NEGATIVE EFFECTS OF THE MEDIA

Media coverage of the Green River case was not entirely beneficial. It resulted in certain problems. They included interference with the investigation, the creation of media zones, and media mistakes.

The media swarmed over the Green River case. Three major types of media interference with the investigation included following the police, tampering with witnesses, and "blowing" police stakeouts.

The Green River murders investigation was beset with a close media presence. On one occasion, "The searchers expanded their efforts, searching a number of ravines. The usual media pack was there, waiting. A reporter for the *Times* and one for KIRO stood together on the road not far from the police command post, a van parked along the roadside."[55]

In 1987, Dave Reichert led a search party to Ridgway's house. The media was not caught unawares. "A newspaper reporter beat him to the door."[56]

In the Green River case, after the discovery of the river murders, the police found that they were outnumbered by the reporters who were also working the Sea-Tac strip for information and answers, talking to victims' relatives and friends and generally interfering with the police investigation.[57] The problem posed by this redundant journalistic questioning of witnesses was explained by Smith and Guillen, "The problem was to figure out who really knew something, and who didn't and the uncontrolled publicity was making that task extremely difficult."[58]

Smith and Guillen offered an extended description of how media tampering impaired the police investigation:

The media firestorm was actually increasing, Kraske realized. Already detectives were complaining that it was almost impossible to talk to potential witnesses who hadn't already been interviewed by some reporter from someplace. Worse, the reporters were generally untrained in conducting investigation interviews. Often they inadvertently contaminated the witnesses' recollections by telling them things the witness wouldn't have known. A case in point was *The Times* report a few days earlier about the supposed connection of the women. A reported fact soon had the effect of becoming an actual fact, at least in the minds of potential witnesses. Soon, witnesses were telling police that sure, all the women had known each other, and it was impossible to say who *really* knew that and who had only read or heard it.[59]

Finally, by late August 1982, Kraske lost his patience with the circuslike atmosphere around the investigation. The initial task was to convince the media to reduce the pressure. Kraske told police spokesperson Pat Ferguson to deliver the message.[60]

Ferguson told the *Tacoma News-Tribune*, "Its been the sheer number of reporters on every scene in connection with this story that has us over-whelmed. They have been reaching witnesses and acquaintances of witnesses before we had a chance to get to them."[61] The problem, Ferguson continued, was, "With people like this who have been involved in a crime like this, it changes the way people talk to a police officer if they have been interviewed on television first or if the newspapers have been talking with them. We cringe each time we see a vehicle description or a nickname of a possible suspect on the air before we have a chance to locate the vehicle, or find the subject."[62]

During the Green River serial investigation, the media assisted the killer several times. In August 1982, a stakeout of the killer's dumping grounds was revealed on the evening news. That evening, a Seattle television helicopter over-flew the Green River with a live report on the evening news. The airborne reporter declared that the Green River was under police surveillance. The police were furious. Detectives blamed the media for destroying their only chance to apprehend the murderer before it could be implemented.[63]

More than a year later, the media again complicated the lives of investigators. A sudden change in the killer's dump sites from the river to dry land most likely was the result of the substantial publicity, the FBI agents said.[64] Smith and Guillen noted that the killer undoubtedly did return occasionally to the dumpsites. Or, at least he had until the television reports warned him that it was now too dangerous to continue when it disclosed the recent surveillance operation. Now, no one knew the killer's location.[65]

Scott added, "Police thought they could catch the killer by staking out parts of the dumping area and waiting. But a television newscaster flying overhead reported for all his viewers that he could see the police watching certain areas."[66] Similarly, Brady observed that when the dumpsite stakeouts were arranged, "Almost immediately, the sensationalist media leaked this information to the general public—and presumably to the killer, for he did not return to the scene of the crime this time."[67]

There were numerous instances where media zones were created during the Green River investigation. Smith and Guillen described how on Monday, August 23, 1983, the police decided to release the names of victims Opel Mills and Cynthia Hinds. Almost immediately, members of the media began to swarm all around the families.[68]

When a man named Ernest W. (Bill) McLean was a suspect, his neighbor-hood became a news zone. There was a pack of reporters still gathered outside the local police headquarters and McLean's house in Riverton Heights. They lingered at both locations, sharing information and watching everything and everyone for any new developments in the case.[69]

On February 6, 1986, at about 4:30 in the afternoon, the Green River Task Force searched a house on South 139th Street in Seattle. Within a matter of minutes, television camera crews were setting up in the street outside the house. The entire street was packed with news personnel, the neighbors, and curious sightseers.[70]

Media intrusion also was a factor in the Green River investigation. At one point in the investigation, the police continued their search of the woods on the north side of a road, where they soon discovered a fourth skeleton. The rain stopped, the sun came out, and the narrow country lane was gridlocked with news media vehicles. At least a hundred newspaper reporters, television cameramen, and sound technicians—including a crew from West Germany—filled the road, walking around while the police tried to ignore them.[71]

In the Green River case, journalists elicited confessions from two incarcer-ated persons, Robert Matthias and Richard Carbone. A careful background check, however, would have revealed that they were in prison during many of the crimes, and thus could not be guilty. Instead, headlines in the *San Francisco Chronicle* proclaimed the capture of the Green River killer.

Once the claims were made public, the task force was obligated to go through the exercise of formally determining their validity, for reasons of pub-lic image if nothing else. And, within a few hours, it was easily determined that Matthias and Carbone had absolutely nothing to do with the Green River murders.[72]

PUBLIC RELATIONS ASPECTS

The police used the media to attain law enforcement objectives in this case. Publicity elicited tips. The communication tactical media mix included televi-sion, news conferences, and a public meeting.

Police Urged to Use the Media

There were numerous suggestions for media involvement in the Green River investigation. The FBI recommended that the task force solicit media assis-tance. The police should use the media more, former FBI profiler John Douglas suggested. It was suggested that a newspaper or television station profile an investigator, and use the opportunity to promote the investigator as a "super cop" or as a relentless pursuer, in hopes that the killer might be provoked to contact the police.[73]

The link between case publicity and tips is a common aspect of these crimes. The accelerated investigative pace produced other problems as well as benefits.

One was a steep rise in new tips about the murders, which seemed to depend on the amount of publicity the case received.[74]

A variety of publicity channels was tapped by the task force during the investigation. They included news conferences, news releases, the release of composites of victims, billboards, and even the taping of a segment for the *Crimestoppers* television program.[75]

Until the conviction of Gary Ridgway for the Green River killings, there had been little in the way of investigative success. Wilson and Seaman recalled the one other good early suspect, and how a television program led to his identification. Only one man was arrested and named as a "viable" suspect during the early investigation. He was William Jay Stephens, aged thirty-nine, who was arrested in June 1989 following a tip resulting from a *Manhunt* television segment on the case.[76] According to Publications International Ltd., a televised plea by authorities, coupled with identifying information, led to the identification of a suspect in the Green River killings.[77]

Law enforcement held a special news conference in this case, just as baffled authorities had fifty years earlier in Cleveland, Ohio, when the Mad Butcher of Cleveland preyed upon the homeless. The Green River murders motivated the U. S. Justice Department to call an ad hoc homicide conference in January 1984. This conference was held mainly to inform the public about the gravity of these murders.[78]

Public meetings are frequently conducted as part of the public information efforts during a serial murder campaign. They are an efficient way to solicit public opinion and convey public information. They are also used to apprehend killers.

Serial killers often try to inject themselves into the investigation of their crimes. Public meetings are thought to be a way to identify such undercover offenders. In the Green River case, FBI serial murder expert Douglas recommended that the police should sponsor a community meeting to discuss the murders. There was a good chance the killer might actually attend such a meeting.[79]

A community meeting about the Green River murders was scheduled. The result? Four people attended. The audience was outnumbered five to one by the ten police officials and dozen reporters in attendance.[80]

CONCLUSION

A fugitive for two decades, the Green River killer is behind bars. Gary Ridgway is serving forty-eight consecutive life sentences, without possibility of parole.[81] He was also ordered by Judge Richard A. Jones of King County Superior Court to pay his victims' families restitution, from "any profit Mr. Ridgway might receive from a book or movie deal."[82]

While his exact death total is unknown, it is worth remembering that he confessed to sixty murders. He scattered the bodies in groups located near his home, so he could visit the sites for necrophilia or just reminiscing.

The media coverage of the Green River case was beneficial, in that it motivated the police and informed the public of safety information. But the negative consequences of the media on the investigation were enormous. Relations between the media and law enforcement were shown to be mutually disrespectful and even hostile.

A variety of public relations tactics were used by the task force public information campaign, most notably television and a so-called homicide conference. In addition, public information initiatives in this case included a public meeting, outdoor communication, news releases, and news conferences.

10

ANDREW CUNANAN

ANDREW CUNANAN WAS perceived as a highly intelligent child. He attended an exclusive San Diego prep school, and mingled there with children of some of the wealthiest local citizens. It was at this time, if not earlier, that an alternate fantasy world began to hold an attraction for him.

His entree to most conversations was a personal claim too grandiose, too over-the-top to be believed. But that was Andrew. Was, for example, his bedroom really a shrine to Tom Cruise? His homosexual lifestyle and his use and selling of recreational street drugs placed him at a certain socioeconomic level in the San Diego gay community.

Perhaps his life began to spin out of control when he and his former sugar daddy, wealthy Norman Blanchard, went separate ways. He gained weight and credit-card debt, and lost friends as well as options as his mood darkened and his attitude became pessimistic, even fatalistic. Before killing Gianni Versace in Miami Beach, he killed two lovers who had rejected him, as well as murdering a well-known Chicago-area realtor (who was not known to be gay) and a park service employee.

For the media, the Cunanan case was too good to be true. It was a story (or stories) with legs. There was substantial media interest in the Cunanan case, initially in the location of his murders but later nationwide. This media interest led to misbehavior.

To attain an optimal understanding of these crimes, we will consider eight topics. The criminal and his crimes will be described. The investigation, and the Cunanan resolution will be recalled. Media interest will be documented, along with the positive and negative effects of the media, and the use of public relations functions and tactics.

THE CRIMINAL

Andrew Cunanan was born to Modesto (Pete) and MaryAnn Cunanan on August 31, 1969. Pete was from the Philippines, and MaryAnn was an

American girl from California.[1] Pete fled to his homeland in 1988 after being caught embezzling more than $100,000.[2]

Andrew Cunanan grew up in Rancho Bernardo, California.[3] In San Diego, he attended the prestigious Bishop's School.[4] He had a seemingly normal childhood.

Cunanan's personality was profiled by Michaud and Hazelwood, "Cunanan had also exhibited enough traits of the antisocial personality—lying, substance abuse, promiscuity, disdain for social norms, cruelty, use of aliases, lack of a fixed address—to warrant a curbside opinion that he was a sociopath and a narcissist as well."[5]

He was an extravagant and ostentatious spender. "Cunanan spent lavishly— he reportedly owed Nieman-Marcus forty-six thousand dollars at his death."[6] An attorney who asked to be identified only as Mr. G. was interviewed after Cunanan's death. According to Indiana, "G. describes the rather extravagant taste in clothes and dinners that Cunanan apparently enjoyed."[7]

Cunanan had a decidedly nontraditional sex life. Michaud and Hazelwood observed that according to several sources, Cunanan preferred sadomasochistic pornography. One former sex partner described Cunanan's sexual behavior as "extreme." Daniel Stih knew Cunanan for about half a year, and did not like him very much. Stih described Cunanan as "asexual."[8] Scott added that Cunanan lived off of rich older men, smoked expensive cigars, and was a generally generous and friendly person. That was the public Andrew. The darkness in his soul involved leather straps, sadomasochism, pornographic videotapes, and black latex masks with only a nose opening for bondage.[9] He moved in with Norman Blanchard at 100 Coast Drive of San Diego in summer 1995 as a "kept man."[10]

He sold drugs. Erik Greenman, Cunanan's former roommate, told police investigators that Cunanan sold stolen pharmaceutical drugs.[11] Scott agreed, noting that Cunanan sold prescription drugs on the street, such as Prozac and Xanax.[12] According to Michaud and Hazelwood, Cunanan "dealt and consumed (sometimes injecting) a variety of drugs, including cocaine, methamphetamine, and the male hormone testosterone."[13]

He used drugs, too. He was known in San Diego for his use of recreational drugs. In Miami, prior to the attack on Gianni Versace, he regularly bought crack cocaine from a street dealer named Lyle.[14]

Impression formation was very important to Cunanan, who felt no qualms about intentionally staging events to create a false but beneficial impression. Two incidents revealed this tendency. Jeff Trail told the story of Cunanan's birthday party, held just before Cunanan and Blanchford became lovers. Trail said that Cunanan purchased several expensive presents for himself, then gave them to friends to wrap and present to him in front of Blanchford.[15] According to Indiana, "Trail apparently believed Cunanan's motive for doing this was an effort to impress Blanchford by showing Blanchford that Cunanan's friends liked him so much that they purchased expensive gifts for his birthday."[16]

A second incident similarly revealed Cunanan's desire to stage reality in order to impress his acquaintances. At a dinner party in San Francisco, Cunanan asked Trail to tell guests that Trail was an instructor at the California Highway Patrol academy, not a cadet in training.[17] He reportedly also asked a friend who was an employee of Southwest Airlines to present himself as a country and western singer.[18]

THE CRIMES

What caused Andrew Cunanan to strike out as he did, killing five people in the spring and summer of 1997? Although his death precludes certain knowledge, it appears that something set Cunanan off. "Something we may never know happened in early 1997 that made Cunanan, who had no history of violence, suddenly act like a desperate man. At a talk about safe sex, he made an outburst that indicated he may have thought that he was infected with AIDS."[19] Michaud and Hazelwood added that "By the following spring, Cunanan appears to have gone broke and was drinking heavily."[20] John Semeran, a Cunanan acquaintance, saw him in spring 1997, and recalled, "Something had snapped in him. Now I realize the guy was hunting—he was getting the thrill of the hunt, the thrill of the kill. I saw it in his eyes. I saw it in his body. He had stepped over the edge."[21]

"But then he began to age. His appearance—the essence of his self-esteem—began to fade. He was finding it difficult to attract the rich and appreciative sexual partners he believed he deserved," another Cunanan acquaintance stated. He concluded, "So Andrew Cunanan, I believe, decided to get even. He did so by killing those who represented or symbolized the men who'd ruined and then rejected him."[22]

Cunanan killed five people. The initial victim was Jeffery Trail, who was murdered on April 27, 1997, in Minneapolis, Minnesota. He was battered repeatedly on the head with a hammer, and left wrapped in a rolled-up carpet.[23]

Two days later, on April 29, 1997, David Madson was killed by Cunanan. His body was found by fishermen at a lake an hour north of Minneapolis.[24] He had been shot once in the head, once in the eye, and also once in the back with a .40-caliber firearm.[25]

Lee Miglin was slain on May 3, 1997, at his Chicago residence. The seventy-five-year-old real estate developer was tied up, and his body was partly wrapped in plastic and tape. His head was taped, except for two airholes.[26] Miglin was tortured. Several of his ribs were broken, and he was stabbed, Michaud and Hazelwood recalled.[27] Miglin's "sadistically broken body" was left on the floor in the garage.[28] According to Scott, Miglin's body revealed superficial wounds from a sharp metal tool, probably from being tortured to tell Cunanan where his money and car keys were.[29] Miglin's assailant was careful not to leave behind any fingerprints. That is because he wore gloves.[30]

It has been alleged that Miglin was gay, despite a seemingly successful marriage, and that he knew Cunanan.[31]

Cemetery caretaker William Reese was murdered on May 9, 1997. He worked at the Finn's Point National Cemetery in Pennsville, New Jersey.[32] The forty-five-year-old was shot in the head, and his 1995 Chevy pick-up truck was missing.[33]

The final Cunanan killing claimed the life of Gianni Versace in Miami Beach on July 15, 1997. This crime differed from the four others in two important respects. Versace was clearly the most notable of Cunanan's five murder victims. He was also the only one with whom Cunanan was not intimate, or from whom he did not steal something.[34]

THE INVESTIGATION

The Cunanan serial murder investigation was noteworthy in a couple of ways. It was a difficult case for a number of reasons. Numerous mistakes were made by law enforcement during this multistate probe. In this section, we will consider the investigations, investigative mistakes, and the difficulty of the case.

Local police and federal law enforcement officials pursued Cunanan from coast to coast. Perhaps this led to Clarkson's conclusion that this investigation involved "the biggest manhunt in American criminal history."[35] There were in fact several Cunanan investigations, conducted in a half-dozen jurisdictions by as many police agencies.

In Minneapolis, where the murders began, "With Madsen and Trail dead, and Cunanan missing, Minnesota authorities immediately notified local and federal authorities for help."[36] After Trail's murder, Minneapolis police initiated an investigation. Cunanan became one of their first suspects. Monique Salvetti, a public defender, told police that a man named Greg Nelson might be a prime candidate, but she also mentioned Cunanan as a possible person of interest.[37]

In Chicago, city police began the probe into Miglin's murder. After the discovery of Madsen's Jeep around the corner from the Miglin residence, the link between the Minneapolis murders and Miglin's death became apparent. Chicago police were blamed for numerous leaks of confidential case information.[38]

In Pennsville, New Jersey, local police were on the Reese murder case. They set up a command center for the numerous other police forces already on the case. Airports up and down the East Coast were put under surveillance, as were bus and train terminals and other likely avenues of escape for the fugitive.[39]

The Federal Bureau of Investigation (FBI) had been involved in the case since the Miglin murder. According to Minneapolis police sergeant Steven Wagner, from that time the FBI was deeply involved in the case, it escalated. Clarkson agreed, adding "Now the whole complexion of the case did change. With the FBI in, the investigation would expand—there would be a national manhunt." Six days after the Versace murder, the FBI activated a central command facility in Washington, D.C., to coordinate the investigation.[40]

Various law enforcement agencies were guilty of mistakes during the Cunanan case. Orth noted that the investigation into Cunanan's crimes seems to have been rife with mistakes. There is reason to believe that an insufficient understanding of their prey hampered the police. Police in several jurisdictions, the FBI, and prosecutors were still trying to understand Cunanan and his motives a week into the Miami manhunt, and a full three months after Jeff Trail's murder.[41]

In the Miglin case, for instance, Chicago police were accused of being uncooperative with other police agencies. During the Versace probe, police were accused of "sloppy investigative work." Miami police and the FBI failed to locate where Cunanan had stayed in Miami for three days after the Versace murder. Three people told the FBI that Cunanan would head to Miami and try to contact Versace, but there is no such mention in any FBI files.[42]

Maybe we should not be too critical of law enforcement errors in the Cunanan case. This was an exceptionally difficult investigation, for a number of reasons. For instance, Cunanan changed the license plates on the vehicle he stole from Reese in a Wal-Mart parking lot in Florence, South Carolina. He also used an alias while on the run, Kurt Matthew DeMars.[43]

Cunanan was a cunning criminal. He eluded police at every turn during his murder spree. One source realized that Cunanan had gotten the jump on the police, and he remained ahead of the law until his death.[44]

Chicago police were initially clueless in their probe. According to Orth, for three days after Lee Miglin's murder, until Wednesday afternoon, the Chicago police had no suspects. She concluded that from the beginning of the investigation Cunanan frustrated the police because they had no clues, nothing concrete to guide their probe. Cunanan was never arrested, so law enforcement agencies were unable to identify him or match the fingerprints discovered at the various crime scenes.[45]

THE RESOLUTION OF THE CASE

Cunanan seemingly vanished after murdering Versace. Police believed he had fled from Miami. In fact, he had moved about forty blocks from the Versace crime scene.

On July 23, 1997, Cunanan's clandestine presence was detected on a houseboat in Indian Creek, parked at 5250 Collins Avenue. The houseboat was owned by Torsten Reineck, who resided in Las Vegas, and was being watched by caretaker Fernando Carreira. Carreira, age seventy-one at the time, entered the houseboat after noticing that the lock had been broken, and heard a shot soon thereafter.[46] The first police officers arrived at the scene within four minutes. More than one hundred police officers from several jurisdictions surrounded the houseboat within ten minutes of the initial call to 911.[47]

Police surrounded the houseboat, and told Cunanan to surrender and come out. When there was no reply, Miami-Dade SRT officers sprayed pepper spray and CS gas into the residence at about 8:00 p.m. They entered the houseboat at 8:20, but did not locate Cunanan's body for some time. At 9:00, a police spokesperson misinformed the media, telling them that no bodies were found in the police search.[48]

MEDIA INTEREST IN THE CRIMES

Andrew Cunanan, perhaps best known for the murder of Gianni Versace, killed six people, including himself. Media coverage of his nationwide murder spree drew nationwide attention. According to Indiana, "The scariest aspect of the Andrew Cunanan story was the insensible proliferation of media coverage of it following the shooting of Gianni Versace: the killer, widely ignored while he left a trail of bodies from Minnesota to New Jersey, became, abruptly, a diabolical icon in the circus of American celebrity."[49]

In the Andrew Cunanan case, there were again two stories, or a story within a story, if you will. The murders were the main story, and the true sexual orientation of a wealthy married Chicago businessman, Lee Miglin, was the other. This enhanced the desirability of the Cunanan murders as a news topic.

The existence of both stories was perceived by Orth. The story then became considerably more sensational, launching Cunanan's previous murders that were considered to be "domestic crime," albeit gay ones, into a tale of sordid immorality.[50] As for the second, salacious story, the Chicago media searched all over town, trying to discover whether or not Miglin was gay and if his son Duke knew Andrew, but they were frustrated in these efforts.[51]

POSITIVE EFFECTS OF THE MEDIA

In the present study, it is postulated that there are three potential beneficial consequences of media involvement in serial murder investigations. Media motivates law enforcement, it assists in apprehension of killers, and it disseminates public safety information. Each of these beneficial outcomes was realized to some extent in the Cunanan case.

Motivated Law Enforcement

His exploits received considerable publicity, which the authorities took notice of, it appears. "Absolutely, the press drove it," said Peter Ahern of the San Diego FBI Field Office, referring to the media's effect on the investigation.[52] Orth concluded that "The murder of Versace and the massive amount of coverage it engendered jolted both the FBI and local authorities."[53]

Assisted in Apprehension

During the time that Andrew Cunanan was a fugitive, a plan was developed to assist in his apprehension, based on a personal televised appeal from his old friend Liz Cote. It was hoped that Cunanan might surrender after viewing the segment. The profilers wanted Andrew's old college pal and ex-housemate Cote to make the appeal, because she would seem more independent and less controlled by the FBI than Andrew's family.[54]

Disseminated Public Safety Information

Later in this chapter we will discuss the role of Dan Pryor in the Cunanan case. Pryor is the unsung hero of the case, the only one to broadcast a warning about Cunanan to Miami's gay community. Suffice it to say that the FBI was much more interested in apprehending Cunanan than in warning the public about his presence.

NEGATIVE EFFECTS OF THE MEDIA

It is safe to say that the negative consequences of media coverage of Andrew Cunanan's murders and related exploits easily outweighed the benefits of that mass communication activity. Specific problems included media interference with the investigation, the fact that the media informed the killer, checkbook journalism, the creation of celebrities, the creation of media zones, the motivation of the killer by the media, and finally, direct media involvement in the case.

Interference with the Investigation

The media was very interested in the Cunanan case. This led to behavior considered inimical to the police investigation. Three specific types of media interference in the investigation will be considered: crime scene tampering, eavesdropping on the police, and witness harassment.

Cunanan's Miami hotel room was located by the media before the police found it. Chuck Goudie was a reporter for WLS-TV in Chicago. He not only entered the room, he handled a variety of objects, thereby contaminating the crime scene and any potential evidence located there.[55]

The police reported that during the Cunanan investigation, "the media got in our way. We couldn't use our radios," said Miami Beach Police Department Sergeant Richard Pelosi. Paul Marcus, a detective in the same force, corroborated Pelosi's recollection, "We had to talk on land lines because of the media. The *Herald* and the TV stations could monitor the radio. We had to be very careful—we couldn't even use cell phones."[56]

An extreme example of media eavesdropping can be cited, also from the Cunanan investigation. Sergeant Pelosi recalled, "One day, all of a sudden, a camera and boom mike are outside our window of the third-floor detective bureau. The boom mike was from a local channel. We made them move it."[57]

In the Cunanan case, the media interfered with the investigation in another way. Members of the media harassed witnesses. A former deep-pockets, sugar daddy lover of Cunanan's named Norman Blanchard was chased by the media, all the way across an ocean. Reporters from the *Chicago Tribune* pursued Norman Blanchard via satellite phone records as he and Peter Cooper, a friend, were hoping to escape the media by sailing for London on the QE2. Blanchford refused to comment, but the *Tribune* had its London reporter waiting on the dock like a chauffeur, with a sign saying "Norman Blanchard." Blanchford did not talk to the reporter, but when the aggressive journalist tracked him down to his London hotel room, Blanchford told him in unequivocal terms to leave him alone.[58]

Another witness received similar treatment from the media. Betsy Brazis was a neighbor of the Miglins, who reportedly saw Miglin and Cunanan in conversation. "Betsy Brazis's life was disrupted long after the murders," because reporters would follow her, and try anything to engage her in conversation.[59]

Media Informed the Killer

The investigation into Andrew Cunanan's flight and murders was impaired twice by the media. Initially, as he fled from Chicago to the East Coast, Cunanan was being tracked by the cell phone "triggerfish," or triangulation device, in the victim's Lexus he was driving. An all-news radio station in Philadelphia had broadcast that Cunanan was being tracked, as did numerous other radio and TV stations.[60] When found, much of the inside of the Lexus was destroyed where Cunanan had tried to disable the device after learning about it on the news.

Orth clarified the impact of the disclosure on the investigation. Cunanan was in a state of panic. He knew from news reports that his flight was being followed electronically. "Everyone who was working on (the case) was outraged," said Randall Schwegman, Chicago County Sheriff.[61] The police would never get so close to Andrew again.[62]

In a tragic sequel to this situation, Cunanan was alerted to seek another vehicle by the news reports. This resulted in the death of the owner of the vehicle he stole, as Sergeant Steve Wagner noted. "I still believe that precipitated Reese's death. He [Cunanan] had to get rid of that car."[63]

The media might have assisted Cunanan again, shortly before his death, as he took refuge on a houseboat in Miami Beach. Television station helicopters sent live shots from overhead, giving away the tactical activity of the Metro-Dade SRT team and endangering law enforcement personnel.[64]

Finally, the Miami Beach Police Department public information staff had to take action. Al Boza began to call television stations, saying "Folks, you're giving tactical information, because whoever that is inside is delighted to see we have got three people in front, two on the side." The SRT team and several others were potentially in danger.[65] Miami Beach Police Department officer Bobby Hernandez concluded, "As an officer its a safety issue—there's a huge amount of vulnerability. The media would not back off."[66]

Checkbook Journalism

Checkbook journalism was most evident in the Cunanan case. From Andrew's father's $10,000 *Inside Edition* windfall to his brother and sister's refusal "to speak to the media if they were not paid," greed marked this case.[67] One Cunanan associate, Steven Gomer, received a total of 175 requests from the press and television.[68]

Former Cunanan roommate Erik Greenman accepted $85,000 from the *National Enquirer* to peddle a tale about Cunanan's infatuation with Tom Cruise, and gay activist and drag queen Nicole Ramirez Murray made $5,000 from the *Globe*.[69] Robbins Thompson appeared on *Hard Copy* for $5,000, and he made several thousand more on *Sally Jesse Raphael*.[70] Anne and Rachel Rifat received $20,000 for photographs of Cunanan, and Rachel's twin brother Matthew sold some other photos for $10,000.[71] Andrew White was paid $4,000 by *Hard Copy*, while Karen Lapinski and Evan Wallit received a reported six-figures payment for photographs of Cunanan and one of his victims together.[72] Former prep schoolmates from Bishop's "were willing to talk, but only if they were paid," and the photographer who shot Gianni Versace's bare feet protruding from the back of the ambulance asked $30,000 for the photo.[73]

Celebrity

A celebrity after he killed Gianni Versace, Andrew Cunanan enjoyed reading about himself. Then, he committed suicide on a friend's houseboat. As Indiana recalled, Cunanan found articles about himself in magazines and large metro daily newspapers that called him a "chameleon," and a "master of disguise."[74] According to Douglas and Olshaker, "Cunanan has left newspaper clippings about the other three murders. Many of the serial offenders I talked to told me why they do this—to document their 'accomplishments' and revel in them."[75]

Michaud and Hazelwood concluded that Cunanan knew his murders were a major national news story. Several papers published lengthy articles about the case, including the *New York Times*.[76] He seemed to relish his celebrity status.

In the Cunanan case, not only did the killer achieve a measure of notoriety, but so did many of his former associates in the gay world. Nicole Ramirez Murray said that "I've never been in more limos in two weeks, and I've been in limos. *G.M.A.* [*Good Morning America*] and the *Today Show* fought over me, and tried to make me swear I wouldn't go on the other one."[77]

Media Zones

"I never before experienced anything near the media frenzy that occurred when designer Gianni Versace was murdered outside his home," declared former FBI profiler John Douglas.[78] There were at least four media zones in the Andrew Cunanan case: in Minneapolis, after the first two murders, in Chicago, where he killed Lee Miglin, in the New Jersey town where he killed William Reese, and in Miami, where he killed Gianni Versace and committed suicide.

The initial Cunanan murders were in Minneapolis, and the first media zones appeared there, too. David Madsen's funeral in Barron, Minnesota, drew hordes of reporters, Orth noted. She added that in Barron the local townspeople intentionally made the journalists feel completely unwelcome.[79]

In Chicago, reporters from *Fox News* and the Chicago local TV stations were ringing the Miglin's neighbor's doorbells, asking for any information.[80] The first television truck arrived at the Miglin home twelve minutes after the first police radio call.[81]

In New Jersey, panic swept the countryside, induced by the unfamiliar sight of fifteen or twenty satellite television trucks racing through thinly populated rural townships on route to the crime scene.[82] The murder victim's widow was treated poorly; in the days after her husband's murder, reporters pestered Rebecca Reese incessantly. She was finally forced to call the police to remove the media vans from her neighbor's property. For several weeks they would occasionally drive up to her house at night and shine their light into her windows, "giving the effect of being in a concentration camp," said one observer.[83]

There was a massive media manifestation in Miami, as well. The poles and dishes on satellite television trucks looked like several giant lollipops dotting the Florida sky. The local Miami television stations broadcasted the houseboat scene live in English and Spanish.[84] Police radio transmission transcripts reveal that the media residents of the Miami news zone were a bit aggressive. "We've got the media here at 5101 Seacoast Towers. Would you advise on media? He's trying to get through here," one officer radioed. He was told, "He needs to stay outside the perimeter. He's not to pass that point."[85] Another radio dispatch declared, "I have three media here—they're getting a little hostile. But I'm keeping them back. They're getting real hostile. They're telling me I don't know the law."[86]

Media Motivated Cunanan

There is reason to believe that Cunanan was motivated, in part, by the media coverage of his crimes. That was the opinion of Chicago Police Department Captain Tom Cronin. The publicity was more sexual to him than anything else, Cronin speculated. Right after committing these homicides, Cunanan most likely went to a gay bar in the afternoon when the news was on and his likeness was on television, and he sat there having a drink and relishing his secret, according to Cronin.[87]

Direct Media Involvement

As in many serial murder cases, reporters became part of the story, at times. They occasionally beat the police to key witnesses and undiscovered facts. Chisago County law enforcement officials learned of the discovery of Madsen's Jeep from the local NBC affiliate, not from other police.[88]

PUBLIC RELATIONS ASPECTS

Public relations, or public information, played a major role in this case. In this section, we will assess this public relations activity on two levels. We will examine both public relations functions and tactics.

It is usually possible to identify the purposes or functions being served by public relations activity. In the case of the Cunanan investigation, there were two such purposes behind the public relations. Limiting media access to information and managing the crisis were both evident. Each purpose will be considered.

The media frequently met a stonewall in the Andrew Cunanan case. The *Sun-Times* could elicit very little information from the Chicago Police Department.[89] In general the police divulged as little as possible.

Crisis management is another typical public relations function. Serial murders frequently qualify in this category, as far as local law enforcement and civic leaders are concerned. For instance, when Andrew Cunanan struck in Miami Beach, city public relations officials went into their crisis management mode. The first instinct of the Miami authorities was to defend the municipal image, and the Miami Beach police were effectively muzzled.[90]

Most public relations campaigns and activities use more than one kind of media or communication tactic. The specific mixture of media used in a campaign is called a media mix. In the Cunanan case, the public relations media mix included eight tactics, such as news releases, *Crimestopper*-type television, news conferences, brochures, posters, magazines, the Internet, and fliers.

A series of three releases issued by the Miami Beach Police Department dragged out the admission that their suspect was Andrew Cunanan. Finally, at 8:30 p.m., a third news release admitted what had been known for quite awhile—the police were searching for Cunanan.[91]

Crimestoppers received two valuable tips regarding the whereabouts of Andrew Cunanan in Miami Beach, as police pursued him there. One tip placed Cunanan at the Crystal Beach Club, at 71st and Collins Avenue, and the other located him at the Twist Nightclub.[92] Both times Cunanan was gone before the police arrived.

Families of serial murder victims occasionally conduct news conferences. The family of one of the victims of Andrew Cunanan held a private memorial mass right after the murder. Soon after that, the family convened a press conference.[93]

Bilingual brochures have been employed during serial murder investigations, when dictated by target audience linguistic factors. As Scott observed, in the Andrew Cunanan investigation, responding to possible Cunanan sightings in Florida, the FBI disseminated leaflets in four languages: English, Spanish, French, and Arabic.[94]

There was criticism of the FBI handling of the Andrew Cunanan investigation. Because they wanted to surprise him they conducted undercover surveillance-type operations, instead of using posters as other locales did. Glen Albin, editor of a Miami Beach newspaper, *Ocean Drive*, declared that if posters had been put up, Cunanan would have been caught. In light of the dynamics of the gay community, posters would have worked, Albin alleged.[95]

Magazines were the only publicity source used to warn the gay community. The FBI had decided to try and capture Cunanan without help, FBI agent Keith Evans informed Miami Beach homicide detective Paul Scrimshaw. Evans made it very clear to Scrimshaw that the FBI did not want publicity about Cunanan; the Bureau preferred to keep the investigation low key.[96]

Orth described the magazine publicity in this case. It was not until July 12, 1997, that *Scoop* magazine, a weekly gay publication serving South Florida, published an article with the headline; "Wanted by the FBI! Accused Killer Has Many Faces." This was the first mention of Cunanan, the first time the gay media in South Florida ran anything at all about Cunanan. *Scoop* ran a full-page warning piece by Dan Pryor, a local Miami radio reporter who received his information from an Internet site. He decided to write the story because of "the high concentration of affluent gays in South Florida."[97] No other warnings were issued.[98]

The FBI visited gay organizations on the East Coast after Reese's murder. They distributed fliers with Cunanan's photograph before Gay Pride Week in Philadelphia. In New York and San Francisco, thousands of fliers with Cunanan's picture were distributed and posted in gay neighborhoods.

Later, in Miami, there was considerable controversy over fliers, or the lack thereof. When the FBI chose to pursue Cunanan quietly, without publicity, gay activists like Lilia Doe, who directed the Gay and Lesbian Community Center in Fort Lauderdale, made and distributed their own fliers. The FBI contended after Versace's murder that it had distributed thousands of fliers of Cunanan in the Miami area.[99]

CONCLUSION

In January 2004, a music-theatre piece was going to be produced, dealing with Cunanan's 1997 serial murders. Opposition to the piece was aptly summarized by Bill Peters of the Gay and Lesbian Community Center in Fort Lauderdale, Florida. He declared that "Cunanan was sick, and do you celebrate that? People's lives were gone, and do you celebrate that?"[100]

Andrew Cunanan was a complex individual, one whose precise motivations and needs are forever beyond our understanding. He was intelligent, but he was more "street smart," and he succeeded for a while in living both in the San Diego gay bar scene and as a "kept man" for a wealthy homosexual lover. He had both rags and riches.[101]

The media played a major role in the investigation into Cunanan's crimes. In a positive sense, it motivated the police. And the police tried unsuccessfully to use a televised appeal from an old friend to induce the fugitive to surrender. There was relatively little dissemination of public safety information about the Cunanan case.

Negative consequences of media coverage of the Cunanan case abounded. The media repeatedly interfered with the police during the investigation. Cunanan was informed of police plans and tactics through media coverage of the investigation. Media zones were created on a number of occasions. There were numerous instances of checkbook journalism, as well as the creation of celebrities from a variety of parties in the case.

Media conduct during this case endangered the lives of law enforcement personnel attempting to apprehend Cunanan. Media surveillance of a police meeting was noted, as were repeated media attempts to be allowed access to Cunanan crime scenes. Media coverage helped Cunanan escape the police and kill two other persons. On balance, the media contribution to the Cunanan case must be considered a negative one.

Two purposes or functions of Cunanan case public relations were identified, limiting media access to information, and managing the public relations crisis. Tactics used in the Cunanan case public relations efforts included news releases, *Crimestopper*-type television programs, news conferences, posters, fliers, magazines, and the Internet.

It is no overstatement to describe the Cunanan murders as media events. He was motivated by the media coverage of his exploits. He yearned for celebrity status, which he earned by killing and fleeing. Mass communication played a decisive and multifaceted role in the Cunanan case.

11

⎯•◦•⎯

PAUL BERNARDO AND KARLA HOMOLKA

THE SERIAL MURDERS of Canadians Paul Bernardo and Karla Homolka were few in number, but horrible in execution. Together this husband-and-wife team killed three teenaged girls. One of them was Karla's younger sister Tammy, whom she gave as a Christmas "gift" to Paul. Sedated by her sister and Paul to make the rape easier, Tammy choked on her own vomit and died.

Paul was busy in the early and mid-1990s as the notorious Scarborough Rapist. He may have raped as many as fifty-three women. This was just before he and Karla became a twosome, which is when the killings began. His sex drive, or libido, must have been enormous.

Perhaps the worst individual aspect of these crimes was the videotaping of victims. Paul and Karla produced homemade rape and torture videos, and the action was 100 percent real. The videotapes were considered virtually irrefutable proof that the prosecution's case was correct in accusing Bernardo and Homolka of heinous and fatal misdeeds.

It is difficult to understand the murders committed by Bernardo and Homolka. To enhance our comprehension of these deeds, we will consider ten main subjects. The criminals and their crimes will be described. The investigation, arrests, and trial will be explained, and their communication behavior noted. Public and media interest is shown along with the positive and negative effects of media coverage, and public relations aspects.

THE CRIMINALS

The murders were apparently joint husband-and-wife productions. In this section, we will attempt to form a better understanding of the crimes through the consideration of the criminals, Paul Bernardo and Karla Homolka.

Bernardo was born on August 27, 1964, to Kenneth and Marilyn Bernardo, and named Paul Kenneth Bernardo. His mother was described in the summer of 1965 as a relatively plump woman about thirty with an "obvious lack of dress sense." Kenneth was an accountant and Marilyn a homemaker. When he was sixteen, Bernardo's mother told him that he was the result of an affair with a very successful Canadian businessman. Chidley added that "After that, the distance between son and parents grew wider." Kenneth Bernardo admitted to the *Toronto Globe and Mail* in 1995 that Paul was not his biological son.[1]

By all accounts, Paul Bernardo was an adorable baby. He had bright blue eyes, thick wavy blond hair, and a smile that lit up his cherubic little face, one source recalled. A recent study noted, "Boy scout, good student—on the surface, Paul Bernardo was raised in a typical suburban environment." He grew up in a neighborhood called Guildwood, in Scarborough, a Toronto suburb. "Paul Bernardo, by all accounts, was a cute child," one source noted. A former neighbor recalled, "He looked like this sweet, angelic, Hollywood-type kid."[2]

Another youthful Paul Bernardo can be described, however. "Even at a young age, Paul seemed to have a distant relationship with the rest of the family." He ran away at age five or six, returning home several days later, but "nobody in the family even asked him where he had been," Chidley stated in *Macleans*. It seemed that Paul had trouble playing with others, "The young Paul rarely socialized with other children, and when he did, he would often burst into violent temper tantrums."[3]

He attended Sir Wilfrid Laurier High School, and later Albert Campbell High School. He attended college at the Scarborough branch of the University of Toronto.[4]

His sanity has been questioned. One psychiatrist defended his sanity, "There is nothing I have seen in the evidence so far available that Mr. Bernardo has or has had a major illness of a psychotic type, i.e. he is fully in touch with reality." Another diagnosis perceived "several pathological mental states," including paraphilia, sexual sadism, voyeurism, hebephilia, toucheurism, coprophilia, alcohol abuse, and narcissistic personality disorder.[5]

Despite his problems, Bernardo was a ladies' man. His high school yearbook shared his nickname, "Stud." One study concluded that for whatever reason, women who were attracted to Paul fell deeply in love with him and were willing to do virtually anything to keep him.[6]

Bernardo was a stalker. In July 1991, he stalked Rachel Ferron. She obtained Bernardo's license plate and told police, but nothing happened. Lori Lazurak and Tania Berges were stalked by Bernardo in March and April 1992. *Macleans* reported that "According to police surveillance teams, Bernardo was still stalking young women in the Toronto area in early 1993, in the weeks preceding his arrest." Karla Homolka told the authorities that Bernardo had recently purchased a stun gun to assist in his stalking endeavors.[7]

In 1990, Bernardo became unemployed. He lost his job at the international accounting firm Price-Waterhouse. He later turned to cigarette smuggling as a source of money, the Canadian Broadcasting Corporation (CBC) observed. Another study dated Bernardo's involvement in smuggling to February 1991.[8]

Bernardo was also the Scarborough Rapist. This infamous sexual predator was responsible for at least twenty-eight and as many as fifty-three rapes in

Scarborough in the early and mid-1990s. "Bernardo was a match for three fluid samples taken from victims of the Scarborough Rapist," Chidley recalled.[9]

Was Bernardo a Freemason? If so, were the crimes part of a Masonic conspiracy? These questions have been raised, most notably by Freemasonry Watch. This website referred to the killer as "Grand Lodge of Ontario, Canada Master Mason, Serial Killer and Serial Rapist Paul Bernardo."[10]

Bernardo changed his name. "He later assumed the name Paul Teale," according to Biography.ms.[11] The reason he changed his name is unknown. Karla Leanne Homolka was born on May 4, 1970. Her father Karel was a Czech immigrant, a salesman with a perpetual tan. Her mother worked at St. Catharines's Shaver Hospital.

Karla's relationship with her parents was unusual. Her childhood friend Lisa Stanton recalled that arguments between Karla and her parents over chores, homework, or other topics frequently ended with Karla yelling, "No!" and slamming the door of her room after entering.[12]

She had an enjoyable childhood. The swimming pool in the Homolka back yard became the meeting place for Karla and her friends. She made friends easily, and was popular. She did, however, have the disconcerting habit of yelling "Fuck."[13]

After her elementary education at Ferndale Public School, she attended the prestigious Sir Winston Churchill Secondary School. Karla was a member of the French Club. She did well in school.[14]

Her hair was the focus of her adolescent changes. She changed her hair color from blonde to brunette between her seventh and eighth grade years. Then, a few years later, "A kaleidoscope of colors—greens, blues and reds—appeared on a regular basis in Karla's hair."[15]

She discovered boys between her last year in elementary school and her entry into high school. She, Stanton, and another friend, Mandy Whatling, began taking walks together. They called the walks "SOGGings," for "Searching Out Gorgeous Guys."[16]

Karla's teenage angst led to self-mutilation at times. Stanton asked her about bruises and cuts on her arms. A couple of times she intentionally slit her wrist with a small knife.[17] Her prison psychiatric evaluation diagnosed her with "severe clinical depression, battered spousal syndrome and post traumatic stress disorder."[18]

"The extent of Homolka's involvement in the murders has been controversial. Some believe that she was simply a victim of Bernardo." The CBC reported the "outcry when the true scope of her involvement in murder became clear: not a helpless, manipulated victim, as it turned out, but a willing and enthusiastic participant in some appalling acts." An informed source added, "She implicated herself in first-degree murder as surely as her accomplice," said prosecutor Ray Houlahan, who described Homolka as "definitely, definitely not a victim."[19]

Her time in prison was highlighted by publicity about her love life. It was reported in the *Montreal Gazette* on September 22, 2000, that "Homolka was in a lesbian relationship with convicted child-rapist Christina Sherry." In fact, "Homolka's lesbian relationship was with Lynda Verroneau [sic]."[20] Another source noted that "While at Joliette Homolka was involved in a lesbian relationship with convicted bank robber Lynda Veronneau, who is due to inherit almost $1 million from a family estate."[21]

THE CRIMES

There were comparatively few victims of the Bernardo/Homolka serial murders. However, elements of the crimes made them unusually abhorrent. In this section, we will consider the crimes through examination of five topics. The murders of Tammy Homolka, Leslie Mahaffy, Kristen French, Elizabeth Bain, and others will be explored. If the name sounds familiar, it should. Tammy was Karla's younger sister. How Tammy became their first murder victim is a sad testament to how love can be twisted.

"Bernardo and Homolka were also responsible for the death of Homolka's youngest sister, Tammy. Homolka wanted to 'give' Tammy to Bernardo as a Christmas present. To do so, she drugged her sister Tammy with Halcion-laced drinks and then used a halothane-saturated cloth to further sedate her," according to one recent account. Unfortunately, "As a consequence of the drugs, Tammy died as a result of suffocating on her own vomit."[22]

This crime took place on December 23, 1990. According to one recent report, "During the subsequent rape by Bernardo, taped by Homolka when she herself wasn't sexually assaulting her own sister, Tammy choked on her own vomit and died. The murder was ruled accidental when an autopsy revealed nothing suspicious."[23]

Bernardo and Homolka "began a relationship of sexual perversion marked by escalating fantasies involving Homolka's fifteen-year-old sister Tammy," one source claimed. It added, "Those fantasies were tragically realised on December 23, 1990, when the two drugged the girl unconscious while alone with her in the Homolka family's St. Catherine's [sic] home."[24]

The Halothane was stolen by Homolka from the pet store where she worked. One recent analysis recalled that "Together she and Bernardo administered it to her fifteen-year-old sister Tammy Lyn [sic] Homolka along with a mixture of alcohol and halcion. They raped Tammy in the basement of the Homolka family home while she was unconscious." According to a CBC report, Bernardo told the police that he had attempted to revive her, to no avail, and Tammy's death was declared accidental.[25]

Tammy's death was *initially* ruled accidental. That quickly changed once news of the other murders was made public. Accordingly, "Tammy's body was exhumed by court order and based on the evidence derived from the new autopsy, Bernardo was tried and convicted of Tammy's murder."[26]

The fatal encounter was not the only attempt to use drugs to take sexual advantage of Tammy. Bernardo claimed that in July 1990, he and Karla served

Tammy spaghetti laden with Valium. Bernardo raped Tammy for about a minute or so before she began to awaken.[27]

On June 15, 1991, Bernardo abducted Leslie Mahaffy, whom he then tortured, raped, and killed, contended a recent analysis. It added that Mahaffy's dismembered body floated to the surface of Lake Gibson near St. Catharines, Ontario. Additional details on this terrible crime were provided by another account. It recalled that "The first was fourteen-year-old Leslie Mahaffy, kidnapped during a chance late-night encounter with Bernardo during June of 1991. She was raped and beaten for over 24 hours before being strangled with an electrical cord, dismembered, and encased in blocks of cement."[28]

Wikipedia offered additional information: "Bernardo—while stealing license plates to aid in his cigarette smuggling scheme—discovered Leslie Erin Mahaffy, who was standing at the door of her home because she had been locked out. The two spoke for some time and went back to Bernardo's car for a cigarette, at which point he forced her into the car and drove her to his home. There, Homolka and Bernardo held the girl hostage several days, sexually assaulting her repeatedly."[29] A Canadian media source added that on June 14, 1991, Bernardo kidnapped Leslie Mahaffy from the front porch of her house. He and Homolka raped and killed her.[30]

A final note on the Mahaffy murder. Most authorities mention the ironic fact that Mahaffy's body was discovered on the day that Bernardo and Homolka were married. Not the wedding present they had hoped for, perhaps.[31]

Less than a year after the Mahaffy murder, Bernardo struck again. On April 16, 1992, Bernardo, assisted by Homolka, abducted Kristen French from the parking lot of a church. Once more, Bernardo tortured, raped, and killed a young girl.[32] French was the last of the Bernardo/Homolka murder victims. Her treatment at the hands of her captors was terrible, to say the least.

"Next was Kristen French, 15, nabbed after school by the killer couple on April 16, 1992. The two took turns sexually molesting and raping the innocent girl at their home," noted one recent source. It concluded, "French was subjected to painful humiliations repeatedly before she was finally strangled by Bernardo and his trusty cord more than two days after her abduction. Her body was discarded and discovered in an illegal trash dump near Burlington."[33]

French was abducted from a church parking lot, claimed a recent analysis.[34] Another contemporary report noted that French was taken from the vicinity of her school.[35] It is interesting how even the most basic facts can be obscured by the passage of time and the reporting of different information.

"On April 16, 1992, the couple drove into a church parking lot. Homolka stepped out of the car with a map pretending to be lost and asking for help from 15-year-old Kristen Dawn French. Bernardo then approached from behind and used a knife to force Kristen into the back seat of the car," a recent analysis declared. Investigators searching the scene of the abduction discovered a piece of the map, one of French's shoes and tufts of her hair. This study added, "They brought French to their home where for several days they sexually assaulted, abused and tortured her. They killed her just before going to Easter Sunday dinner at Homolka's parent's home." French's remains were discovered in a ditch in Burlington, Ontario, on April 30, 1992.[36]

A slightly different perspective on this crime was offered by a Canadian source. In a much briefer account, the CBC noted that on April 16, 1992, "Bernardo, with the assistance of Homolka, kidnaps Kristen French from a church parking lot. After raping, torturing and killing her, they leave her body naked in a ditch, her hair cut off."[37]

Some believe that Tammy Homolka, Leslie Mahaffy, and Kristen French were not Bernardo's only murder victims. They point to the murder of Elizabeth Bain.

Bain was an acquaintance of Bernardo's. A man named Robert Baltovich was convicted of Bain's murder. However, "The discovery of new evidence pointing to Bernardo as the murderer led to Baltovich's release from prison."

"Some people including the defense attorneys for Robert Baltovich, think that Elizabeth Bain, a 22-year-old female in the Scarborough area of Toronto was abducted and murdered by Paul Bernardo in 1990," according to one recent source. It added that "There are numerous other links between Bernardo and Bain," which is why the Ontario Court of Appeals on December 2, 2004, set aside Baltovich's conviction and issued an order for a new trial. A recent book by Derek Finkle, *No Claim to Mercy,* reportedly presents the case that Bernardo killed Bain.[38]

Were there any additional Bernardo/Homolka slayings, or Bernardo murders? The trouble with determining precise body counts when it comes to serial murderers is that they sometimes keep secrets. In this case, one analysis reported that Bernardo "is also suspected of other murders."[39]

THE INVESTIGATION

The investigation into this pair's crimes began on June 21, 1991, when William Grekul and his wife found part of Leslie Mahaffy's body while canoeing on Lake Gibson. More pieces were located the following day. Within an hour a dozen officers with the Niagara Regional Police were on the scene. Police agencies in Niagara, Hamilton-Wentworth, and Halton carefully examined missing persons reports to help identify the dismembered body.[40]

French vanished on April 16, 1992. Police immediately questioned her family and friends for any clues to her disappearance. Michele Tousignant found one of French's shoes at the scene of her abduction, which the police cordoned off as a crime scene at a little after 10:30 the next morning. Investigators then located part of a map of Canada, and a tiny lock of French's curled hair.[41]

Police searched for a Camaro, based on an eyewitness account of the abduction. Halton Police Department Detective Sergeant Bob Waller "focused on a Camaro, based mainly on Packham's sighting. It was a good lead." After the discovery of French's remains by Roger Boyer, Constable Ken DeBoer was at the site and took command of the investigation within minutes.[42]

The investigation into the apparent accidental death of Tammy Homolka was led by David Weeks. He had been with the Niagara Regional Police for less than two months. The only sign of foul play was a mysterious red mark around Tammy's mouth and nostrils.[43]

A psychological profile of the killers was prepared by Gregg McCrary of the FBI Behavioral Sciences Unit. By February 17, 1993, Bernardo was a prime suspect in the murders. Earlier, in spring 1992, a friend of Bernardo's named Van Smirnis had told police he might be a killer.[44]

The big break in the investigation was in early February 1993. Karla Homolka told her family and Toronto Metro Sex Assault Squad about the murders. As a result, Paul was placed under around-the-clock surveillance until his arrest.[45]

THE ARREST

Bernardo was arrested on February 17, 1993, at about 3:30 in the afternoon by Detective Constables Brent Symonds of the Niagara Regional Police and Jim Kelly with the Toronto Police Department. The apprehension occurred at his home, 57 Bayview Drive. He was charged with the murders and the Scarborough Rapist crimes. He was interrogated by Gary Beaulieu, a sergeant with the Niagara police, and Toronto police detective Steve Irwin. He requested a lawyer, but the request was ignored as "vague."[46]

He was remanded to police custody until March 2 at a February 18 hearing. During this time he was incarcerated at the Metro East Detention Centre. Ironically, at about the same time his father was also in custody, facing rape charges.[47]

THE TRIALS

Karla was tried first, her trial starting on June 28, 1993. She was offered a plea bargain by Murray Segal, a plea-bargain negotiator with the Crown's Law Office. In return for her testimony against Paul, she was allowed to plead guilty and receive a ten-year sentence. She was on the witness stand for sixteen days.[48]

Paul's trial began on May 18, 1995. An unusually large venire, or jury pool, was selected because of fears of excessive pretrial publicity. However, the jury was not sequestered once the trial was underway.[49]

A total of twenty-four witnesses took the stand against Bernardo. The most damaging evidence against him might have been the videotapes he and Karla made to record the French murder and rapes. In addition, Karla testified against him for nine days, beginning on June 19, 1995. Then she was cross-examined for seven days by John Rosen, Bernardo's defense counsel.[50]

Bernardo testified on his behalf. He was questioned by his attorney for three hours. Then Crown attorney Ray Houlihan cross-examined him for nearly six days, with Bernardo standing the entire time. The jury began deliberations on August 31, at 3:30 p.m., and ended before noon the next day. He received nine guilty verdicts, and a minimum twenty-five year prison sentence.[51]

THE COMMUNICATION

Videotapes were the murderers' mass media mode salient to this case. They were created during the rapes, torture, and murders. The videotapes played a very important role in the investigation, trial, and aftermath of this case.

Bernardo and Homolka made videotapes of murders they committed, perhaps in part to mutually incriminate each other. As Burnside and Cairns recalled, Bernardo told a friend about the tapes. "Karla's not as innocent as you think. Tammy's death was not an accident. I don't know if you know this or not, but Karla's a lesbian and she's not that innocent. Tammy's death wasn't an accident, and I have it on tape to prove it."[52]

"Capturing the assault on tape," the murderers made a souvenir of the French murder that wound up being very incriminating.[53] Michaud and Hazelwood explained why the videotapes were so important, "The videos also implicated Karla, because they were explicit and damning." They added that Paul Bernardo's "own little way of hiding things" was to secrete the six "highly incriminating videocassettes of his assaults" in a bathroom light fixture.[54]

The playing of the tapes in court caused victims' loved ones enormous pain. Debbie Mahaffy, Leslie's mother, had been devastated by her daughter's kidnapping, killing, and subsequent dismemberment. The screams and anguished cries audible on the tape were the last sounds made by her daughter. The tape's stark reality overpowered her and left her slumped on the shoulder of a friend, nearly unable to stand and leave when court recessed. After the day's trial proceedings were over, she had to be assisted from the court building.[55]

Several analyses have noted the importance of the videotapes, personally to Bernardo and Homolka and to the ensuing investigation and trial.[56] One of the important issues surrounding the videotapes was the question of why they were not turned over to the court sooner. The tapes, which Bernardo had hidden above "a ceiling light fixture," were overlooked by police searching the house. Bernardo's lawyer, Ken Murray, recovered them but said nothing about having the videotapes. "Murray held on to the tapes for 16 months, until quitting as Bernardo's attorney in September, 1994." At that point his replacement, John Rosen, "immediately handed them over to Crown prosecutors."[57]

Besides killing three victims, Bernardo stalked countless other women. Videotapes played a role in this stalking, as well. This fact was brought to the attention of the authorities by Lori Lazurak and Tania Berges, who nearly became Bernardo victims.

"Then they noticed the lens of a video camera pointed at them through the doughnut shop window," *Macleans* reported. Lazurak and Berges had been sitting in a St. Catharines doughnut shop at about midnight on March 29, 1992, when this incident occurred. There were several other incidents like that, until Lazurak got Bernardo's license plate numbers a month later, on April 18, 1992. She turned the information over to the Niagara police prior to the abduction of Kristen French, but to no avail.[58]

One recent account reported how the pair recorded their rape of French. "This they recorded on videotape, including one scene where Homolka pretties herself for the camera before raping the girl."[59] A second study provided a similar account.[60]

The tapes no longer exist, officially. "The six videotapes depicting the rape and torture of Bernardo and Homolka's victims are destroyed," declared the CBC. The destruction took place in December 2001.[61] "This footage has since been destroyed," added another account.[62]

Despite the official tape eradication, "bootleg" copies are available over the Internet. For instance, in June 2005 eBay offered three copies of the Bernardo/Homolka murder tape, along with two copies of their wedding videotape and nine copies of other items.[63]

MEDIA AND PUBLIC INTEREST

The Canadian husband-and-wife serial killers, Paul Bernardo and Karla Homolka, elicited both substantial public and media interest and activity. The interaction between these two serial murder stakeholders created problems for a third stakeholder, law enforcement. It seemed that whenever public tipsters failed to receive satisfaction or were given insufficient attention by the police, they called the media. Soon the media, not civic leaders or the police, were determining the public agenda.[64]

In this section, we will examine two factors in this case, public interest and media interest. As in most cases, there were complex and multifaceted relationships between serial murder stakeholders.

Not only has there been considerable public interest in the Bernardo and Homolka murders, there are passionate feelings among some members of the public. Canadians were horrified and angry after Mahaffy's body was found. Later, at Homolka's trial, there was a festive, carnival-like feeling outside of the St. Catharines courthouse. Hopeful trial spectators and reporters were in line well before dawn trying to get in.[65]

The CBC in-depth feature story identified two levels of public interest. Initially, it reported, "The story riveted our attention, even as we were repelled by the details. There were books, TV specials, a movie and too many front pages to count." And now, with Homolka's release from prison in the immediate future, "The imminent release from prison of Karla Homolka has served to reignite a public fury that's been simmering just below the surface for as long as the whole story's been known."[66]

The existence of fan sites dedicated to Homolka and Bernardo are a sign of continuing public interest in the case. The *Toronto Star* reported on April 9, 2005, that there was an "Internet frenzy" of fan sites. However, a recent analysis concluded that "Only one could be classified as a fan-site." A web page named, "Paul Bernardo News and Information," is hosted by Hot News 360.[67]

One way to gauge public interest is through sales. Bernardo and Homolka continue to demonstrate commercial appeal. According to one study, "A number of books have been written about the Bernardos and in October of 2005, the Hollywood motion picture story will be released under the title *Deadly*." Quantum Entertainment has refused requests for advance review by attorneys for the families of victims French and Mahaffy, and some Canadians have called for a boycott of the movie.[68]

Bernardo business is brisk on eBay. According to *The Internet Tourbus News Service,* fourteen Bernardo/Homolka items were available as of June 9, 2005. The items include the murder and wedding videotapes and Canadian government documents.[69]

The sex-murders by Paul Bernardo and Karla Homolka became widely publicized. Reporters from across Canada and from as far away as upstate New York invaded St. Catharines to cover the missing-schoolgirl case. After their initial interviews with the friends and neighbors of the French family, the media targeted the police for additional information on the Kristin French kidnapping.[70]

"Like every other chapter in the saga of Homolka and her ex-husband, Paul Bernardo, Thursday's hearing to determine whether her movements should be restricted once she's out of jail was a media spectacle that featured at least one reporter gazing at her through binoculars," LaSalle and Wyatt noted. The CBC has acknowledged the longevity of the Bernardo/Homolka story.[71]

When Mahaffy's body was discovered, "Tipped to something newsworthy happening at Lake Gibson, reporters and photographers swooped to the area." Later, after Bernardo's arrest, police telephones were constantly ringing. There were literally hundreds of calls from reporters, and not just the Canadian media, but reporters from throughout the United States, Great Britain, and other countries. Before the trials, preparations were begun to handle the massive media presence that was expected to inundate the small town.[72]

POSITIVE EFFECTS OF THE MEDIA

The police tried to use the media in their investigation into the crimes of Bernardo and Homolka. In this case, there were two major beneficial outcomes of media coverage of the crimes. The media was used in the apprehension of the killers, and it motivated the police.

Assisted in Apprehension of the Killers

The investigation into the Bernardo and Homolka serial crimes was assisted by publicity. A television show was aired on the crimes, which served the dual purposes of exerting psychological pressure on the killers while also soliciting tips from the public. Police estimated that approximately 44,000 calls from across Canada were stimulated by the show.[73]

Media publicity assisted law enforcement in this case. At dinner time one night, Barbara Joan Packham was watching the Global-TV news at home when she noticed a story about a missing schoolgirl. Video footage was aired of Grace Lutheran Church and Linwell Road. She changed channels quickly to CHCH-TV, her local station, to see if she could find more comprehensive coverage of the story on that station's newscast. She was horrified to realize that the incident she witnessed in the church parking lot was most likely the abduction of Kristen French. She immediately called a friend who was a police officer in the nearby town of Grimsby.[74]

Motivated Law Enforcement

Sustained and critical coverage of serial murder cases tends to motivate the police. This is often the case in serial killing investigations. In the Bernardo/Homolka crimes, one study referred to "the hounding media articles."[75]

NEGATIVE EFFECTS OF THE MEDIA

It is difficult to find a serial murder case with more negative consequences of substantial and sustained media interest than this one. We have already learned about the considerable public and media interest in the case, which led to a number of meaningful media missteps. Six such serious consequences will be discussed, including the media motivation of the killers, interference with the investigation, checkbook journalism, creation of media zones, influence on case outcome, and the creation of celebrities.

Motivated by the Media

Paul Bernardo and Karla Homolka watched television accounts and read newspaper stories on their crimes. They shared these media products with their victims. The night that CHCH aired the television special on their crimes, which described their FBI profile, Paul and Karla viewed the program from their bed. Paul was so happy and excited that he was literally dancing with glee. With French still alive at his house, Bernardo went out to acquire The *St. Catharines Standard* to learn the details and developments about the police investigation into the Kristen French kidnapping.[76]

In a bizarre and evil twist, Bernardo and Homolka allowed French to watch the news coverage of her own abduction. Karla claimed that Kristen French was permitted to view television updates on her own kidnapping case. French reportedly became upset when video footage of her family was shown, and Bernardo decided she could not watch such broadcasts any more.[77]

Media Interfered with the Investigation

The media interfered with this investigation in one main way. They followed the police. This forced the police to change their plans and apprehend Bernardo before they felt they were ready to do so.

Paul Bernardo's arrest was moved up, because of the media following the police. Global TV reporter Sue Sgambati forced the police to act quickly, after her surveillance of a Metro police detective led her to the Green Ribbon Task Force headquarters in Beamsville, just north of St. Catharines. Sgambati was informed that a major development in the case was imminent, and her presence threatened to reveal this critical stage of the Bernardo investigation.[78]

Checkbook Journalism

In the case of Bernardo and Homolka, media interest in obtaining photographs was high. The *Toronto Sun* bought and published some of Paul and Karla's wedding photographs.[79] This is sometimes called "pay for play."

In addition the couple's wedding video was sold. One news show broadcast a segment of video footage taped at the wedding. Karla declared that it was probably offered and sold to the television station by an uncle and aunt who had just departed on a month-long vacation.[80]

Homolka testified that she and Bernardo had discussed book and movie rights and royalties. According to their scheme, "That's what I would live off of," she recalled. Homolka's plea bargain contains a clause prohibiting her from granting media interviews, and another expressly preventing her from profiting in any way from media treatments of the murders.[81]

Creation of Media Zones

The Bernardo and Homolka case produced several media zones. When French's body was discovered, approximately fifty reporters staked out the police roadblocks that blocked access to the crime scene.

Paul Bernardo's mother, Marilyn, complained about the media. She was under medication to soothe her frayed nerves, but when she went to get the prescription filled she was followed by reporters. She asked no one in particular, "What do they want to take pictures of me for?" After receiving crank phone calls and having the traffic constantly slow down and stop in front of their house, sometimes shining car lights through the window, they had requested police protection, Marilyn said.[82]

The parents of a victim saw their home become a media zone. When Doug and Donna French returned home, what was once a comfortable sanctuary had now become a kind of prison. Daily, reporters walked up to the door requesting an interview, another quote, or more video footage. At one point, Donna French ran from her home into the street, screaming "The reporters are driving us crazy." One study referred to "the throng of reporters" camped outside the French home.[83]

"The tiny courtroom was jammed with the press" at a Bernardo court appearance. At the trial, the media presence was overwhelming. Never before had a Canadian trial compelled such media attention and caused such a media presence.[84]

At the Homolka home, there was a media zone. Journalists hung around the quiet residential neighborhood street much like birds gathered together on a telephone wire. The Homolka telephone was constantly ringing, with reporters requesting an interview. And, the Homolkas laughed at the reporters who were camped out behind the Homolka's backyard fence.[85]

Influence on Case Outcome

The defense strategies in the case of Paul Bernardo and Karla Homolka were similar, but individual. Each party tried to pin the blame on the other. Public opinion seemed to exonerate Karla and blame Paul.

Paul's attorney commented that the media was being fueled through deliberately orchestrated leaks from the police. They continued to depict Karla Homolka as the victim of Paul Bernardo, who was the real killer.[86] The defense felt this to be a bit unfair and one-sided.

The Creation of Celebrities

Some parties to serial murder cases become celebrities as a result of the case publicity, and this was true in the Bernardo/Homolka case. According to one account, "Paul Bernardo and his accomplice/wife Karla Homolka have achieved notoriety normally reserved for the world's worst of the worst."[87]

PUBLIC RELATIONS ASPECTS

Public relations, or public information, played an important role in the Bernardo/Homolka investigation. Ineffective police media relations practices hindered the investigation and created problems for law enforcement. In general, the authorities favored limited information disclosure policies. The police were confronted with difficult choices to make in their public information messages.

Police Media Relations

Police media relations policies angered the media. Police released a statement that "The charges had been put on hold and that they would answer no more questions." Reporters were irritated with the repetitive police replies of "no comment." Confronted with an impenetrable barrier when attempting to obtain information, reporters looked for and found their own new story angles. In fact, police would not even say if there was one suspect or two involved in these serial crimes.[88]

Police media relations attitudes and practices were suboptimal and not very sophisticated. *Toronto Sun* reporter Alan Cairns tried to reason with Police Inspector Vince Bevan about the need for some disclosure. "Vince, do you realize that if another dead girl shows up the media is going to come down here and shit on your head—and I'll be the first one! Are you prepared to accept that?" Bevan fired back, "You do your job, and I'll do mine."[89]

Limited Disclosure Policies Favored

As is often the case in serial murder probes, the police favored minimal information release. While case publicity has advantages, investigators generally try to limit uncontrolled publicity of any kind. In this case, there was disagreement between the Niagara and Helton police about whether basic autopsy information ought to be disclosed to the public.[90]

Public Information Choices

Canadian authorities investigating the Bernardo/Homolka murders received different identifications by eyewitnesses of the suspect vehicle; one specified a Camaro, the other did not. Burnside and Cairns described the investigator's decision, "If police had not trusted witness accounts of the abductor's car being a Camaro and instead broadcast an unidentified two-door sports car, would the likes of stalking victims Lori Lazurak and Rachel Farron have come forward with more formal tips, or would the 44,000 tips on Camaros simply have swollen to 440,000 tips on assorted two-door sports cars?" [91]

Television

A Niagara police spokesperson appeared on a Canadian CHCH-TV special on the serial murders being committed by Paul Bernardo and Karla Homolka. On the July 21, 1992, program, the police revealed that they were looking for two persons, not a sole killer as had been assumed. Inspector Vince Bevan reportedly stated, "The odds are good" that "the killers watched the TV show on which the two-abductors theory was announced."[92]

Radio

The serial murders of Paul Bernardo and Karla Homolka received extensive radio publicity. According to one study, news of the Kristen French abduction spread rapidly all through the Golden Horseshoe area on radio newscasts.[93] Radio is an effective local medium.

Posters

Some posters are designed, printed, and distributed by family or friends of serial murder victims. There were substantial family efforts to find victims of Paul Bernardo and Karla Homolka. Debbie and Robert Mahaffy, along with Leslie's grandmother and some of her school friends, put up approximately five hundred posters of Leslie in hotels, motels, doughnut shops, bars, convenience stores, laundromats, and numerous other businesses in the Burlington area.[94]

News Conferences

One of the most basic serial murder public information tactics, news conferences, are a typical tactical response in these situations. At a media conference in the winter of 1993, Bevans disclosed that ten innocent people had thus far confessed to the serial slayings. A frustrated detective depicted the lack of leads, "We're essentially just waiting for another body to turn up."[95]

News Releases

News or media releases, like conferences, are commonplace communication tactics in these cases. In the Bernardo/Homolka crimes, the media was dissatisfied with police news releases. They were largely public relations exercises, void of value.

"The two-sentence media release the police offered every day," was criticized by Burnside and Cairns. They added that "The release normally said little more than 'the investigation is continuing' and 'police are searching for witnesses.'"[96] The media did not find these releases helpful.

Media Ban

Judge Frances Kovacs sought to minimize the media encroachment on his courtroom, and preserve defendants' rights. His solution? He imposed a ban on media coverage of most information, "the most sweeping ban in Canadian history." One recent account added, "One of the more controversial aspects of the Homolka and Bernardo saga was the media publication ban." The stated rationale behind the ban was to preserve Bernardo's legal rights, but the actual reason was to protect the families.

Although meant to protect victim families, "It signally failed in that aim," according to Burnside and Cairns. In fact, the ban was actually counterproductive. "The ban almost single-handedly assured that this sensational case became even more sensational."[97]

There have been attempts to enforce the ban. When author Stephen Williams sought to publish his book, *Invisible Darkness and Karla: A Pact with the Devil*, he became the second person convicted and sentenced under the terms of the ban in January 2005. He was originally cited on May 4, 2003. Ontario Provincial Police charged Williams with ninety-four additional counts in October of 2003.[98]

CONCLUSION

The Bernardo/Homolka murders had a disproportionate impact on Canada. These crimes were considered among the darkest deeds done in that land. They were terrible.

Communication was at the heart of the crimes, and resulted in convictions. Videotapes of the French rape, torture, and murder took the guesswork out of the verdict. These tapes were graphic, pornographic, and quite incriminating.

There were numerous negative consequences of media coverage of the Bernardo/Homolka murders. In addition, there was considerable public information activity. Police relations with the media were ineffective, and information was not divulged. The result was an adversarial relationship between the media and law enforcement.

12

WESTLEY ALLAN DODD

WESTLEY ALLAN DODD killed a relatively small number of victims, three. And the victims were small in size, too. He was a child molester and killer.

Dodd said that he was molested by cousins at eight or nine years of age. When he was thirteen he began "flashing," first from his bedroom window and then from his bicycle, as a mobile molester of sorts. As an adult, he liked to frolic naked at night in children's playgrounds.

The media played a major role in this case. Publicity about this case motivated law enforcement, promoted public safety, and assisted in Dodd's arrest. But it also motivated the killer, created chaotic media zones, and informed the killer. And there were numerous public information initiatives, including one by Dodd himself.

He built a homemade torture rack for use on his juvenile victims. His future plans, according to his diary, included cannibalism, decapitation, dismemberment, and mutilation of the children's corpses. Thankfully, those plans never came to fruition.

There was considerable communication surrounding this case. Dodd kept a detailed diary, and made written crime plans to guide his criminal efforts. He photographed one victim, and kept a photo album of photos, newspaper clippings of his crimes, and related memorabilia. He even produced a brochure for the media to use in preventing future sexual predators. The media played both positive and negative roles during the investigation.

To better comprehend what Dodd did and why he did it, nine main topics will be explored. The criminal and his crimes will be described. The investigation, arrest, and trial are examined. Dodd's communication, and the positive and negative effects of the media, are covered, with the public relations aspects of the investigation and aftermath.

THE CRIMINAL

Dodd's crimes were especially terrible, in part because of his choice of victims. They were children, unable to defend themselves. To best understand Dodd, eight subjects should be considered. His badness, his goodness, and his social isolation will be discussed, along with his problems. We will note that he desired death. His last moments will be recounted, along with his sexual deviancy and Dodd's early criminal history.

He was called "a particularly vicious predator."[1] According to another report, Dodd was "the Northwest's most notorious and vicious child killer."[2] Scott called him "one of the most calculating predators to prowl the playgrounds."[3]

He was born on July 3, 1961, in Toppenish, Washington.[4] He had a younger brother named Doug, and a sister Kathy. According to his father, Jim Dodd, his eldest son was a good boy.

"The eldest of three kids, Westley was otherwise well-behaved. 'He never did drugs, he never drank, he never smoked'," said the elder Dodd of his son Westley.[5]

Dodd himself traced part of his trouble to his inability to play well with others, especially girls. According to Scott, "Dodd has described himself as socially isolated, intimidated by girls. While others began dating and going to high school dances, Dodd stayed at home, thinking of ways to instigate sexual activity with children."[6]

It seems that Dodd's childhood was unhappy, from his statements and the recollections of others. There were two major issues. One was his parent's fighting, and the other was being bullied at school.

His home life as a child was not ideal, by any means. "Lousy" was how he later described his parent's relationship, and he said there was nightly yelling and fighting between his parents. "They fought all the time, they were vicious. They fought over dumb things. There was no love there at all, we were never close," Dodd declared. Scott recalled that Dodd "later blamed his unhappiness as a child on his parent's constant fighting and their lack of emotional support."[7]

Things were not much better for Dodd at school. He was bullied on numerous occasions. It is understandable how this might affect a young person's attitudes toward others.

"I conducted interviews with some of his classmates in Richland [Washington]. They told me horrific stories of Dodd being bullied in school. There were too many to recount here, but a single example shows how far things went. Two boys grabbed Dodd, one by each leg . . . and dragged him spread-eagled into a flagpole," according to a recent study of bullying. It concluded that "Every former classmate recalls numerous incidents of his suffering at the hands of the larger, stronger, tougher kids. . . . And each person I spoke to expressed regret at having stood by in silence."[8]

Once he was apprehended and convicted, Dodd expressed the desire to die for his crimes. One source described it this way, "Less than four years elapsed between the murders and Dodd's execution because he felt he deserved the punishment. He said that he 'should be punished to the fullest extent of the law, as should all sex offenders and murderers.'"[9]

Scott agreed that Dodd wanted to die. "As his execution date approached, Dodd professed remorse for what he had done. 'I have confessed all my sins,' he told a reporter in his interview. 'I believe what the Bible teaches. I'll go to Heaven.'"[10]

Dodd's last moments are well-chronicled, occurring as they did within prison walls. For instance, for his last meal he had salmon, scalloped potatoes, mixed vegetables and cole slaw, with lemonade to drink. Dodd's company for much of his last day and evening was his attorney and a clergyman.[11]

There was an unusual aspect to Dodd's execution. He chose hanging, which was a rarity among death modes at the time. According to one study, "His execution on January 5, 1993, was the first legal hanging in the United States since 1965." Another report added, "His was the first hanging in 25 years."[12] Scott's account agrees with these conclusions.[13]

The key to comprehending Dodd's deeds lies in his deep sexual deviance. In this section, we will explore his lengthy history of dangerous and predatory sexual behavior against children. His was a complex and twisted sexuality.

Dodd himself was molested on July 3, 1970. It was the weekend of his ninth birthday, and his brother and sister were in the hospital for tonsillectomies. He was dropped off at his cousin's house, where he was assaulted by two older male cousins.[14]

He began exposing himself at age thirteen. Dodd would stand naked in his second-floor bedroom, hiding his face in the curtain. The police were informed, but showed little concern. Neither did Dodd's parents.[15] "After realizing that exposing himself from his own house would get him in trouble, Dodd 'took his show on the road,' as he called it, and pedaled his bike around the neighborhood, looking for children, 10 or younger. He would ride by, yell at them, and expose himself when he got their attention," Scott recalled.[16]

He began molesting children at thirteen or fourteen years of age. According to one account, "Dodd began sexually abusing children when he was 13 years old; his first victims were his own cousins."[17] Scott's version differs slightly, on the age when Dodd began his criminal sexual behavior: "At 14 he molested his own 8-year-old cousin in a closet, her six-year-old brother later that day, and another male cousin weeks later. Dodd later molested the kids of a woman his father was dating."[18] Subsequently, he offered to babysit for neighborhood children, and at sixteen he molested several children as they slept, while substituting for their usual sitter.[19]

His sexual misbehavior resulted in his less-than-honorable discharge from the United States Navy. He was arrested by military police after offering young boys money for sexual favors.[20] Scott provided additional details; Dodd had offered some boys $50 apiece to play strip poker with him. Under questioning by the police, Dodd admitted that he had planned on molesting the boys, but "the charges were mysteriously dropped." He was convicted of attempted indecent liberties, and received a general discharge. He also served nineteen days in the brig and was ordered to receive counseling, which he never did.[21]

At times in his life, he enjoyed nocturnal naked jaunts in public. Scott recalled that "Sometimes Dodd went out on bizarre 'nude excursions,' rollicking in a children's playground, naked, in the middle of the night."[22] But not all of his behavior was so childlike and innocent, albeit strange. It is estimated that he molested more than fifty children over the years.[23] All of his victims were very young, between two and ten years of age.[24]

It seemed that Dodd's crimes increased in intensity and depravity over time. A recent study noted, "Dodd became more deranged the older he became (he wrote about wanting to castrate his victims and eat their genitals)."[25] Dodd reportedly masturbated frequently while looking at his photo album.[26]

We have already learned that Dodd was usually treated quite leniently by law enforcement and the judiciary when apprehended. One person tried to change that, though. Dr. Kenneth Van Cleve at one point tried to get misdemeanor charges against Dodd raised to a felony. He wrote, "Mr. Dodd's history of deviant assaults on minors is the most extensive I have ever encountered in an offender his age." The doctor referred to Dodd as an "extremely high risk for future re-offense." Van Cleve described Dodd's perspective and communication behavior and demeanor, "He was like a child. When he talked about the offenses, he did it in baby talk, like a kid. He fit right in with them. He didn't want to hurt them."[27]

How did Dodd explain his sexual behavior? He blamed his parents. "Dodd said he began exposing himself because he had hit puberty, and wasn't educated about sex."[28]

By the time he was fifteen, Dodd had been arrested for exposing himself, although he was never prosecuted for the offense.[29] Dodd was arrested again, in May of 1984, and charged with sexually molesting a ten-year-old boy. He was again treated leniently, given a one-year probation term, and although he was twice arrested for driving without a valid license, his probation was not revoked.[30]

Dodd decided to kill in 1987. His intended initial victim was an eight-year-old boy he knew. He intended to lure the lad into a deserted building. The boy escaped, and Dodd was convicted of committing a "gross misdemeanor," resulting in a 118-day prison term and another year of probation.[31]

THE CRIMES

Dodd's dark deeds, terrible as they were, thrilled him. He enjoyed thinking about them. The police realized this during Dodd's initial interrogation. As Dodd talked, the detectives thought, he manifested a mild amount of fear but an even greater degree of self-satisfaction and enjoyment while confessing to his crimes.[32] To understand these crimes, we will consider the murder of the Neer brothers and Lee Iseli, his future murder plans, and his torture rack.

The Murders

Cole Neer was an eleven-year-old, and his brother William (who was called Billy) was a year younger. On September 4, 1989, they encountered Dodd in David Douglas Park. They took a shortcut with tragic consequences.[33]

A website set up to honor the brothers explained the fatal encounter: "They were stopped by Westley Alan [sic] Dodd, ordered into an isolated spot, tied up and molested. Dodd stabbed them after he was done and left them for dead in the woods. Billy was still alive when found, but was too injured to tell what had happened or even identify himself. He died in the hospital. Cole died in the woods where he was stabbed. He was not found until Billy was identified and searchers realized his brother was missing."[34]

Here is another account of the incident. Dodd ordered the Neer brothers to get off their bikes. "I want you to come with me," he said. The boys challenged him, and Dodd responded firmly, "Because I told you to."[35]

Little Lee Iseli, age four, was killed by Dodd about a month and a half later, on October 29, 1989. When Dodd returned to his apartment after abducting the youngster from the Richmond School playground a little after 11:30 that morning, he showed the boy his pornographic photograph album.[36]

Dodd molested Lee Iseli all night long, as the boy fitfully slept. He told the boy at 3:15, "I'm going to kill you in the morning," and the defiant little boy said "No, you're not."[37]

An excellent extended explanation of the horrible end-of-life and death of Lee Iseli at the hands of Westley Dodd is available to readers of Court TV's Crime Library. Two pages are devoted to detailed description of the interactions between Dodd and his captive. Lee and his older brother Justin had gone to the school playground that sunny October afternoon, and Dodd abducted Lee when Justin was momentarily distracted.[38] Some authorities spell this victim's last name Islei.[39]

Future Murder Plans

Frightening indications of Dodd's worsening pathology were left in his diary. He was getting sicker, and only more savage atrocities would sate his blood lust. He dreamt of future mutilations, even dismemberment.

The Dodd jury had to observe and listen to the evidence incriminating Dodd, much of it disgusting and abhorrent to normal sensibility. At the trial, the prosecutor acquainted the jurors with Dodd's self-confessed future plans, as taken from his diary. A juror almost passed out as he listened to excerpts of Dodd's diary read aloud. The jury also heard about Dodd's plans for his future victims, including mutilation, dismemberment, decapitation, and death.[40]

The Torture Rack

Like many serial murderers, Dodd was not content to merely kill his prey. He wanted to play with them, sexually and psychologically. He even wanted to torture them.

An organization called Vancouver Eastside Missing Women took cognizance of the Dodd case. According to this group, "In late 1989, Dodd tortured and murdered three little boys in a ten-week span near Vancouver, Washington. He was in the process of abducting a fourth child when he was captured."[41] And the worst was yet to come, as Dodd was building a torture machine for use on future victims.

Dodd described the work he was doing on his torture rack in his last diary entry. He wrote, "Will now prepare ropes as I had for Incident #2, tied to bed and hidden under it—to use on victims as soon as wanted or needed—needing only to tie loose rope ends to the victim, other ends already attached to bed, or my 'rack,' my wood framework already built for this purpose."[42]

Dodd built the torture rack the day of Lee Iseli's funeral. Investigators had hoped the killer would attend the funeral, and perhaps thereby be discovered. Instead, Dodd "built a 'torture rack' out of boards and ropes."[43] When the police searched Dodd's lodging after his arrest, they discovered Dodd's self-made torture device, which was never actually used.[44] Other sources confirmed the authenticity of Dodd's homemade torture technology, "When he was arrested, the police found him with a homemade torture rack. Thankfully unused."[45]

THE INVESTIGATION

This was an unusually difficult investigation. In spite of the efforts of four local law enforcement agencies and several detectives to end his perverted homicidal behavior, however, Dodd had murdered with calculation and cold-bloodedness, frightening whole communities, and he virtually turned the population of two states into panicked publics before being apprehended, King noted. He added that the officers from the Vancouver Police Department tracked down one false lead after another during an investigation that taxed them mentally and physically. Before long detectives were working eighteen-hour days.[46]

One problem confronting investigators was the volume of tips received from the public. After police released a composite sketch of a suspect, more than one hundred tips were offered by citizens. After the Iseli murder, four to five hundred tips were received in three or four days. The task force at one point developed a list of 160 possible suspects.[47]

Three different psychological profiles of the offender were produced during the investigation. The FBI profiled the killer, at the request of the Vancouver Police Department. Later, a local psychologist specializing in sexual abuse and homicide cases provided another profile. Finally, Dr. Ronald Turco, who was a medical doctor and a policeman, provided an uncannily accurate profile when asked to do so by the task force.[48]

The Neer brothers crime scene was discovered by a local youth shortly before seven o'clock on the evening of September 4, 1989. Billy Neer's body was immediately located. Clair Neer, the boy's father, called police to report them missing at about 9:00 p.m. A search was immediately organized, and Cole's body was discovered at 2:00 a.m. the next morning.[49]

Vancouver Police Department Lieutenant Roy Brown and a team of officers responded to the 911 call. They were at the scene within minutes. The Vancouver police immediately issued a news release, to alert the community to the potential danger.[50]

The Neer case was taken very seriously by the police. King suggested that "From its outset, the double murder case took on a marked intensity like none that Vancouver had ever seen before. . . . The intensity was evident throughout much of Tuesday, September 5." Initially, two teams of three detectives apiece worked twelve-hour shifts, later increased by 50 percent.[51]

The boys' clothes were sent to the Washington State Crime Laboratory for forensic analysis. At about the same time, searches were underway. King referred to "the many investigators who literally combed David Douglas Park with metal detectors right after the murders in their search for evidence." A boy who had seen a suspicious man in the park that day was located, and the result was a composite sketch of the suspect.[52]

Police initially suspected the boy who claimed to have stumbled onto the crime scene. In fact, he was the focus of the investigation for nearly nine weeks, as police interviewed and re-interviewed him and his family, friends, and classmates. Because of this experience, he was diagnosed with Post-Traumatic Stress Disorder, and wound up receiving Social Security disability payments. At the same time, "Detective Jeff Sundby and his colleagues also looked at the Neer family's background."[53]

Robert L. Iseli called 911 on October 29, 1989, at 1:30 p.m. to report his son Lee's disappearance. Officer W. F. Brown, from the Portland Police Bureau East Precinct, responded to the call.[54]

Brown filed the report on Case Number 89-100170. The report was teletyped to all area police agencies. Police and volunteers conducted "a coordinated grid search," from Southeast Twenty-eighth Avenue to Southeast Forty-fourth Street, and between Southeast Harrison Street and Southeast Taggart Street. In the grid search, police examined the exterior of every building, and made door-to-door contact with all residents. "It was an all-out effort to find Lee Iseli, one of the most intense search efforts ever conducted by the Portland Police Bureau."[55]

At 9:00 p.m. that evening, two missing persons detectives, M. D. Tellinghusen and C. L. Lovenborg, were assigned to the case and dispatched to the Iseli home. The next day, Portland Police Bureau Sergeant Larry Neville requested the assistance of homicide detective Charles "C. W." Jensen. Police questioned the family extensively, concentrating on Justin, Lee's older brother, who was watching Lee the day of his abduction.[56]

Lee Iseli's body was discovered on November 1, 1989, in the Washington State Game Preserve. Deputy Dave Lundy was first on the scene, at 9:41 a.m., and he called his supervisor, Detective Sergeant Bob Rayborn, to report the body. Detectives Dave Trimble and Rick Buckner were assigned to the case, arriving at the dumpsite at 10:20 a.m. with their supervisor, Sergeant Mike Kestner. Since this case seemed to cross police jurisdictions, an informal task force including the Vancouver Police Department, the Portland Police Bureau and the Clark County Sheriff's Department was created.[57]

A thorough search of the Iseli dumpsite was conducted by Clark County Sheriff's Department evidence technician Sergeant Craig Hogman and detective Melanie Kenoyer. They created a 122-quadrant grid emanating outward from the body. Searchers included the Portland Police Bureau, the Mountain Wilderness Search Dog Rescue team, the Washington State Police Explorers, Silver Star Search and Rescue, Clark County Search and Rescue, and the Clark County Explorers and Reserves.[58]

THE APPREHENSION

The irony of the circumstances of Dodd's capture are self-evident. "He was apprehended while trying to abduct still another little boy," recalled the website set up to honor Cole and Billy Neer.[59] His sexual obsession with children led to his arrest.

On Monday, November 13, 1989, Dodd sat in the New Liberty Theatre in Camas, Washington, viewing "Honey I Shrunk the Kids," while actually prowling for victims. He tried to kidnap a six-year-old child from the bathroom, but the child's cries and screams as Dodd took him from the theatre led to the boy's escape and Dodd's apprehension. As Dodd tried to flee the scene, the stepfather of the boy he'd tried to abduct confronted and captured him, holding him until the police arrived.[60]

William "Ray" Graves was that stepfather. He ran after Dodd, and found him a few blocks away because Dodd's Ford Pinto station wagon was having engine trouble. He physically detained Dodd until the police arrived.[61]

Officer R. L. Strong of the Camas Police Department arrived at the theater shortly thereafter. After taking statements, he told Dodd, "I'll have to place you under arrest and take you in for questioning." He was taken to the Camas Police Department for booking and detention.[62]

Camas Police Department Sergeant Don Chaney realized that Dodd was most likely the area child murderer. So he contacted the police forces involved. Dodd was turned over to the Clark County Sheriff's Department on November 14, at midnight.[63]

It is sometimes reported that Dodd confessed immediately after his arrest. That is not true. He initially denied the murders, before admitting to his deeds under police questioning.

"In custody, 28-year-old Dodd denied any involvement in the murder of other boys," Scott noted.[64] Similarly, according to the same writer, "He admitted to his history of molestations but left out the murders."[65]

His protestations and denials were unconvincing. It was only a matter of time until he capitulated. One source noted, "In less than an hour of custody, Dodd confessed."[66] Another source reported, "Eventually, Dodd confessed that he had killed Billy and Cole Neer, and Lee Iseli, and went into graphic detail."[67]

THE TRIAL

The courtroom was completely filled. The chambers were packed beyond capacity, King noted. He added that several of the spectators who were previously admitted had to be turned away for lack of seating.[68]

Dodd surprised everyone on June 11, 1990, by changing his plea to "Guilty." He did so at a hearing before Clark County Superior Judge Robert Harris. This eliminated the need for a trial, but there was still the matter of a jury sentence recommendation. A jury of six men and six women was empanelled.[69]

The jury heard victim impact statements from the parents of the murdered children. Iseli's mother's statement read, in part, "You have taken my whole world apart—my family's whole world apart. You are the scum of the Earth. You get on the news and the radio and tell everyone how you felt when you did these unspeakable crimes . . . and you get a high just by talking and going over what you did. You make me sick. I hate your guts . . . you are a sick, cruel, and ugly person. . . . I will never rest until the day your life is taken. . . . I hope you rot in Hell." The Neer brothers' father said, "How did we allow *this* (points at Dodd) to end up where he is today? It is sad to take a life."[70]

The penalty phase of the trial ended on July 15, 1990. The jury deliberated for fourteen hours over Dodd's fate—life in prison, or death. They chose death.[71]

On July 26, 1990, Judge Harris passed sentence on Dodd. Harris told Dodd, "You have an ongoing, sadistic desire to hurt, injure and maim others. To you, it is clear that murder is the ultimate goal—the ultimate satisfaction." He concluded, "I am able to sign your death decree without looking back."[72]

THE COMMUNICATION

There were two important communication behaviors of Dodd's salient to the murders. These were his diary and a brochure. The diary in particular probably played a major role in Dodd's incarceration. The brochure will be discussed later in this chapter, in the section on Public Relations. Dodd kept an explicit, detailed diary, which recounts in great detail the planning, execution, and aftermath of his crimes. He described his crime plans in his diary:

Murder Methods:
Fastest: Stabbing, Slicing Throat. Too Messy!!!
Slowest: Bleeding to death (blood could be caught in jars)
Medium: Suffocation, Drowning
Uses/Possibilities:
   1) Drown; 2) hang by neck; 3) plastic bag over face; 4) strangle (with hands or rope); 5) pillow tight over face; 6) hog-tie and tape over nose and mouth;

7) amputate privates a little at a time until bled dead; 8) stab; 9) slice throat (too messy!); 10) no food and/or water; 11) drugs (full bottle sleeping pills?); 12) start experimental surgery on live, conscious, blindfolded, tied down victims.

For my first incident, knife would be best choice as my kill would have to be quick and easy for the chosen location.[73]

He also wrote: "I bought a set of X-acto knives and tweezers last night, giving me the necessary tools for my 'exploratory surgeries.' I've now asked Satan to provide me with a 6-10 year old boy to make love to, suck and fuck, play with, photograph, kill, and do my exploratory surgery on. On my legs and groin, I wrote, 'I now have needed tools for surgery.' And I took a nude nap from 4:00–5:30, and dozed until about 6:30 this afternoon."[74]

Investigators searching Dodd's home discovered the diary. Police observed several large manila envelopes, which contained a number of handwritten documents that they recognized as the journal or diary that Dodd continually referred to during his confession. They were carefully organized and titled "Incident 1," "Incident 2," and "Incident 3."[75]

Prosecutor Roger Bennett emphasized Dodd's diary during the trial. One diary entry, he said, described how he inserted a plastic tube into little Lee Iseli's penis. Contrary to Dodd's diary, the prosecutor said, this must have caused excruciating pain for the child to endure.[76]

Another diary entry noted that "Lee's happy and cheerful." This was after "Dodd removed his clothes, too, and for the next hour proceeded to molest Lee Iseli by performing oral sex on the boy. Afterward, he allowed Lee to dress . . . together they watched Yogi Bear cartoons on television, after which Dodd placed the two photos of Lee inside his photo album."[77] A different diary entry proclaims, "If I can get it home, I'll have more time for various types of rape, rather than just one quickie before murder."[78]

Publicity seemed to at least partly stimulate this diary entry:

4:50 p.m. Will now go take a leak and take the naked body of 4-year-old Lee Joseph Iseli out of the closet. I'll log everything as I go now. The paper article, labeled "The Oregonian, 10/30/89," was on page 5 of Section B, like it was no major deal he's missing. Looks like a perfect kidnapping.

5:05 p.m. Now getting Lee out of closet. Oh yeah—I knew for sure this morning he was dead. I'd heard of muscles relaxing and it's normal to "go potty" after dying—he peed on me twice as I hid his body in the closet, and once more on the shelf in the closet.

5:10 p.m. He is rather gross-looking—cold, stiff and purple.

5:16 p.m. See photos # 8 and # 9. . . . These photos show the position he's stuck in from being in a small closet area.

5:35 p.m. I'm going to get some garbage bags now to put his bundled-up body into. Then I'll figure out a place to dump the "garbage." I'll wear gloves when handling the bags—no chance of fingerprint if anyone discovers contents of the bags.

6:50 p.m. Now wearing gloves (after shower) to handle trash bags to put Lee in . . . shed his underwear in shower—Will now go dump his naked body.

8:00 p.m. Home. Dumped 7:35 p.m. on 10-30.[79]

POSITIVE EFFECTS OF THE MEDIA

The media coverage of the Dodd case reflected a "mixed bag" of consequences. The media made mistakes and created a number of problems for
other serial murder stakeholders. On the other hand, three benefits of media
coverage of the case can be cited; dissemination of public safety information,
motivation for law enforcement, and assistance in the apprehension.

Dissemination of Public Safety Information

Westley Allan Dodd was a child molester and murderer, who kept a scrap-
book about his crimes. He recorded his thoughts and events in a detailed personal diary about the murders. The police used the media to warn parents
about the necessity of protecting their children from the serial child killer in
their midst, prior to Dodd's capture.

The specifics of law enforcement warnings in the Dodd case might be considered. The Vancouver police issued cautionary and detailed warning messages using newspapers, radio, and television, urging parents to use
considerable caution in caring for their small children. Police emphasized that
children of virtually all ages should never be left unattended anywhere in public, and they should not be permitted to walk or play outdoors unsupervised
by an adult until the child murderer was apprehended.[80]

Motivation for Law Enforcement

Law enforcement officials diligently investigated the child abductions of
Westley Dodd. They were confronted with considerable public and media pressure. Police Captain Ray Anderson recalled that the police felt extreme pressure
from the public and media to apprehend the child killer.[81]

Assistance in Apprehension of Killer

The Vancouver police used the media to assist in the apprehension of
Westley Dodd. Vancouver police detectives emphasized the necessity of citizen
involvement and assistance. "Citizens who have information about other people who they might have seen in the park need to come forward. That's how
these cases are made," one declared.[82]

Early in the Dodd investigation, a boy saw a suspicious-looking man in the
park, and he got a good look at him and saw him quite clearly. As a result,
forensic artist Jean Boylan was recruited to create a composite drawing of the
suspicious stranger. This sketch of the suspect was circulated among police
departments and to the Vancouver media.[83]

Dodd admitted that the newspaper pleas to the captor of Lee Iseli made an
impression on him, although obviously an insufficient one. He remarked during
his post-arrest interrogation that "I think reading those articles was when I started
feeling guilty about it and I thought a couple of times about going in."[84]

NEGATIVE EFFECTS OF THE MEDIA

Despite these benefits of media serial murder coverage in the Dodd case, there were also a number of negative consequences. These included motivation for the killer, creation of media zones, information for the killer, and media notification of death.

Media Motivation for Killers

Westley Dodd, a pedophile and serial killer, kidnapped a young boy named Lee and killed him. As King recalled, "Dodd 'played' with Lee's genitals for the next hour while waiting for the 11:00 p.m. news, which was the first news broadcast since Lee 'disappeared.'"[85] Later, after his arrest, he was asked during the interrogation, "Did you keep the newspaper articles about the murders?" Dodd replied, "I kept all the newspaper articles that I found about it."[86]

Earlier, after his initial murders, the same phenomenon had occurred. Dodd had relished television coverage of the double murder. In fact, his careful scrutiny of media coverage of his crimes had a dual purpose: allowing him to relive his crimes and enjoy them all over again, and keeping tabs on the police investigation.[87]

Creation of Media Zones

At Westley Dodd's execution, the parking area at the Walla Walla State Prison that was allocated to the media was filled beyond capacity, primarily with media vans and trucks with satellite up-link dishes for the major television network affiliates from all parts of the country. Several of the eager news teams, some from as far away as New York, showed up early, way before the stated 9:00 p.m. arrival time.[88]

An observer described the media zone at the execution, "Outside, in the parking lot we just left, sit dozens of satellite trucks and secondary crews. Everyone is waiting. Earlier that night one pizza delivery car after another pulled up to the fence and handed off stacks of steaming pizza to hungry crews. It was the strangest scene. The huge and quiet penitentiary. The chanting protestors. And the steady stream of delivery cars."[89]

Media Provided Information to Dodd

Westley Dodd carefully monitored news reports of his pedophile murders. One evening in Vancouver, Washington, Dodd had watched the evening news and seen the composite sketch of the man observed talking to Lee Iseli at the school before he was abducted. Dodd wrote in his diary that it "looked a lot like me." He decided to watch the news regularly and read the newspaper daily for the foreseeable future and stay inside and out of public places for a while. Dodd also gathered up Lee's clothes that night and burned them.[90]

In September 1989, the media coverage definitely influenced Dodd. Until Thursday, September 7, none of the news stories on the Neer murders caused him any real concern. Until then the media reports had produced only minor worries. But the article in the *Columbian,* the Vancouver daily newspaper, that day had concerned him. It reported that the police had talked with witnesses who were at the park on the day of the Neer brothers killings, and how a police artist had drawn a sketch of the unknown man seen that day at the park. Dodd observed as he looked at the drawing that it actually resembled him. He decided to spend most of his time at home for a while. He would go outside only when he absolutely had to so he could avoid anyone recognizing him. He also decided to change his appearance in a substantial way.[91]

Media Notification of Death

Portland Police Bureau Detectives Mike Hefley and Tom Nelson stood by, prepared to deliver the tragic news to Lee Iseli's family after the positive identification was made of the child's remains. They sought to do so as sensitively as was possible. They also made arrangements for volunteer chaplain Elaine Caldwell to accompany them. But, when they arrived at the Iseli home, they discovered that a reporter for The *Oregonian* had already contacted Robert Iseli and tried to get an interview about his reaction to the discovery of his son's body.[92]

PUBLIC RELATIONS ASPECTS

A considerable number of communication tactics were used in the Dodd serial murder public information campaign. These included television, fliers, radio, telephone tiplines, news releases, and news conferences. Additionally, a brochure by Dodd will be discussed.

Television

In the serial murder case of Westley Dodd, television was used as a publicity tool. Dodd's photograph, and one of his car, were shown on television screens throughout Oregon and Washington, and appeared in almost all major metro daily newspapers on the West Coast.[93] We have already learned that Dodd took cognizance of the television coverage of his crimes.

Fliers

Westley Dodd's serial murders resulted in flier production and distribution. Fliers with Lee Iseli's picture and a detailed recent description were prepared and disseminated in the Vancouver area and to the Vancouver local media.[94] Fliers are typically used in serial murder cases.

Radio

Radio was used by Vancouver police searching for their child serial rapist and killer. A description of the suspect appeared in the newspaper. It was also broadcast by virtually every television and radio station in Vancouver.[95]

Telephone Tiplines

Special police telephone arrangements are not unusual in serial murder public information efforts. In the Dodd case, neither a police telephone tipline nor a $10,000 reward could stop the child molester for some time. He kept walking the streets while frustrated police exhausted their leads.[96]

News Releases

Dodd's crimes caused panic in Vancouver. Because of concern for the public's safety, the Vancouver Police Department distributed a news release concerning the Dodd homicide victims. Since the implication of the release was that a child molester and murderer was active in Vancouver, the police sought to emphasize the necessity for residents to take all reasonable precautions with their children.[97]

News Conferences

Westley Dodd kidnapped, molested, and murdered the man's two sons. An understandably distraught and mourning Clair Neer nevertheless convened a news conference. He told reporters that the public should know what had happened to his sons. Neer said that it was personally important for him to share this message. It was a moving experience hearing it from a man who had just lost most of his family to a serial killer.[98]

News conferences were conducted by the authorities, as well. For instance, a public relations official at the Walla Walla State Penitentiary fully briefed reporters covering Dodd's execution about the convicted man's final meal. He answered questions about what would happen if the noose failed to fully snap Dodd's neck.[99]

Brochures

Dodd wrote a pamphlet or brochure while incarcerated in prison. Throughout May, Dodd had discussed writing something to help kids protect themselves from sexual predators like him. Dodd wrote occasionally, whenever he felt like it and when he was not occupied masturbating in his cell. He finished at the end of May, when he mailed a document he called a pamphlet to The *Columbian* newspaper in Vancouver.[100] Here is the text of the pamphlet:

WHEN YOU MEET A STRANGER Westley A. Dodd
    Introduction—written by a professional—who I am, what I've done, why this was written. There *are* things that *work* that kids *can* do to protect themselves. I have never molested or harmed any child that resisted me. WHAT DO YOU DO?

Many boys and girls are told "don't take candy from strangers," or "don't get in a stranger's car." But what should you do when you're alone, and someone you don't know wants you to go with him, or wants you to pull down your pants, or do something else you know is bad? What do you do if there is no grown-up around that can help you? Do you do what a stranger wants, and hope he'll go away soon? NO!

The stranger is bigger and stronger than you, and you might be scared, but *you* can make *him* run away! Sometimes the stranger is just as scared as you are. He's afraid you might do something to get him caught. He'll leave you alone and run away from you.

How can a boy or girl make a grown-up run away when he wants to do something bad to you? *What do you do?* JUST SAY NO!

You may have been told "just say no" to drugs. You can also say *no* to someone who wants you to go somewhere with him. You can say *no* to a person who tells you to pull down your pants, or take your clothes off. There are other people like me. We make you take your clothes off. Some of us tell you to get in our cars. We can be nice to you, or we can be very mean. Sometimes, some of us want to hurt, or even kill you. But you can still get away.

A boy said *no*. Then, before I could say or do anything else, he ran away! I ran away, too—I went the other way. I didn't want anyone to see me chasing him, and I was afraid he'd send the police back to get me. Say *NO!*, then *RUN!* YELL! SCREAM!

Okay. You said *no*, but he held you so you *couldn't run*, or he caught you when you did run. Now what? Do you let the stranger do what he wants to you and hope it won't hurt? NO!

Another boy said no, then tried to run. I grabbed his arms and wouldn't let go. He finally pulled his pants down and let me touch him, so I'd let him go. Is there anything else he could have done to protect himself. What?

I met another boy—he was 6-years-old. I told him, "You have to come with me." He said NO and tried to get away from me, but I picked him up and started to carry him away. He knew he couldn't get away, but he didn't give up. He started yelling and screaming, "Someone help me—he's killing me."

He kept screaming and yelling for help. I was afraid someone would hear him, so I let him go and ran away. I didn't want to get caught, but the boy ran and told someone what happened and the police caught me ten minutes later. The 6-year-old boy didn't know what I was going to do. He only knew I was trying to take him away, and something real bad could happen. Instead of being scared and going with me, he yelled for help! He's a hero now because even though he was afraid of me, he screamed and yelled for help when he needed it.

Just say NO! Then RUN! SCREAM—it will scare him away! YELL for HELP! Get away fast and tell someone what happened! Always tell someone! Be a HERO!

Opinions on this document were mixed. Skeptics saw it as an attempt by Dodd to stave off execution by assisting law enforcement. It did nevertheless offer children and their parents useful information from the offender's perspective.

Dodd Case Polygraph Keys

"Polygraph key" is police jargon for information withheld from the media and public about a serial murder crime scene. If police hold back certain facts, they can weed out phony confessors and help ascertain who is truly guilty, as in this case.

Dodd was surprised by omissions in media coverage of the Neer boys' murders. Then, Dodd figured out that the police had deliberately held back certain information. Some of the facts were graphic, others mere details.[101]

CONCLUSION

Dodd, a molested child, grew up to molest at least fifty other children, and killed three. Sometimes that happens. But why did it happen in this case?

Dodd's early life certainly was no bed of roses. His parents bickered constantly, and eventually divorced. Dodd said his home life was loveless. And he was mercilessly bullied at school.

His pathological sexuality was the cause of his crimes. Media coverage of those crimes both benefited and hindered the investigation in a number of ways. There were several communication tactics used in the public information efforts.

The media kept Dodd informed of important facts about the investigation. This led to the destruction of evidence and the taking of precautions by Dodd. It lengthened his murder spree. On the other hand, however, public information provided important public safety information, motivated law enforcement, and assisted in Dodd's apprehension.

13

———•◦•———

CONCLUSION

AT THIS POINT, a dozen cases of serial killer mass communication behavior have been studied. Each of these serial murder cases included both rhetorical and mass communication as an integral aspect of the crimes. This warrants our serious attention, as this rhetorical penchant of serial killers may be useful in determining their motivations and developing additional means of apprehension, taking advantage of their interest in the media.

MEDIA ANALYSIS FINDINGS

The media play an important, if controversial, role in serial murder investigations. There are three sets of findings to share regarding the role and behavior of the media in these crimes. We will consider positive findings, negative findings, and media misbehavior.

The media can have a positive effect on serial murder investigations, and it can actually assist law enforcement efforts. There are three positive effects of media coverage of serial murder:

1. Media coverage of these cases can disseminate vital public safety information. This occurred in the Nelson, Buono and Bianchi, Ridgway, Cunanan, and Dodd cases.
2. Media coverage of serial murder cases can motivate the authorities involved in the investigation. That was perceived in the Buono and Bianchi, Puente, Ridgway, Cunanan, Dodd, and Bernardo and Homolka cases.
3. Media coverage of serial murder can facilitate apprehension of the murderer(s). That was observed in the Nelson, Buono and Bianchi, Puente, Cunanan, Bernardo and Homolka, and Dodd cases.

Unfortunately, media coverage of serial murder cases frequently results in negative consequences. Despite the positive potential of such coverage, instead there are often negative effects of media coverage of these crimes. Eight such recurrent types of negative consequences have been documented:

1. Media coverage of serial murder motivates the killer(s). This happened in the Nelson, Manson, Buono and Bianchi, Cunanan, Bernardo and Homolka, and Dodd cases.
2. Media coverage of serial murder interferes with the investigation. There are four subtypes of interference:
    — The media followed the police in the Manson, Brady and Hindley, Buono and Bianchi, Puente, Ridgway, Cunanan, and Bernardo and Homolka cases.
    — Harassment of witnesses occurred during the Buono and Bianchi, Ridgway, Puente, and Cunanan cases.
    — Police stakeouts were "blown" in the Buono and Bianchi and Ridgway cases.
    — Crime scene contamination occurred in the Dahmer and Cunanan cases.
3. Media coverage of serial murder also results in checkbook journalism. This was observed in the Manson, Buono and Bianchi, Dahmer, Puente, Cunanan, and Bernardo and Homolka cases.
4. Media coverage of serial murder creates celebrities. The Landru, Manson, Buono and Bianchi, Dahmer, Puente, Cunanan, and Bernardo and Homolka cases manifested this tendency.
5. Media coverage of serial murder results in the creation of media zones. Every case except the Axeman of New Orleans case was marked by media zones.
6. Media coverage of serial murder influences case outcome. This was evident in the Nelson and Bernardo and Homolka cases.
7. Media coverage of serial murder leads to direct media involvement in the case. The Manson, Puente, and Cunanan cases witnessed this media behavior.
8. Media informs the killer. Puente, Cunanan, and Dodd all benefited from media-disseminated case information.

It has frequently been alleged that media involvement in serial murder cases results in a variety of specific forms of misbehavior. Eleven types of specific media misbehavior are manifested in serial murder cases, including:

1. The premature naming of innocent suspects, as was seen in the Nelson and Manson cases that involved publicized arrests of innocent suspects.
2. The harassment and pursuit of people, as occurred in the Nelson and Cunanan cases.
3. The introduction of story errors and mistakes, which was seen in the media's coverage of the Ridgway and Buono and Bianchi case.
4. Biased coverage, as was noted in the Nelson case.

5. Sensationalized reporting, as in both the Dahmer and Buono and Bianchi cases.
6. Civil and criminal misconduct, as occurred in the Dahmer and Cunanan cases.
7. The insensitive treatment of people, which was clearly manifested in the Dahmer case.
8. Death notification by the media, as exhibited in the Dodd case.
9. The invention of facts, which transpired in the Nelson case.
10. Pressure exerted on the police for information, as was demonstrated in the cases of Buono and Bianchi and Bernardo and Homolka.
11. The creation of malicious stories by the media, as was illustrated in the Manson case.

PUBLIC POLICY RECOMMENDATIONS

Certain recommendations for serial killer public policy can be offered, based upon the results of this study. Two types of recommendations are offered, serial murder investigation policies and media relations policies:

1. Media personnel should be interviewed, or surveyed, to determine their values, attitudes, and beliefs toward serial killer communication and investigations. This study has identified several areas of conflict between the media and law enforcement during serial murder investigations, and it is important to understand why journalists act as they do during serial murder cases.
2. Protocols for responding to serial killer communication need to be developed. At the present time it is quite likely that much bona fide serial killer communication is disregarded by the authorities as mere "crank communications," when they are in fact important messages emanating from offenders. When messages are understood to be from serial killers, there are no standardized guides or response procedures to assist law enforcement officials in understanding and responding effectively to the offenders.
3. Education and training should be provided to federal, state, and local law enforcement officials likely to engage in serial murder cases. If we expect law enforcement to understand the rights and information needs of the media, education ought to be provided to facilitate the process of perceiving, comprehending, and responding to media needs, when appropriate.

Steps might be taken to rehabilitate and professionalize the relationship between the media and law enforcement. We have noted numerous instances of friction between the members of the media covering serial murder cases and the authorities responsible for solving the crimes. In some cases it has been alleged that media coverage interfered with or damaged serial murder investigations. In other cases, law enforcement seems not to have appreciated the right of the media to cover stories.

Four media relations policy recommendations are suggested, including:

1. Reciprocal and mutual understanding and appreciation for the rights and responsibilities of self and the other between law enforcement and the media. If necessary, Memoranda of Understanding between the two parties can specify any particular items desired by law enforcement and the media in any part of the country, under whatever specialized local conditions and circumstances may exist.

2. Two policies might create respect and understanding between the media and police, such as the convening of editorial conferences. When serious misunderstandings or disagreements between law enforcement and the media occur, they can be minimized or solved by editorial conferences. Simply put, law enforcement officials and media editors and news directors get together, either on their own or under the supervision of a mediator or other disinterested third party, and respectfully and professionally discuss their differences, their perceived stake, and their unhappiness with the other party. Another tactic would be the use of media briefings. Although similar to news conferences they typically involve far fewer media representatives than do press conferences, and the information divulged is frequently "off-the-record," either not for media use at all or not for attribution to any particular source.

3. Education and training should be provided for the media in serial murder investigative techniques. It is possible that members of the media are unaware that some of their behaviors make it difficult for the authorities to successfully conduct serial murder investigations. Providing reporters with this information would improve the quality of their serial murder reporting, as well as lessen the likelihood of accidental or unintentional media misbehavior during these cases.

4. If necessary, mediation or some other method of conflict resolution can be used. When law enforcement media relations deteriorate to the point where the two parties are incapable of interacting, this might be necessary.

RESERVATIONS AND CAVEATS

It is possible to find fault with any scholarly endeavor, and this one is no exception. Two specific reservations ought to be expressed. Neither is especially serious.

First, histories of serial murder cases and biographies of serial murderers have been relied upon to a considerable extent, in the information gathering process used for this book. This was a deliberate choice I made, in addition to liberally using Internet sources. Ordinarily, I would avoid secondary sources like these and use primary sources such as autopsy and police reports, and contemporary newspaper accounts, but that would have severely restricted the information available for analysis, as alternate information gathering processes are exceptionally slow.

Furthermore, no detailed, rigorous statistical procedures were employed in the analysis of the data in this book. Of course, this book is not quantitative in nature, unlike the broader study from which it came, a study of one thousand serial murderers.

But, as was suggested in the Introduction, it is desirable to add communication-based insight to more traditional serial murder indices, to enhance the informational basis upon which the typical investigation is conducted. The richer and fuller the serial murder information that is available to law enforcement, the better in terms of likelihood of offender apprehension.

IMPLICATIONS

I conclude this book with some suggested implications. What does this book mean? If this analysis is correct, so what? Does it really matter? I believe that it does, for three reasons:

1. The initial and perhaps most important implication of this study is the importance of mass communication to serial killers and to serial murder investigations. So many serial killers have contacted the media or police, decade after decade, crime after crime, that it cannot be an accident or coincidence. Nor is their media craving spontaneous or unimportant. The rhetorical behavior of serial murderers deserves closer analysis, because it seems to be so important to serial murderers. Communication with the authorities increases their risk of apprehension, yet serial killers persist in communicating. This is especially true with the media.

2. A second implication of this work involves the salience of serial murderer mass communication behavior to the investigation. I have argued that if the authorities better understand serial killer communication, they will better understand serial killers. That is an important subgoal for law enforcement officials in serial murder investigations, as it promotes attainment of the main goal, immediate apprehension of the serial murderer(s). Many serial killers need to say something to someone, and they choose to engage in this communication during and after serial murders. It is likely that clues to offender motives, values, perceptions, attitudes, and behavior can be discerned through effective interpretation of serial killer rhetorical and mass communication. The mass communication motivation and behavior of serial killers needs to be explored in greater detail.

3. The relationship between serial murder stakeholders, particularly that between the murderer and the media, are critically important for understanding the serial murder phenomenon. The media motivates some killers, and enables others. But in each of the dozen cases analyzed in this book, mass communication played a central role in the crimes, in some way. Recognition and better understanding of the role of the media in these cases would be beneficial to the smooth functioning of the process. Media coverage is a critical factor.

We have noted both good and bad effects of media coverage of serial murder. A large variety of types of media misbehavior have been identified. On balance, it must be conceded that media involvement in serial murder cases has generally been detrimental to the public and investigative good.

Most important, in a sense, is the impact of serial murder upon the community, and each member therein. In a sense, everyone is a victim of serial murderers when they prey upon a community. The pervasive and unreasonable fear uniquely resulting from serial murder has been documented in case after case.

It must be acknowledged that the serial murder problem is a serious one, likely to remain so far into the future. Given this situation, it behooves us as rational citizens and policymakers to enhance our understanding of serial murderers. By adding the mass communication dimension of serial murder to our psychological and sociological insight, it might be possible to more effectively combat this source of social stress and sorrow.

NOTES

—•—

CHAPTER 1

1. Rotten.com, "Henri Desire Landru: AKA the French Bluebeard," http://www. rotten.com, 1 (accessed May 23, 2005).

2. Publications International Ltd., *Murder and mayhem* (Lincolnwood, IL: Publications International Ltd., 1991), 172.

3. Publications International Ltd., *Murder and mayhem,* 172.

4. Publications International Ltd., *Murder and mayhem,* 172.

5. Court TV, "Henri Landru," http://www.crimelibrary.com, 1 (accessed May 23, 2005).

6. Explore Dictionary of Famous People, "Henri Desire Landru," http://www. explore-biography.com/biographies/H/Henri_Desire_Landru.html, 1 (accessed May 23, 2005).

7. Court TV, "Henri Landru," 1.

8. Court TV, "Henri Landru," 1.

9. News of the Odd, "French Bluebeard guillotined," http://www.newsoftheodd.com, 1 (accessed June 4, 2005).

10. Publications International Ltd., *Murder and mayhem,* 173.

11. Court TV, "Henri Landru," 3.

12. Explore Dictionary, "Henri Desire Landru," 1.

13. Court TV, "Henri Landru," 1–2.

14. News of the Odd, "French Bluebeard," 1.

15. Trivia Library.com, "Henri Desire Landru the Bluebeard: Part 2," http://www.trivia-library.com/a/henri-desire-landru-the-bluebeard-part-2.htm, 1 (accessed June 4, 2005).

16. Court TV, "Henri Landru," 2.

17. Court TV, "A unique killer," http://www.crimelibrary.com, 1 (accessed May 23, 2005).

18. Explore Dictionary, "Henri Desire Landru," 1.

19. Trivia Library.com, "Part 2," 2.

20. Publications International Ltd., *Murder and mayhem,* 173.

21. Court TV, "Henri Landru," 2.

22. News of the Odd, "French Bluebeard," 1.

23. Court TV, "Henri Landru," 2.

24. Court TV, "Henri Landru," 3.

25. Rotten.com, "Henri Desire Landru," 1.

26. Explore Dictionary, "Henri Desire Landru," 1.

27. Trivia Library.com, "Part 2," 1–2.

28. Explore Dictionary, "Henri Desire Landru," 1.

29. Court TV, "Henri Landru," 2.

30. Dennis Bardens, *The ladykiller* (Middlesex, U.K.: Senate, 1972), 104.

31. Trivia Library.com, "Part 2," 1; Bardens, *Ladykiller,* 283; and Court TV, "Unique killer," 2.

32. Trivia Library.com, "Part 2," 1; Court TV, "Henri Landru," 1.

33. Trivia Library.com, "Henri Desire Landru the Bluebeard: Part 1," http://www.trivia-library.com/a/henri-desire-landru-the-bluebeard-part-1.htm, 1 (accessed June 4, 2005); "Maigret—Landru," http://www.trussel.com, 1 (accessed June 4, 2005).

34. Nationmaster.com, "Encyclopedia: Henri Desire Landru," http://www.nation-master.com, 1 (accessed May 23, 2005); Court TV, "Bluebeard's 'wives'," http://www.crimelibrary.com, 3 (accessed May 23, 2005); Explore Dictionary, "Henri Desire Landru," 1; and Rotten.com, "Henri Desire Landru," 1.

35. Court TV, "The arrest and investigation of Landru," http://www.crimelibrary.com, 3 (accessed May 23, 2005); Court TV, "Unique killer," 2.

36. Explore Dictionary, "Henri Desire Landru," 1; Rotten.com, "Henri Desire Landru," 1.

37. Bardens, *Ladykiller,* 186.

38. Court TV, "Arrest and investigation," 3.

39. Rotten.com, "Henri Desire Landru," 1; Trivia Library.com, "Part 1," 2.

40. Explore Dictionary, "Henri Desire Landru," 1; Bardens, *Ladykiller,* 115.

41. Bardens, *Ladykiller,* 176.

42. Bardens, *Ladykiller,* 176.

43. Biography.ms, "Henri Desire Landru," http://henri-desire-landru.biography.ms, 1 (accessed May 23, 2005).

44. Publications International Ltd., *Murder and mayhem,* 174.

45. Explore Dictionary, "Henri Desire Landru," 1. Does crime pay? At Landru's trial, the presiding justice declared that from the beginning of 1915 until April, 1919, Landru had lived almost entirely off the revenues generated by the disappearances of Andre Cuchet, Mesdames Cuchet, Laborde-Line, Guillin, Henn, Collomb, Babelay, Buisson, Jaume, Pacscal, and Mlle. Marchadier. See Bardens, *Ladykiller,* 138. On the other hand, there are indications that the effort was not justified by the relatively paltry reward. According to one source, "Ironically, it didn't pay much—about $250 a victim—it was later estimated." See Trivia Library.com, "Part 2," 2.

46. Bardens, *Ladykiller,* 176.

47. "Maigret—Landru," 1; Biography.ms, "Henri Desire Landru," 1.

48. Rotten.com, "Henri Desire Landru," 1; Court TV, "Unique killer," 2.

49. Bardens, *Ladykiller,* 104, 117.

50. Bardens, *Ladykiller,* 110.

51. Bardens, *Ladykiller,* 119, 283.

52. Bardens, *Ladykiller,* 75–81.

53. Bardens, *Ladykiller,* 104–5.

54. Bardens, *Ladykiller,* 107.

55. Bardens, *Ladykiller,* 107–8.

56. Bardens, *Ladykiller,* 110–12.

57. Bardens, *Ladykiller,* 108.

58. Publications International Ltd., *Murder and mayhem,* 173.

59. Bardens, *Ladykiller,* 82–83.

60. Bardens, *Ladykiller,* 86.

61. Bardens, *Ladykiller,* 132.

62. Bardens, *Ladykiller,* 110, 145–46.

63. Bardens, *Ladykiller,* 147–48.

64. Bardens, *Ladykiller,* 149.

65. Bardens, *Ladykiller,* 185.

66. Bardens, *Ladykiller,* 149, 166, 196, 198.

67. Bardens, *Ladykiller,* 186, 189.

68. Bardens, *Ladykiller,* 192–93.

69. Bardens, *Ladykiller,* 196–97.

70. Bardens, *Ladykiller,* 143.

71. Bardens, *Ladykiller,* 197.

72. Bardens, *Ladykiller,* 118.

73. Bardens, *Ladykiller,* 143.

74. Court TV, "The trial of Landru," http://www.crimelibrary.com, 1 (accessed May 23, 2005); Publications International Ltd., *Murder and mayhem,* 172.

75. Trivia-Library.com, "Henri Desire Landru the Bluebeard: Part 3," http://www. trivia-library.com/a/henri-desire-landru-the-bluebeard-part-3. htm, 1 (accessed June 4, 2005); Bardens, *Ladykiller,* 143.

76. Publications International Ltd., *Murder and mayhem,* 175; Bardens, *Ladykiller,* 143.

77. Bardens, *Ladykiller,* 189, 98; Publications International Ltd., *Murder and mayhem,* 175.

78. Bardens, *Ladykiller,* 19; Court TV, "Arrest and investigation," 3.

79. Rotten.com, "Henri Desire Landru," 1; Publications International Ltd., *Murder and mayhem,* 173.

80. Court TV, "Henri Landru," 3.

81. News of the Odd, "French Bluebeard," 2.

82. Trivia Library.com, "Part 1," 1; Bardens, *Ladykiller,* 57–58.

83. Bardens, *Ladykiller,* 46.

84. Bardens, *Ladykiller,* 51.

85. Bardens, *Ladykiller,* 152.

86. Bardens, *Ladykiller,* 66. Others received suspicion-arousing missives supposedly from their loved ones, but actually composed by Landru. Bardens recalled that Mme. Lacoste, Mme. Buisson's only surviving sister, had received a postcard allegedly signed by Mme. Buisson but in a different handwriting. Mme. Simon also received a similar letter purportedly from Buisson. But it seemed oddly cold and vague, mentioning no date for the wedding and overlooking the fact that Mme. Simon had previously been asked to serve as a witness. The handwriting was strange, too, resembling a man's. See Bardens, *Ladykiller,* 54.

Mme. Heon was another of Landru's victims. Bardens noted that within a day or so, three friends of Mme. Heon received postcards written by Landru—on her behalf, he said, as she was so happily busy caring for her home and preparing for her planned travel abroad. That was the last they heard from her, so they assumed she had gone on her trip and then her new, happy life. See Bardens, *Ladykiller,* 40.

Mme. Jaume was another Landru would-be wife who was turned into a victim, and again Landru's correspondence was a factor. Bardens explained that Mme. Lherault, Mme. Jaume's employer, became concerned over Jaume's absence, but Landru sent her a letter by pneumatic tube explaining that Mme. Jaume had gone to America. See Bardens, *Ladykiller,* 61.

87. Court TV, "Unique killer," 3; Court TV, "Arrest and investigation," 1.

88. Bardens, *Ladykiller,* 28.

89. Bardens, *Ladykiller,* 31.

90. Bardens, *Ladykiller,* 52.

91. Bardens, *Ladykiller,* 173.

92. Court TV, "Arrest and investigation," 2.

93. Rotten.com, "Henri Desire Landru," 1; Publications International Ltd., *Murder and mayhem,* 175; and Bardens, *Ladykiller,* 115.

94. Trivia Library.com, "Part 2," 2. Landru attempted to lose his carnet during his arrest while being taken into custody. A policeman who accompanied Landru in the automobile to the Surete noticed Landru attempting to secretly remove something from his pocket and throw it away outside. What was Landru trying to dispose of so quietly? It was a relatively small black notebook. See Bardens, *Ladykiller,* 84.

95. Explore Dictionary, "Henri Desire Landru," 1. On one day, for example, his notebook listed appointments at 9:30, 10:30, 11:30, 2:30 and 3:30, with Mademoiselle Lydee, Madame B, Mademoiselle L, Mademoiselle L, and Mademoiselle D, respectively. See Bardens, *Ladykiller,* 37.

96. Publications International Ltd., *Murder and mayhem,* 175.

97. Bardens, *Ladykiller,* 2.

98. Bardens, *Ladykiller,* 108.

99. Bardens, *Ladykiller,* 116, 174.

100. Bardens, *Ladykiller,* 104.

CHAPTER 2

1. Harold Jeffers, *With an axe* (New York: Kensington, 2000), 14. The solution to their panic as the Axeman preyed on fellow New Orleans residents? Humor. Everitt explained that levels of hysteria reached the point where sardonic humor (called thanahumor, or dark humor) was a means for reducing the fear. See David Everitt, *Human monsters: An illustrated encyclopedia of the world's most vicious murderers* (Chicago: Contemporary Books, 1993), 77. According to another report, "To cope with their fears, citizens resorted to morbid humor, throwing raucous New Orleans-style 'Axeman parties' and singing along to a popular tune called 'The Mysterious Axeman's jazz'." See Harold Schechter and David Everitt, *The A-Z encyclopedia of serial killers* (New York: Simon & Schuster, 1996), 20.

2. Brian Lane and Wilfred Gregg, *The encyclopedia of serial killers* (New York: Berkeley Books, 1992), 38.

3. Lane and Gregg, *Encyclopedia of serial killers,* 38.

4. Lane and Gregg, *Encyclopedia of serial killers,* 38.

5. Everitt, *Human monsters,* 78.

6. Colin Wilson and Damon Wilson, *The killers among us: Sex, madness, and mass murder,* vol. 2 (New York: Warner Books, 1995), 171.

7. Eric W. Hickey, *Serial murderers and their victims* (Belmont, CA: Wadsworth, 1997), 133.

8. Court TV, "The Axeman of New Orleans: From Hell," http://www.crimelibrary.com, 2, 3 (accessed May 8, 2005).

9. AmaZon, "Axeman of New Orleans," http://www.crimezzz.net, 2 (accessed May 8, 2005).

10. Schechter and Everitt, *A-Z encyclopedia,* 20.

11. "The Axman," http://www.geocities.com/area51/Dimension/2724/oddstory1.html? 20058, 2 (accessed May 8, 2005).

12. "Axman," www.geocities.com, 2.

13. "Axman," www.geocities.com, 2.

14. Troy Taylor, "The Axeman's Jazz: The 'Boogeyman' Comes to New Orleans," http://www.prairieghosts.com, 4 (accessed May 8, 2005).

15. Lane and Gregg, *Encyclopedia of serial killers,* 38.

16. Schechter and Everitt, *A-Z encyclopedia,* 20.

17. Everitt, *Human monsters,* 78.

18. Court TV, "Justice," http://www.crimelibrary.com, 1 (accessed May 8, 2005).

19. Court TV, "From Hell," 3.

20. Everitt, *Human monsters,* 78.

21. Lane and Gregg, *Encyclopedia of serial killers,* 38.

22. Taylor, "Axeman's jazz," 4.

23. Court TV, "The Axeman of New Orleans: The dark figure," http://www.crimelibrary.com, 2 (accessed May 8, 2005).

24. Taylor, "Axeman's jazz," 1–2.

25. Court TV, "The Axeman of New Orleans: Jekyll and Hyde," http://www.crimelibrary.com, 1 (accessed May 8, 2005).

26. Court TV, "The Axeman of New Orleans: The Devil," http://www.crimelibrary.com, 1 (accessed May 8, 2005).

27. Wilson and Wilson, *Killers among us,* 168–69.

28. Michael Newton, *Hunting humans: The encyclopedia of serial killers* (New York: Avon Books, 1990), 18; Schechter and Everitt, *A-Z encyclopedia,* 19.

29. Jeffers, *With an axe,* 14.

30. Taylor, "Axeman's jazz," 1; Everitt, *Human monsters,* 76.

31. Jeffers, *With an axe,* 14.

32. Taylor, "Axeman's jazz," 1.

33. Newton, *Hunting humans,* 18.

34. Lane and Gregg, *Encyclopedia of serial killers,* 35.

35. AmaZon, "Axeman," 1; Newton, *Hunting humans,* 18.

36. Wilson and Wilson, *Killers among us,* 168.

37. Wilson and Wilson, *Killers among us,* 168.

38. Lane and Gregg, *Encyclopedia of serial killers,* 36.

39. AmaZon, "Axeman," 1.

40. Taylor, "Axeman's jazz," 2.

41. Taylor, "Axeman's jazz," 1.

42. AmaZon, "Axeman," 1.

43. Taylor, "Axeman's jazz," 2.

44. Wilson and Wilson, *Killers among us,* 169.

45. "Axman," www.geocities.com, 1.

46. AmaZon, "Axeman," 1.

47. Wilson and Wilson, *Killers among us,* 168.

48. Lane and Gregg, *Encyclopedia of serial killers,* 36.

49. Lane and Gregg, *Encyclopedia of serial killers,* 36.

50. Jeffers, *With an axe,* 15.

51. Wilson and Wilson, *Killers among us,* 176.

52. Lane and Gregg, *Encyclopedia of serial killers,* 37.

53. Lane and Gregg, *Encyclopedia of serial killers,* 37. Taylor observed that the Laumann attack occurred on August 3, 1919. See Taylor, "Axeman's jazz," 3.

54. Jeffers, *With an axe,* 15.

55. Wilson and Wilson, *Killers among us,* 170.

56. Taylor, "Axeman's jazz," 4.

57. Wilson and Wilson, *Killers among us,* 170.

58. Lane and Gregg, *Encyclopedia of serial killers,* 37.

59. Jeffers, *With an axe,* 15. There were a number of other attacks, prior to 1918 and during 1918–19, attributed to the Axeman.

60. Wilson and Wilson, *Killers among us,* 171.

61. Court TV, "The Axeman of New Orleans: The black hand," http://www.crimelibrary.com, 2 (accessed May 8, 2005).

62. Schechter and Everitt, *A-Z encyclopedia,* 20.

63. Everitt, *Human monsters,* 78.

64. Everitt, *Human monsters,* 77.

65. Jeffers, *With an axe,* 14.

66. Schechter and Everitt, *A-Z encyclopedia,* 19–20.

67. Wilson and Wilson, *Killers among us,* 169.

68. Taylor, "Axeman's jazz," 2.

69. "Axman," www.geocities.com, 1.

70. Jeffers, *With an axe,* 14.

71. Taylor, "Axeman's jazz," 1; Lane and Gregg, *Encyclopedia of serial killers,* 35.

72. Court TV, "Black hand," 1.

73. Michael Newton, *The encyclopedia of serial killers: A study of the chilling criminal phenomenon, from the "Angels of Death" to the "Zodiac" killer* (New York: Checkmark Books, 2000), 9–10.

74. Taylor, "Axeman's jazz," 1; Court TV, "The Axeman of New Orleans: The next attack," http://www.crimelibrary.com, 3 (accessed May 8, 2005); and Newton, *Encyclopedia of serial killers,* 10.

75. Court TV, "Next attack," 2; Lane and Gregg, *Encyclopedia of serial killers,* 36; and Newton, *Encyclopedia of serial killers,* 10.

76. Court TV, "The Axeman of New Orleans: Copycat or mistaken identity?" http://www.crimelibrary.com, 1–2 (accessed May 8, 2005); Lane and Gregg, *Encyclopedia of serial killers,* 37–38; and Newton, *Encyclopedia of serial killers,* 10.

77. Taylor, "Axeman's jazz," 2.

78. Court TV, "Dark figure," 1.

79. Court TV, "From Hell," 2.

80. Court TV, "Dark figure," 1.

81. Kathleen Ramsland, "The Axeman of New Orleans: He came in the night," http://www.crimelibrary.com, 2 (accessed May 8, 2005).

82. Lane and Gregg, *Encyclopedia of serial killers,* 36.

83. "Axman," www.geocities.com, 1.

84. Newton, *Hunting humans,* 18.

85. Taylor, "Axeman's jazz," 1.

86. Court TV, "Black hand," 1.

87. Court TV, "Black hand," 1.

88. Wilson and Wilson, *Killers among us,* 168.

89. Newton, *Hunting humans,* 19.

90. Newton, *Hunting humans,* 19.

91. Newton, *Hunting humans,* 19–20.

92. Wilson and Wilson, *Killers among us,* 169.

93. AmaZon, "Axeman," 1.

94. "A Mysterious Letter," *New Orleans Times-Picayune,* March 14, 1919, 1. This letter has been reprinted in several places. See Court TV, "From Hell," 2; Taylor, "Axeman's jazz," 3.

95. Court TV, "From Hell," 2.

96. Taylor, "Axeman's jazz," 3.

97. Taylor, "Axeman's jazz," 3.

98. Schechter and Everitt, *A-Z encyclopedia,* 19–20.

CHAPTER 3

1. Wilson and Wilson, *Killers among us,* 175; Gini G. Scott, *Homicide: 100 years of murder in America* (Los Angeles: Lowell House, 1998), 61; Schechter and Everitt, *A-Z encyclopedia,* 197; John Burchill, "The Strangler," Winnipeg Police Service, http://www.winnipeg.ca/police, 1 (accessed May 11, 2005); and Harold Schechter, *Bestial: The savage trail of an American monster* (New York: Pocket Books, 1998), 363.

2. Scott, *Homicide,* 61; Mark Gribben, "Growing up bad," http://www.crimelibrary. com, 2 (accessed May 11, 2005); and Schechter and Everitt, *A-Z encyclopedia,* 196.

3. Schechter and Everitt, *A-Z encyclopedia,* 196; Scott, *Homicide,* 62.

4. Burchill, "Strangler," 2; Everitt, *Human monsters,* 90.

5. Fortune City.com, "Earle Nelson, the Gorilla Murderer," http://www.fortune city.com, 1 (accessed May 11, 2005); Wilson and Wilson, *Killers among us,* 175.

6. Scott, *Homicide,* 61; Burchill, "Strangler," 2.

7. Gribben, "Growing up bad," 2; Mark Gribben, "Descent to madness," http://www.crimelibrary.com, 1 (accessed May 11, 2005).

8. Wilson and Wilson, *Killers among us,* 175; Gribben, "Descent to madness," 1–2; and Everitt, *Human monsters,* 89.

9. Schechter and Everitt, *A-Z encyclopedia,* 196.

10. Everitt, *Human monsters,* 90; Burchill, "Strangler," 2.

11. Gribben, "Growing up bad," 3.

12. Answers.com, "Earle Nelson," http://www.answers.com, 1 (accessed May 11, 2005).

13. Everitt, *Human monsters,* 90; Scott, *Homicide,* 62; and Serial Killers A-Z, "Earle Nelson," http://www.geocities.com/verbal_plainfield/i-p/nelson.html, 1 (accessed May 1, 2005).

14. Burchill, "Strangler," 3; Mark Gribben, "The dark strangler," http://www. crimelibrary.com, 2–3; Mark Gribben, "A phantom," http://www.crimelibrary.com, 2; and Mark Gribben, "Room to kill," http://www.crimelibrary.com, 2 (all accessed May 11, 2005).

15. Everitt, *Human monsters,* 90; Gribben, "Growing up bad," 2–3. Nelson was very strange. As Gribben observed, "Nelson carried on conversations with invisible friends and enemies, was known to walk around the house on his hands and increasingly came home battered and bruised, as if he had been in a fight." See Gribben, "Descent to madness," 2; Gribben, "Growing up bad," 3.

16. Gribben, "Growing up bad," 3; Schechter and Everitt, *A-Z encyclopedia,* 196.

17. Gribben, "Descent to madness," 1.

18. Schechter, *Bestial,* 233, 247.

19. Serial Killers A-Z, "Earle Nelson," 1; Gribben, "Growing up bad," 3; and Answers.com, "Earle Nelson," 1.

20. Wilson and Wilson, *Killers among us,* 173; Scott, *Homicide,* 62.

21. Gribben, "Descent to madness," 2.

22. Serial Killers A-Z, "Earle Nelson," 1.

23. Schechter, *Bestial,* 310–11.

24. Everitt, *Human monsters,* 91; Schechter and Everitt, *A-Z encyclopedia,* 196; Fortune City.com, "Earle Nelson," 1; and Colin Wilson and Donald Seaman, *The serial killers: A study in the psychology of violence* (New York: Carol Publishing Group, 1997), 71.

25. Burchill, "Strangler," 6.

26. Wilson and Wilson, *Killers among us,* 173; Scott, *Homicide,* 62.

27. Serial Killers A-Z, "Earle Nelson," 1; Schechter and Everitt, *A-Z encyclopedia,* 196; and Burchill, "Strangler," 1.

28. Wilson and Wilson, *Killers among us,* 172.

29. Scott, *Homicide,* 62; Wilson and Seaman, *Serial killers,* 71; Serial Killers A-Z, "Earle Nelson," 1; Everitt, *Human monsters,* 90; and Burchill, "Strangler," 1.

30. Wilson and Wilson, *Killers among us,* 174.

31. Fortune City.com, "Earle Nelson," 1; Answers.com, "Earle Nelson," 2.

32. Schechter, *Bestial,* 83.

33. Schechter, *Bestial,* 232.

34. Schechter, *Bestial,* 76.

35. Schechter, *Bestial,* 76.

36. Schechter, *Bestial,* 78.

37. Schechter, *Bestial,* 110.

38. Schechter, *Bestial,* 109–10.

39. Schechter, *Bestial,* 112–13.

40. Schechter, *Bestial,* 113–14.

41. Schechter, *Bestial,* 124–25.

42. Schechter, *Bestial,* 285–87.

43. Schechter, *Bestial,* 287.

44. Schechter, *Bestial,* 260–61, 267.

45. Schechter, *Bestial,* 273, 277.

46. Schechter, *Bestial,* 292, 304.

47. Schechter, *Bestial,* 303.

48. Schechter, *Bestial,* 316–17.

49. Schechter, *Bestial,* 316–17.

50. Schechter, *Bestial,* 320, 323–24.

51. Schechter, *Bestial,* 335, 358.

52. Schechter, *Bestial,* 315. Schechter referred to "the public's insatiable hunger for any tidbits about Nelson." See Schechter, *Bestial,* 294.

53. Schechter, *Bestial,* 351.

54. Schechter, *Bestial,* 73.

55. Schechter, *Bestial,* 305.

56. Schechter, *Bestial,* 87. It must be admitted that the public's attention span is a short one, and the public interest in serial murder wanes. Gribben noted that "Frightened as they were, it didn't take long for Bay-area residents to put the Dark Strangler, as the papers dubbed Nelson, out of their minds." See Gribben, "Dark strangler," 3.

57. Schechter, *Bestial,* 85.

58. Schechter, *Bestial,* 96.

59. Schechter, *Bestial,* 162.

60. Schechter, *Bestial*, 189.
61. Schechter, *Bestial*, 167.
62. Burchill, "Strangler," 7.
63. Schechter, *Bestial*, 306–7.
64. Schechter, *Bestial*, 314–15.
65. Schechter, *Bestial*, 363–64.
66. Schechter, *Bestial*, 292.
67. Schechter, *Bestial*, 292–95.
68. Schechter, *Bestial*, 281.
69. Schechter, *Bestial*, 146.
70. Schechter, *Bestial*, 194.
71. Schechter, *Bestial*, 249.
72. Schechter, *Bestial*, 219.
73. Schechter, *Bestial*, 252.
74. Schechter, *Bestial*, 248–49.
75. Schechter, *Bestial*, 194.
76. Burchill, "Strangler," 7.
77. Schechter, *Bestial*, 261.
78. Schechter, *Bestial*, 233.
79. Everitt, *Human monsters*, 91.
80. Schechter, *Bestial*, 110, 294.

CHAPTER 4

1. It is unfortunate that space limits preclude consideration of all of the Manson "Family" murder participants. There were simply too many individuals involved.

2. Joel Norris, *Serial killers* (New York: Doubleday Books, 1988), 105, 161–63; Douglas O. Linder, "The Charles Manson trial: A chronology," http://www.law.umkc.edu/faculty/projects/ftrials/Manson/Mansonchrono.html, 1 (accessed May 24, 2005); and Explore Dictionary of Famous People, "Charles Manson," http://www.explore-biography.com/biographies/C/Charles_Manson.html, 1 (accessed May 25, 2005).

3. Linder, "Chronology," 1; Explore Dictionary, "Charles Manson," 1.

4. Norris, *Serial killers*, 161–63.

5. Linder, "Chronology," 1; Explore Dictionary, "Charles Manson," 1; and Norris, *Serial killers*, 105, 162–63.

6. Linder, "Chronology," 1; Norris, *Serial killers*, 164.

7. Rotten.com, "Charles Manson," http://www.rotten.com/library/bio/crime/serial-killers/charles-manson/, 1 (accessed May 24, 2005); Linder, "Chronology," 1; and Norris, *Serial killers*, 165–66.

8. Rotten.com, "Charles Manson," 2; Linder, "Chronology," 1; and Explore Dictionary, "Charles Manson," 2.

9. Linder, "Chronology," 1; Rotten.com, "Charles Manson," 1.

10. Norris, *Serial killers*, 164.

11. "Charles Manson," http://www.members.tripod.com/~SerialKillr/SerialKillers Exposed/manson.html, 1 (accessed May 25, 2005); Douglas O. Linder, "The Charles Manson (Tate-LaBianca murder) trial: The defendants," http://www.law.umkc.edu/faculty/projects/ftrials/manson/mansondefendants.html, 1 (accessed May 24, 2005); Linder, "Chronology," 1; Explore Dictionary, "Charles Manson," 2; and Norris, *Serial killers*, 168.

12. Norris, *Serial killers,* 169–70; Linder, "Defendants," 3; and Linder, "Chronology," 1.

13. Everitt, *Human monsters,* 191.

14. Jennifer Furio, *Team killers: A comparative study of collaborative criminals* (New York: Algora, 2001), 196.

15. Explore Dictionary, "Charles Manson," 3; Norris, *Serial killers,* 172; and Lane and Gregg, *Encyclopedia of serial killers,* 253.

16. The Zodiac Manson Connection, "Introduction," http://www.zodiacmurders.com, 1 (accessed May 24, 2005).

17. Publications International Ltd., *Murder and mayhem,* 200. According to an academic report, a music teacher named Gary Hinman was found in his home, stabbed to death. On the wall near his mutilated body, in Hinman's own blood, was printed "political piggy." See Linder, "Chronology," 2; Religious Tolerance.org, "The family (Charles Manson)," http://www.religioustolerance.org, 3 (accessed May 24, 2005).

18. Lane and Gregg, *Encyclopedia of serial killers,* 200, 254; Explore Dictionary, "Charles Manson," 3; and Publications International Ltd., *Murder and mayhem,* 200.

19. Everitt, *Human monsters,* 190; "Charles Manson," tripod.com, 1. The correct spelling of Frykowski's first name is Wojciech, not Voytek. See Explore Dictionary, "Charles Manson," 3.

20. Linder, "Chronology," 1. Levin and Fox claimed that Parent was stabbed once. See Jack Levin and James Alan Fox, *Mass murder: America's growing menace* (New York: Plenum Press, 1985), 88.

21. Levin and Fox, *Mass murder,* 88.

22. The Sixties, Manson, and Helter Skelter, "Death on Cielo Drive," http://www.users.adelphia.net/~mansonmurders/discovery.htm, 1–6 (accessed May 24, 2005). "One hundred and two stab wounds riddled the bodies. Thirty minutes, one stab every twenty seconds," noted Sanders. See Ed Sanders, *The family: The story of Charles Manson's dune buggy attack* (New York: E. P. Dutton, 1971), 268; The Sixties, Manson, and Helter Skelter, "May 25, 2005," http://www.users.adelphia.net/~mansonmurders/the%20murders.htm, 5 (accessed May 24, 2005).

23. Internet Crime Archives, "Tex Watson," http://www.mayhem.net, 2 (accessed May 24, 2005). The group also intended to kill Polish novelist Jerzy Kosinski, but he was not present. See Explore Dictionary, "Charles Manson," 3.

24. Scott, *Homicide,* 200; "Testimony of Virginia Graham in the Charles Manson trial," http://www.law.umkc.edu/faculty/projects/ftrials/manson/mansontestimony-g.html, 2 (accessed May 24, 2005); Publications International Ltd., *Murder and mayhem,* 200–201; Lane and Gregg, *Encyclopedia of serial killers,* 254; and Explore Dictionary, "Charles Manson," 3.

25. Los Angeles Police Department (LAPD), "LaBianca Homicide Report," First Homicide Investigation Progress Report DR 69-586 381 (August 10, 1969), http://users.adelphia.net/~mansonmurders/new_page_21.htm, 1 (accessed May 24, 2005).

26. "Charles Manson," tripod.com, 1; Scott, *Homicide,* 200.

27. Sanders, *Family,* 292–93; Furio, *Team killers,* 195; and Levin and Fox, *Mass murder,* 89. Bugliosi and Gentry described the media interest in the Manson case. The headlines dominated the front pages of the newspapers, and was equally big news on radio and TV, and they called these crimes "probably the most publicized murder case in history." See Vince Bugliosi and Curtis Gentry, *Helter skelter* (New York: W. W. Norton, 1974), 28.

28. LAPD, "LaBianca Homicide Report," 16–17.

29. LAPD, "LaBianca Homicide Report," 7.

30. LAPD, "LaBianca Homicide Report," 8, 10–11.

31. Publications International Ltd., *Murder and mayhem*, 201; Scott, *Homicide*, 200; and Linder, "Chronology," 2. According to Lane and Gregg, Manson, Watson, Atkins, Krenwinkle, Van Houten, and Grogan participated. Scott mentioned Manson, Watson, Van Houten and Krenwinkle. The list included Manson, Watson, Atkins, Krenwinkle, Kasabian, and Grogan, according to Publications International Ltd. According to the UMKC law study, Manson, Watson, Krenwinkle, Van Houten and Kasabian were the second night war party.

32. Rotten.com, "Charles Manson," 1.

33. Douglas O. Linder, "The Charles Manson (Tate-LaBianca murder) trial: Other key figures," http://www.law.umkc.edu/faculty/projects/ftrials/manson/mansonothers.html, 3 (accessed May 24, 2005); Linder, "Chronology," 3.

34. Religious Tolerance.org, "Family: Charles Manson," 3.

35. Linder, "Chronology," 3; Lane and Gregg, *Encyclopedia of serial killers*, 255.

36. Scott, *Homicide*, 200.

37. Everitt, *Human monsters*, 190.

38. Furio, *Team killers*, 193.

39. Linder, "Defendants," 1.

40. Levin and Fox, *Mass murder*, 89.

41. Explore Dictionary, "Charles Manson," 3–4.

42. Furio, *Team killers*, 196.

43. Scott, *Homicide*, 200.

44. Levin and Fox, *Mass murder*, 45.

45. Norris, *Serial killers*, 161.

46. Sanders, *Family*, 275–76, 279.

47. Sanders, *Family*, 277, 305.

48. Sanders, *Family*, 281–82.

49. Sanders, *Family*, 284, 299.

50. Sanders, *Family*, 305.

51. Sanders, *Family*, 305.

52. Sanders, *Family*, 304.

53. Sanders, *Family*, 304.

54. Sanders, *Family*, 310–11.

55. Sanders, *Family*, 305.

56. Sanders, *Family*, 305.

57. Religious Tolerance.org, "Family: Charles Manson," 3.

58. "Charles Manson," tripod.com, 1–2.

59. Lane and Gregg, *Encyclopedia of serial killers*, 255.

60. Furio, *Team killers*, 195.

61. "Testimony of Virginia Graham," 1.

62. Sanders, *Family*, 347, 357–58.

63. Bugliosi and Gentry, *Helter skelter*, 411.

64. Bugliosi and Gentry, *Helter skelter*, 417.

65. Bugliosi and Gentry, *Helter skelter*, 421, 429.

66. Bugliosi and Gentry, *Helter skelter*, 419, 435.

67. Bugliosi and Gentry, *Helter skelter*, 621.

68. Bugliosi and Gentry, *Helter skelter*, 46.

69. Publications International Ltd., *Murder and mayhem*, 200.

70. Everitt, *Human monsters*, 190.

71. Lane and Gregg, *Encyclopedia of serial killers*, 254.

72. Linder, "Chronology," 2.

73. The Sixties, Manson, and Helter Skelter, "Death on Cielo Drive," 1–4.

74. Sanders, *Family*, 293–94.

75. Bugliosi and Gentry, *Helter skelter*, 89–90.

76. Lane and Gregg, *Encyclopedia of serial killers*, 254.

77. LAPD, "LaBianca Homicide Report," 2.

78. Scott, *Homicide*, 200.

79. Sanders, *Family*, 293–94; Everitt, *Human monsters*, 190.

80. Bugliosi and Gentry, *Helter skelter*, 224–25.

81. Bugliosi and Gentry, *Helter skelter*, 224.

82. Lane and Gregg, *Encyclopedia of serial killers,* 254; Publications International Ltd., *Murder and mayhem*, 201; and LAPD, "LaBianca Homicide Report," 1–5.

83. Sanders, *Family*, 293.

84. Publications International Ltd., *Murder and mayhem*, 201; Everitt, *Human monsters*, 191.

85. Charlie Manson.com, http://www.charliemanson.com (accessed May 24, 2005); Furio, *Team killers*, 196.

86. Explore Dictionary, "Charles Manson," 1; Bugliosi and Gentry, *Helter skelter*, 375.

87. Furio, *Team killers*, 38.

88. Bugliosi and Gentry, *Helter skelter*, 296; Norris, *Serial killers*, 4.

89. Bugliosi and Gentry, *Helter skelter*, 22, 23.

90. Bugliosi and Gentry, *Helter skelter*, 15, 253. At the Tate crime scene, just beyond the front gate the reporters and photographers now constituted a crowd, with more arriving in a steady stream of scribes. Police and media vehicles so completely obstructed Cielo Drive that several LAPD officers were sent to try and untangle them. See Bugliosi and Gentry, *Helter skelter*, 18, 78.

91. Bugliosi and Gentry, *Helter skelter*, 78–79.

92. Bugliosi and Gentry, *Helter skelter*, 264–65.

93. Bugliosi and Gentry, *Helter skelter*, 286.

94. Bugliosi and Gentry, *Helter skelter*, 357.

95. Bugliosi and Gentry, *Helter skelter*, 488.

96. Bugliosi and Gentry, *Helter skelter*, 97.

97. Bugliosi and Gentry, *Helter skelter*, 29.

98. Bugliosi and Gentry, *Helter skelter*, 29.

99. Bugliosi and Gentry, *Helter skelter*, 74. In this case, so much confidential information was already given out, in fact, that LAPD detectives would have great difficulty in finding 'polygraph keys' for questioning suspects. See Bugliosi and Gentry, *Helter skelter*, 28. At the LaBianca crime scene, investigators discovered a likely polygraph key, the knife imbedded in Leno LaBianca's throat. "There are many polygraph interrogation keys, but this appears to be an outstanding one." See LAPD, "LaBianca Homicide Report," 6.

CHAPTER 5

1. Ian Brady, *The gates of Janus: Serial killing and its analysis* (Los Angeles: Feral House, 2001), 86.

2. Guardian Unlimited, "Timetable of Moors Murders case," http://www.guardian.co.uk, 1 (accessed May 24, 2005); Absolute Astronomy, "Ian Brady," http://www.

absoluteastronomy.com/encyclopedia/I/IA/Ian_Brady.htm, 1–2 (accessed May 24, 2005); and Newton, *Hunting humans,* 49. "Ian Brady born out of wedlock in Glasgow," recorded the Guardian Unlimited. See Guardian Unlimited, "Timetable," 1.

3. Greg Taylor, "The Moors Murders," http://www.freespace.virgin.net/greg. taylor1/moors.html, 1 (accessed May 24, 2005); Wilson and Seaman, *Serial killers,* 232.

4. Wilson and Seaman, *Serial killers,* 232.

5. Absolute Astronomy, "Ian Brady," 1; Taylor, "Moors murders," 1; Wilson and Seaman, *Serial killers,* 232; and Newton, *Hunting humans,* 49. Seaman and Wilson added that Brady became obsessed with Nazi history and memorabilia. He also became very interested in the ideas of the Marquis de Sade. See Wilson and Seaman, *Serial killers,* 232.

6. Fortune City.com, "Ian Brady and Myra Hindley: The Moors Murders," http://www.fortune city.com, 1 (accessed May 24, 2005); Wilson and Seaman, *Serial killers,* 232; and Newton, *Hunting humans,* 49. Brady served four years of probation for additional burglaries. After another theft, he received a one-year sentence in Borstal. See Wilson and Seaman, *Serial killers,* 232.

7. Wilson and Seaman, *Serial killers,* 232–33; Newton, *Hunting humans,* 49.

8. Taylor, "Moors murders," 3–4; Chris Summers, "Moors murderers," http://www.bbc.co.uk, 3–4 (accessed May 25, 2005).

9. Murder in the UK, "Ian Brady and Myra Hindley: Moors Murderers," http://www.murderuk.com, 3 (accessed May 24, 2005).

10. Guardian Unlimited, "Timetable," 1.

11. Taylor, "Moors murders," 1; Wilson and Seaman, *Serial killers,* 233.

12. Summers, "Moors murderers," 2; Wilson and Seaman, *Serial killers,* 233; and Newton, *Hunting humans,* 49. "By virtually all accounts, Hindley was an eager participant in Brady's nefarious activities. She changed her look to match that of his ideal woman: high boots and mini-skirts. She bleached her hair and the whole ensemble was created so that she would appear more German." See Taylor, "Moors murders," 1.

13. Absolute Astronomy, "Ian Brady," 4; Wilson and Seaman, *Serial killers,* 233–34. "Hindley always portrayed herself as a gullible, easily-led and totally manipulated young woman—she was 19 when she met Brady—who fell under the spell of an evil man and simply went along for the ride." See Summers, "Moors murderers," 2.

14. Summers, "Moors murderers," 2, 4; Wilson and Seaman, *Serial killers,* 234–36.

15. Murder in the UK, "Brady and Hindley," 4; Guardian Unlimited, "Timetable," 1; and Summers, "Moors murderers," 4.

16. Murder in the UK, "Brady and Hindley," 1; Taylor, "Moors murders," 1; Absolute Astronomy, "Ian Brady," 1; Summers, "Moors murderers," 2; and Newton, *Hunting humans,* 49.

17. Murder in the UK, "Brady and Hindley," 1; Wilson and Seaman, *Serial killers,* 233; and Newton, *Hunting humans,* 51.

18. Publications International Ltd., *Murder and mayhem,* 29; Summers, "Moors murderers," 3.

19. Taylor, "Moors murders," 1.

20. Absolute Astronomy, "Ian Brady," 1.

21. Wilson and Seaman, *Serial killers,* 232.

22. Absolute Astronomy, "Ian Brady," 4.

23. Fortune City.com, "Brady and Hindley," 1.

24. Fortune City.com, "Brady and Hindley," 1.

25. Absolute Astronomy, "Ian Brady," 1–2.

26. Newton, *Hunting humans,* 51–52.

27. Nicholas Christian, "Di Stefano linked to Hindley murder claim," http://www. news.scotsman.com, 1 (accessed May 24, 2005).

28. Publications International Ltd., *Murder and mayhem,* 28.

29. Summers, "Moors murderers," 3.

30. Publications International Ltd., *Murder and mayhem,* 28.

31. Absolute Astronomy, "Ian Brady," 2.

32. Summers, "Moors murderers," 1.

33. Summers, "Moors murderers," 4.

34. Guardian Unlimited, "Timetable," 1.

35. Ananova, "Moors murders: The victims," http://www.ananova.news.com/news/ story/sm_710249.html, 1–2 (accessed May 24, 2005).

36. Absolute Astronomy, "Moors murders," http://www.absoluteastronomy.com/ encyclopedia/M/Mo/Moors_murders.htm, 2 (accessed May 24, 2005).

37. Newton, *Hunting humans,* 50.

38. Absolute Astronomy, "Moors murders," 2.

39. Summers, "Moors murderers," 2.

40. Wilson and Seaman, *Serial killers,* 234.

41. Guardian Unlimited, "Timetable," 1.

42. Ananova, "Moors murders," 1.

43. Absolute Astronomy, "Ian Brady," 2.

44. Ananova, "Moors murders," 3.

45. Absolute Astronomy, "Moors murders," 1.

46. Summers, "Moors murderers," 2.

47. Wilson and Seaman, *Serial killers,* 235.

48. Newton, *Hunting humans,* 50–51.

49. Guardian Unlimited, "Timetable," 1.

50. Ananova, "Moors murders," 3.

51. Absolute Astronomy, "Ian Brady," 2.

52. Wilson and Seaman, *Serial killers,* 235.

53. Newton, *Hunting humans,* 50.

54. Guardian Unlimited, "Timetable," 1.

55. Absolute Astronomy, "Ian Brady," 3.

56. Newton, *Hunting humans,* 50.

57. Guardian Unlimited, "Timetable," 1.

58. Publications International Ltd., *Murder and mayhem,* 28.

59. Absolute Astronomy, "Moors murders," 3.

60. "Ian Brady and Myra Hindley," http://www.webukonline.co.uk/ruth.buddell/ brady.htm, 1 (accessed May 24, 2005).

61. Fortune City.com, "Brady and Hindley," 1.

62. Absolute Astronomy, "Ian Brady," 3; Summers, "Moors murderers," 3.

63. Wilson and Seaman, *Serial killers,* 236; Newton, *Hunting humans,* 50.

64. "Ian Brady and Myra Hindley," www.webukonline.co.uk, 1.

65. Summers, "Moors murderers," 2; Wilson and Seaman, *Serial killers,* 235.

66. Newton, *Hunting humans,* 50–51; Wilson and Seaman, *Serial killers,* 19.

67. Absolute Astronomy, "Moors murders," 3. An Internet source added, "The attack was recorded on audiotape by Hindley and the 16 minute 21 second tape of the girl's last desperate moments formed part of the harrowing defense." See Ananova, "Moors

murders," 3; Fortune City.com, "Brady and Hindley," 1; and Murder in the UK, "Brady and Hindley," 1.

68. Fortune City.com, "Brady and Hindley," 1.

69. Fortune City.com, "Brady and Hindley," 1; Murder in the UK, "Brady and Hindley," 1.

70. Newton, *Hunting humans,* 51; Wilson and Seaman, *Serial killers,* 234–35.

71. Emlyn Williams, *Beyond belief* (New York: Random House, 1968), 13–14.

72. Williams, *Beyond belief,* 16.

73. Williams, *Beyond belief,* 22.

74. Williams, *Beyond belief,* 341.

75. Williams, *Beyond belief,* 31.

76. Taylor, "Moors murders," 2.

77. Summers, "Moors murderers," 3; Wilson and Seaman, *Serial killers,* 232, 237; and Newton, *Hunting humans,* 50.

78. Williams, *Beyond belief,* 28, 30.

79. Williams, *Beyond belief,* 31.

80. Williams, *Beyond belief,* 33.

81. Williams, *Beyond belief,* 34–35, 39, 273.

82. Williams, *Beyond belief,* 276, 282.

83. Williams, *Beyond belief,* 297, 350.

84. Williams, *Beyond belief,* 358, 363.

85. Williams, *Beyond belief,* 363.

86. Brady, *Gates of Janus,* 84.

87. Murder in the UK, "Brady and Hindley," 1; Summers, "Moors murderers," 1.

88. Williams, *Beyond belief,* 321.

89. Williams, *Beyond belief,* 325.

90. Williams, *Beyond belief,* 23.

91. Brady, *Gates of Janus,* 73.

92. Williams, *Beyond belief,* 325, 348.

93. Williams, *Beyond belief,* 342, 350.

94. Williams, *Beyond belief,* 315.

95. Williams, *Beyond belief,* 22.

96. Williams, *Beyond belief,* 23.

97. Williams, *Beyond belief,* 14, 23.

98. Williams, *Beyond belief,* 343.

CHAPTER 6

1. It is unclear precisely who coined the nickname "Hillside Strangler."

2. NNDB, "Kenneth Bianchi," http://www.nndb.com, 1 (accessed June 13, 2005).

3. Explore Dictionary of Famous People, "Kenneth Bianchi," http://www.explore-biography.com/biographies/K/Kenneth_Bianchi.html, 1; "Kenneth Bianchi," http://www.hillside-strangler.com, 1 (both accessed June 13, 2005).

4. Kari and Associates, "The Hillside Stranglers: Kenneth Bianchi and Angelo Buono," http://www.karisable.com, 1 (accessed June 13, 2005); Darcy O'Brien, *Two of a kind: The Hillside Stranglers* (New York: New American Library, 1985), 91; and "Kenneth Bianchi," www.hillside-strangler.com, 1.

5. O'Brien, *Two of a kind,* 103, 108–9.

6. Ted Schwartz, *The Hillside Strangler: A murderer's mind* (New York: New American Library, 1981), 232, 249; O'Brien, *Two of a kind*, 91–92, 262.

7. "Angelo Buono, Jr.," http://www.hillside-strangler.com, 1 (accessed June 13, 2005); O'Brien, *Two of a kind*, 41.

8. Schwartz, *Hillside Strangler*, 37, 218; History Channel, "The Hillside Stranglers," http://www.thehistorychannel.co.uk, 1 (accessed May 23, 2005); Chris Summers, "The Hillside Stranglers," http://www.bbc.co.uk, 2 (accessed May 23, 2005); and "Kenneth Bianchi," www.hillside-strangler.com, 1.

9. "Hillside Stranglers," http://www.geocities.com/schoolgirlsadist/hillsidestranglers.html?200523, 1 (accessed May 23, 2005); O'Brien, *Two of a kind*, 41.

10. "Kenneth Bianchi," www.hillside-strangler.com, 1; Summers, "Hillside Stranglers," 2.

11. Schwartz, *Hillside Strangler*, 40; O'Brien, *Two of a kind*, 93.

12. "Hillside Stranglers," www.geocities.com, 1; History Channel, "Hillside Stranglers," 1.

13. Brady, *Gates of Janus*, 274; O'Brien, *Two of a kind*, 108–9; "Kenneth Bianchi," www.hillside-strangler.com, 1; and New Criminologist, "Obituary: Angelo Buono," http://www.newcriminologist.com, 1 (accessed June 13, 2005).

14. Answers.com, "Angelo Buono, Jr.," http://www.answers.com, 1 (accessed June 13, 2005).

15. New Criminologist, "Obituary," 1.

16. Court TV, "Angelo," http://www.crimelibrary.com, 1 (accessed May 23, 2005); O'Brien, *Two of a kind*, 72.

17. "Angelo Buono, Jr.," www.hillside-strangler.com, 1; O'Brien, *Two of a kind*, 7; and Court TV, "Angelo," 1.

18. New Criminologist, "Obituary," 1; Court TV, "Angelo," 2.

19. Brady, *Gates of Janus*, 278; "Hillside Stranglers," www.geocities.com, 1.

20. History Channel, "Hillside Stranglers," 1; Summers, "Hillside Stranglers," 2.

21. Brady, *Gates of Janus*, 278; New Criminologist, "Obituary," 1; Court TV, "Angelo," 1; History Channel, "Hillside Stranglers," 1; "Angelo Buono, Jr.," www.hillside-strangler.com, 1; and Summers, "Hillside Stranglers," 2.

22. Kari and Associates, "Hillside Stranglers," 1; Brady, *Gates of Janus*, 273; New Criminologist, "Obituary," 1; Court TV, "Angelo," 1–2; and O'Brien, *Two of a kind*, 76–80, 196.

23. Brady, *Gates of Janus*, 274; Summers, "Hillside Stranglers," 2; and "Hillside Stranglers," www.geocities.com, 1.

24. Brady, *Gates of Janus*, 278; O'Brien, *Two of a kind*, 73, 76, 97; "Angelo Buono, Jr.," www.hillside-strangler.com, 1; and Court TV, "Angelo," 1.

25. "Hillside Stranglers," www.geocities.com, 1; Brady, *Gates of Janus*, 273; and Summers, "Hillside Stranglers," 2.

26. O'Brien, *Two of a kind*, 82, 86; New Criminologist, "Obituary," 1; and Court TV, "Angelo," 2.

27. History Channel, "Hillside Stranglers," 2; Kari and Associates, "Hillside Stranglers," 1; and Answers.com, "Angelo Buono, Jr.," 1.

28. History Channel, "Hillside Stranglers," 1; Jane Caputi, *The age of sex crime* (Bowling Green, OH: Bowling Green State University Press, 1999), 42.

29. Court TV, "Early victims," http://www.crimelibrary.com, 1–2 (accessed May 23, 2005); Summers, "Hillside Stranglers," 2.

30. Brady, *Gates of Janus,* 255; True Crime.com, "The Hillside Strangler," http://www. jonray0tripod.com, 1 (accessed May 23, 2005).

31. Brady, *Gates of Janus,* 274.

32. Brady, *Gates of Janus,* 255.

33. Answers.com, "Hillside Strangler," http://www.answers.com, 1 (accessed May 23, 2005); "The Hillside Strangler: Timeline of events," http://www.hillside-strangler.com, 1 (accessed June 13, 2005); and Court TV, "Early victims," 1–2.

34. True Crime.com, "Hillside Strangler," 2; Answers.com, "Hillside Strangler," 1.

35. "Timeline," www.hillside-strangler.com, 1; Court TV, "Early victims," 2; and O'Brien, *Two of a kind,* 48.

36. "Timeline," www.hillside-strangler.com, 1; Schwartz, *Hillside Strangler,* 67.

37. "Timeline," www.hillside-strangler.com, 1; Schwartz, *Hillside Strangler,* 67.

38. Caputi, *Age of sex crime,* 42; History Channel, "Hillside Stranglers," 1.

39. Court TV, "Two killers," http://www.crimelibrary.com, 1 (accessed May 23, 2005); True Crime.com, "Hillside Strangler," 3; and Answers.com, "Hillside Strangler," 1.

40. Court TV, "Two killers," 2; Summers, "Hillside Stranglers," 2.

41. True Crime.com, "Hillside Strangler," 3; Answers.com, "Hillside Strangler," 2.

42. "Timeline," www.hillside-strangler.com, 1.

43. Court TV, "Kenny," http://www.crimelibrary.com, 1 (accessed May 23, 2005).

44. Court TV, "Two killers," 2; Answers.com, "Hillside Strangler," 2.

45. Schwartz, *Hillside Strangler,* 67; O'Brien, *Two of a kind,* 58.

46. Court TV, "A witness," http://www.crimelibrary.com, 1 (accessed May 23, 2005).

47. Answers.com, "Hillside Strangler," 2; Schwartz, *Hillside Strangler,* 67.

48. Court TV, "Three more," http://www.crimelibrary.com, 1 (accessed May 23, 2005).

49. Answers.com, "Hillside Strangler," 2; Brady, *Gates of Janus,* 264–65.

50. Court TV, "Three more," 1–2; Court TV, "Kenny," 1; Answers.com, "Hillside Strangler," 2; Kari and Associates, "Hillside Stranglers," 1; and "Hillside Stranglers," http://www.allserialkillers.com, 1 (accessed May 23, 2005).

51. "Hillside Stranglers," www.allserialkillers.com, 1.

52. Kari and Associates, "Hillside Stranglers," 2.

53. True Crime.com, "Hillside Strangler," 1; New Criminologist, "Obituary," 1.

54. O'Brien, *Two of a kind,* xi–xii.

55. Answers.com, "Hillside Strangler," 2; Schwartz, *Hillside Strangler,* 102.

56. Summers, "Hillside Stranglers," 6.

57. Kari and Associates, "Hillside Stranglers," 1; Answers.com, "Hillside Strangler," 1; New Criminologist, "Obituary," 1; and "Hillside Stranglers," www.geocities.com, 1.

58. Mark Fuhrman, *Murder in Spokane* (New York: Cliff Street Books, 2001), 73; Marilyn Bardsley, "The rampage begins," http://www.crimelibrary.com, 1 (accessed May 23, 2005); and Caputi, *Age of sex crime,* 42.

59. Court TV, "Witness," 1; Summers, "Hillside Stranglers," 3; Answers.com, "Hillside Strangler," 1–2; New Criminologist, "Obituary," 1; and "Kenneth Bianchi," www.hillside-strangler.com, 1.

60. Court TV, "Witness," 1; Bardsley, "Rampage begins," 1; Fuhrman, *Murder in Spokane,* 73; O'Brien, *Two of a kind,* 127; and Summers, "Hillside Stranglers," 2.

61. Summers, "Hillside Stranglers," 3; History Channel, "Hillside Stranglers," 1.

62. Kari and Associates, "Hillside Stranglers," 1; Summers, "Hillside Stranglers," 3.

63. Fuhrman, *Murder in Spokane,* 73; "Timeline," www.hillside-strangler.com, 1.

64. "Kenneth Bianchi," www.hillside-strangler.com, 1.

65. O'Brien, *Two of a kind*, 288.

66. Schwartz, *Hillside Strangler*, 72, 83, 93, 111.

67. Schwartz, *Hillside Strangler*, 95–97.

68. Schwartz, *Hillside Strangler*, 80, 106.

69. Schwartz, *Hillside Strangler*, 69; O'Brien, *Two of a kind*, 298.

70. Schwartz, *Hillside Strangler*, 71.

71. Schwartz, *Hillside Strangler*, 21–23.

72. Schwartz, *Hillside Strangler*, 25, 160, 162.

73. Schwartz, *Hillside Strangler*, 148, 179.

74. Schwartz, *Hillside Strangler*, 20, 27.

75. Schwartz, *Hillside Strangler*, 240; O'Brien, *Two of a kind*, 300.

76. O'Brien, *Two of a kind*, 328.

77. Schwartz, *Hillside Strangler*, 262.

78. Schwartz, *Hillside Strangler*, 269; O'Brien, *Two of a kind*, 346.

79. O'Brien, *Two of a kind*, 356.

80. Schwartz, *Hillside Strangler*, 30.

81. Schwartz, *Hillside Strangler*, 252; O'Brien, *Two of a kind*, 328, 395.

82. O'Brien, *Two of a kind*, 407–8.

83. O'Brien, *Two of a kind*, 412–3.

84. Schwartz, *Hillside Strangler*, 179, 238–39, 240.

85. O'Brien, *Two of a kind*, 127–28; Schwartz, *Hillside Strangler*, 68, 102.

86. Court TV, "The Hillside Strangler," http://www.crimelibrary.com, 1 (accessed May 23, 2005); Bardsley, "Rampage begins," 1; and Fuhrman, *Murder in Spokane*, 73.

87. Court TV, "Witness," 2; Summers, "Hillside Stranglers," 2–3; Brady, *Gates of Janus*, 262; True Crime.com, "Hillside Strangler," 3; and "Timeline," www.hillside-strangler.com, 1.

88. O'Brien, *Two of a kind*, 17–18, 401.

89. Schwartz, *Hillside Strangler*, 102; O'Brien, *Two of a kind*, 128; and Summers, "Hillside Stranglers," 3.

90. Schwartz, *Hillside Strangler*, 56.

91. O'Brien, *Two of a kind*, 186.

92. History Channel, "Hillside Stranglers," 1; Caputi, *Age of sex crime*, 42.

93. History Channel, "Hillside Stranglers," 1.

94. Schwartz, *Hillside Strangler*, 161.

95. Publications International Ltd., *Murder and mayhem*, 144.

96. Court TV, "Early victims," 2.

97. O'Brien, *Two of a kind*, 172–73.

98. Schwartz, *Hillside Strangler*, 24.

99. O'Brien, *Two of a kind*, 172–73.

100. Schwartz, *Hillside Strangler*, 103.

101. O'Brien, *Two of a kind*, 301, 340.

102. O'Brien, *Two of a kind*, 300.

103. O'Brien, *Two of a kind*, 27, 40, 149–50, 154, 158.

104. Fuhrman, *Murder in Spokane*, 73; Brady, *Gates of Janus*, 262.

105. Schwartz, *Hillside Strangler*, 61.

106. Schwartz, *Hillside Strangler*, 92; True Crime.com, "Hillside Strangler," 2.

107. Schwartz, *Hillside Strangler*, 92.

108. O'Brien, *Two of a kind*, 177–78, 211–12.

109. O'Brien, *Two of a kind*, 35; Schwartz, *Hillside Strangler*, 63.

110. Schwartz, *Hillside Strangler*, 76.

111. Court TV, "Hillside Strangler," 1; Kari and Associates, "Hillside Stranglers," 1; True Crime.com, "Hillside Strangler," 1; and Schwartz, *Hillside Strangler*, 67.

CHAPTER 7

1. Anne Schwartz, *The man who could not kill enough* (New York: Birch Lane Books, 1992), 70.

2. Schwartz, *Man who could not kill enough*, 210.

3. Don Davis, *The Milwaukee murders: Nightmare in apartment 213—the true story* (New York: St. Martin's Press, 1991), 20.

4. Davis, *Milwaukee murders*, 20.

5. Davis, *Milwaukee murders*, 22.

6. Davis, *Milwaukee murders*, 23.

7. Davis, *Milwaukee murders*, 24.

8. Everitt, *Human monsters*, 268.

9. Davis, *Milwaukee murders*, 21.

10. Newton, *Hunting humans*, 102.

11. Everitt, *Human monsters*, 268.

12. Davis, *Milwaukee murders*, 35.

13. Davis, *Milwaukee murders*, 26. Norris referred to Dahmer's "high I.Q. scores in the Army." He attended Hazel Harvey Elementary School and Revere High School. See Joel Norris, *Jeffrey Dahmer* (New York: Windsor, 1992), 116, 60, 70.

14. Davis, *Milwaukee murders*, 54.

15. Davis, *Milwaukee murders*, 81.

16. Lane and Gregg, *Encyclopedia of serial killers*, 128–29.

17. Davis, *Milwaukee murders*, 101.

18. Davis, *Milwaukee murders*, 60–61, 70. According to Norris, "Other friends remembered that Jeffrey had begun drinking regularly when he was a twelve-year-old in the seventh grade." In high school he began drinking at 7:30 in the morning, where he was once caught with a glass of Scotch by a teacher. Later, in his sole quarter at Ohio State University, "Dahmer was a full-blown alcoholic." He spent so much money on alcohol that he was reduced to selling his blood to finance his drinking. See Norris, *Jeffrey Dahmer*, 74–75, 82, 102–3, 111.

19. Davis, *Milwaukee murders*, 70.

20. Davis, *Milwaukee murders*, 24.

21. Newton, *Hunting humans*, 103.

22. Davis, *Milwaukee murders*, 36.

23. Davis, *Milwaukee murders*, 283.

24. Norris, *Jeffrey Dahmer*, 51.

25. Norris, *Jeffrey Dahmer*, 140–41; Davis, *Milwaukee murders*, 285.

26. Norris, *Jeffrey Dahmer*, 140–41.

27. Norris, *Jeffrey Dahmer*, 146–47.

28. Davis, *Milwaukee murders*, 285.

29. Norris, *Jeffrey Dahmer*, 151–53.

30. Davis, *Milwaukee murders*, 285.

31. Norris, *Jeffrey Dahmer*, 172–74.

32. Davis, *Milwaukee murders,* 286.

33. Norris, *Jeffrey Dahmer,* 198–203.

34. Norris, *Jeffrey Dahmer,* 198.

35. Davis, *Milwaukee murders,* 286.

36. Norris, *Jeffrey Dahmer,* 196–97.

37. Davis, *Milwaukee murders,* 286.

38. Norris, *Jeffrey Dahmer,* 212–13.

39. Davis, *Milwaukee murders,* 286.

40. Norris, *Jeffrey Dahmer,* 216–17.

41. Davis, *Milwaukee murders,* 287.

42. Norris, *Jeffrey Dahmer,* 270–71.

43. Davis, *Milwaukee murders,* 287.

44. Norris, *Jeffrey Dahmer,* 224–25.

45. Davis, *Milwaukee murders,* 287.

46. Norris, *Jeffrey Dahmer,* 226–30.

47. Davis, *Milwaukee murders,* 287.

48. Norris, *Jeffrey Dahmer,* 230–39.

49. Davis, *Milwaukee murders,* 288.

50. Norris, *Jeffrey Dahmer,* 252–53.

51. Davis, *Milwaukee murders,* 288.

52. Norris, *Jeffrey Dahmer,* 253–55.

53. Newton, *Hunting humans,* 104.

54. Norris, *Jeffrey Dahmer,* 255–56.

55. Davis, *Milwaukee murders,* 145, 288. But were there other Dahmer murders? He confessed to a total of seventeen slayings; according to Lane and Gregg, Dahmer confessed to, and reportedly expressed remorse over, seventeen murders. See Lane and Gregg, *Encyclopedia of serial killers,* 128; Wilson and Wilson, *Killers among us,* 298; and Everitt, *Human monsters,* 268.

But there were rumors of five deaths in Germany when Dahmer was stationed there, being investigated by the West German police. Davis added that one of Dahmer's army friends stated that Dahmer killed a hitchhiker in Germany. See Davis, *Milwaukee murders,* 61.

56. Norris, *Jeffrey Dahmer,* 257–58.

57. Newton, *Hunting humans,* 104; Lane and Gregg, *Encyclopedia of serial killers,* 126–27; and Davis, *Milwaukee murders,* 288. Neighbors heard someone yell "Faggot" loudly during the arrest. Sounds of a scuffle, and a loud, long scream were also heard. See Norris, *Jeffrey Dahmer,* 30–31.

58. Wilson and Wilson, *Killers among us,* 297–98.

59. Everitt, *Human monsters,* 260.

60. Davis, *Milwaukee murders,* 157–58.

61. Lane and Gregg, *Encyclopedia of serial killers,* 126.

62. Lane and Gregg, *Encyclopedia of serial killers,* 128.

63. Davis, *Milwaukee murders,* 108.

64. Wilson and Wilson, *Killers among us,* 298. According to Davis, Dahmer cut out Lacy's heart for one reason—a snack. Dahmer removed the heart of his sixteenth victim and put it in the refrigerator. He subsequently told police that he intended to eat it at a later time. See Davis, *Milwaukee murders,* 143.

65. Davis, *Milwaukee murders,* 108.

66. Norris, *Jeffrey Dahmer*, 11. Dr. Frank Berlin of Johns Hopkins Medical School noted that "Dahmer suffered from necrophilia." Another mental health professional, Dr. Judith Becker, suggested that Dahmer was "obsessed with necrophilia." See Norris, *Jeffrey Dahmer*, 276, 278, 66. See also Davis, *Milwaukee murders*, 241.

67. Davis, *Milwaukee murders*, 154; Norris, *Jeffrey Dahmer*, 13.

68. Davis, *Milwaukee murders*, 154–55.

69. Norris, *Jeffrey Dahmer*, 29.

70. Davis, *Milwaukee murders*, 155.

71. Davis, *Milwaukee murders*, 155–56; Norris, *Jeffrey Dahmer*, 30–31.

72. Norris, *Jeffrey Dahmer*, 50.

73. Norris, *Jeffrey Dahmer*, 50.

74. Davis, *Milwaukee murders*, 289–90.

75. Norris, *Jeffrey Dahmer*, 272.

76. Norris, *Jeffrey Dahmer*, 9.

77. Norris, *Jeffrey Dahmer*, 273.

78. Newton, *Encyclopedia of serial killers*, 48.

79. Davis, *Milwaukee murders*, 242.

80. Schwartz, *Man who could not kill enough*, 136.

81. Davis, *Milwaukee murders*, 127.

82. Schwartz, *Man who could not kill enough*, 140–41.

83. Schwartz, *Man who could not kill enough*, 140.

84. Schwartz, *Man who could not kill enough*, 187.

85. Norris, *Jeffrey Dahmer*, 11.

86. Schwartz, *Man who could not kill enough*, 201–2.

87. Schwartz, *Man who could not kill enough*, 201.

88. Schwartz, *Man who could not kill enough*, 201.

89. Joseph C. Fisher, *Killer among us: Public reaction to serial murder* (Westport, CT: Praeger, 1997), 121.

90. Schwartz, *Man who could not kill enough*, 28.

91. Schwartz, *Man who could not kill enough*, 134.

92. Schwartz, *Man who could not kill enough*, 134. Alvin R. Urgent, Session's attorney, defended his client's actions. The custodian, the attorney argued, sincerely believed that he was rendering a public service by giving the purloined information to the media. The *New York Times* reporter explained to Sessions that he had a moral obligation to share the information with the public. See Schwartz, *Man who could not kill enough*, 134. The Milwaukee District Attorney released a statement, which began, "Shame on the *New York Times*."

93. Schwartz, *Man who could not kill enough*, 143.

94. Schwartz, *Man who could not kill enough*, 139.

95. Schwartz, *Man who could not kill enough*, 114–15.

96. Schwartz, *Man who could not kill enough*, 26.

97. Schwartz, *Man who could not kill enough*, 141.

98. Schwartz, *Man who could not kill enough*, 141.

99. Schwartz, *Man who could not kill enough*, 141.

100. Schwartz, *Man who could not kill enough*, 27.

101. Schwartz, *Man who could not kill enough*, 26.

102. Schwartz, *Man who could not kill enough*, 34–35.

103. Norris, *Jeffrey Dahmer*, 41.

104. Schwartz, *Man who could not kill enough,* 135–36.

105. Schwartz, *Man who could not kill enough,* 103.

106. Schwartz, *Man who could not kill enough,* 6.

107. Schwartz, *Man who could not kill enough,* 128.

108. Schwartz, *Man who could not kill enough,* 190.

109. Davis, *Milwaukee murders,* 185–86.

110. Schwartz, *Man who could not kill enough,* 158.

111. Schwartz, *Man who could not kill enough,* 143.

112. Schwartz, *Man who could not kill enough,* 187.

113. Schwartz, *Man who could not kill enough,* 53.

114. Schwartz, *Man who could not kill enough,* 216.

115. Davis, *Milwaukee murders,* 108.

116. Norris, *Jeffrey Dahmer,* 7.

117. Norris, *Jeffrey Dahmer,* 45, 263.

118. Norris, *Jeffrey Dahmer,* 22, 285.

119. Newton, *Encyclopedia of serial killers,* 48.

CHAPTER 8

1. Daniel J. Blackburn, *Human harvest: The Sacramento murder story* (New York: Knightsbridge, 1990), 29.

2. Michael D. Kelleher and C. L. Kelleher, *Murder most rare: The female serial killer* (New York: Dell, 1998), 141.

3. Blackburn, *Human harvest,* 29. An Internet encyclopedia was less kind but probably more accurate in describing the discrepancy in Puente origin tales, "She was born in San Bernardino County, California, to two alcoholics." But, "In later life she lied about her childhood, saying that she was one of eighteen children who were all born and raised in Mexico." See "Dorothea Puente," http://www.wikipedia.org, 2 (accessed August 19, 2005).

4. Blackburn, *Human harvest,* 29.

5. Kelleher and Kelleher, *Murder most rare,* 141.

6. Blackburn, *Human harvest,* 29.

7. Newton, *Hunting humans,* 278. According to NNDB, Puente was married in 1946 for two years to an unknown man who died of a heart attack. She married Axel Johanson in 1952 and divorced in 1966. She married Roberto Puente in 1966, and Pedro Montalvo in 1976. See NNDB, "Dorothea Puente," http://www.nndb.com, 1 (accessed August 19, 2005). Biography.ms also noted the initial two-year marriage, followed by one with Axel Johanson. "In 1952, she married a Swede named Axel Johanson and had a violent 14-year marriage. . . . She divorced Johansen in 1966 and married Roberto Puente in Mexico City." Finally, Biography.ms recalled that "Puente married for the third time in 1976 to Pedro Montalvo who was a physically abusive alcoholic. The marriage lasted only a few months." See Biography.ms, "Dorothea Puente," http://dorothea-puente.biography.ms, 1–2 (accessed August 19, 2005).

8. Newton, *Hunting humans,* 277.

9. Kelleher and Kelleher, *Murder most rare,* 141–42.

10. Newton, *Hunting humans,* 277.

11. Newton, *Hunting humans,* 277.

12. Newton, *Hunting humans,* 277.

13. Lane and Gregg, *Encyclopedia of serial killers,* 294.

14. Blackburn, *Human harvest,* 11.

15. Blackburn, *Human harvest,* 58.

16. Kelleher and Kelleher, *Murder most rare,* 142.

17. Newton, *Hunting humans,* 277.

18. Blackburn, *Human harvest,* 8.

19. Blackburn, *Human harvest,* 35.

20. "Dorothea Puente," www.wikipedia.org, 1.

21. NNDB, "Dorothea Puente," 1.

22. Blackburn, *Human harvest,* 55.

23. Kelleher and Kelleher, *Murder most rare,* 145.

24. Kelleher and Kelleher, *Murder most rare,* 141.

25. Kelleher and Kelleher, *Murder most rare,* 141.

26. Newton, *Hunting humans,* 278; Kelleher and Kelleher, *Murder most rare,* 144. A relatively broad range of possible victims was explained by the *Sacramento News and Review* in 2001: "Some say she did in two dozen this way, but only the eight are confirmed." See Umberto Tosi, "Mr. Bizarro's sactoland tour," *Sacramento News and Review,* September 20, 2001.

27. Kelleher and Kelleher, *Murder most rare,* 144.

28. Lane and Gregg, *Encyclopedia of serial killers,* 294.

29. Newton, *Hunting humans,* 277.

30. Kelleher and Kelleher, *Murder most rare,* 142.

31. Lane and Gregg, *Encyclopedia of serial killers,* 294.

32. Kelleher and Kelleher, *Murder most rare,* 143. An Internet encyclopedia added, "Every month Puente collected all the tenant's mail before they saw it and gave them only a small amount of their money. Invariably, the tenants squandered what little money they had at the nearest bar and were picked-up by the police and jailed for 30 days following anonymous tips. Puente then pocketed the rest of the tenant's money." See "Dorothea Puente," www.wikipedia.org, 2. Similarly, *Sacramento News and Review* reported that Puente's boardinghouse was a place "where pensioners checked in, but not out." Tosi added, "The grey-haired Puente liked to take in pensioners, poison them and bury them in her back yard. Then, she'd continue cashing their Social Security checks." See Tosi, "Mr. Bizarro's sactoland tour," 1.

33. Newton, *Hunting humans,* 279.

34. Newton, *Hunting humans,* 278. Was Florez culpable? An Internet study says no: "Handyman Ismael Florez constructs a six-foot-long wooden box for Dorothea Puente, and assists her dumping it in a river, without actually knowing what is inside the box. He thinks this is somewhat strange but Dorothea is a nice lady." See Rotten.com, "Dorothea Puente," http://www.rotten.com/library/, 1 (accessed August 19, 2005). An Internet encyclopedia provides a different version of this tale. Florez was asked to construct a wooden box, six feet by three feet by two feet in dimension. Puente said it was to store "books and other items." Next, "She then asked Florez to transport the filled and nailed shut box to a storage depot. Florez agreed and Puente joined him. On the way, however, she told him to stop while they were on the Garden Highway in Sutter County and dump the box in the river. Puzzled, Florez questioned why, but Puente told him that the contents of the box were just junk." See "Dorothea Puente," www.wikipedia.org, 2. We might consider a third version of the box incident, to ascertain the likeliest truths. Biography.ms basically corroborated Wikipedia, in very similar

language. But Biography.ms went on to describe the consequences of the clandestine and spontaneous box-dumping incident, which occurred in November 1985. "On January 1, 1986, two fishermen found a foul smelling, half-submerged box in the river and informed police. Investigators found a badly decomposed and unidentifiable body of an elderly man inside." See Biography.ms, "Dorothea Puente," 1.

35. Newton, *Hunting humans*, 278.

36. Lane and Gregg, *Encyclopedia of serial killers*, 294.

37. Kelleher and Kelleher, *Murder most rare*, 274.

38. Newton, *Hunting humans*, 279.

39. Newton, *Hunting humans*, 279. According to Rotten.com, the body was identified as Everson Gillmouth. See Rotten.com, "Dorothea Puente," 1. Puente had met Gillmouth as her pen-pal, while she was incarcerated. When she was released from prison, he met her in his red 1980 Ford pickup. They soon were making wedding plans, opening a joint bank account, and buying a boardinghouse at 1426 F Street in Sacramento. See Biography.ms, "Dorothea Puente," 2. The relationship between Puente and Gillmouth was confirmed by NNDB. It named her "boyfriend" as being "Everson Gillmouth." See NNDB, "Dorothea Puente," 1.

40. Blackburn, *Human harvest*, 41.

41. Rotten.com, "Dorothea Puente," 1; Biography.ms, "Dorothea Puente," 2.

42. Newton, *Hunting humans*, 278.

43. Blackburn, *Human harvest*, 113.

44. Newton, *Hunting humans*, 279.

45. Blackburn, *Human harvest*, 99, 106.

46. Blackburn, *Human harvest*, 109–11.

47. Blackburn, *Human harvest*, 112.

48. Blackburn, *Human harvest*, 112–13.

49. Blackburn, *Human harvest*, 115–17, 119.

50. Blackburn, *Human harvest*, 118.

51. Blackburn, *Human harvest*, 181.

52. Blackburn, *Human harvest*, 181.

53. Lane and Gregg, *Encyclopedia of serial killers*, 295.

54. Blackburn, *Human harvest*, 119, 192.

55. Blackburn, *Human harvest*, 120–21.

56. Blackburn, *Human harvest*, 121.

57. Blackburn, *Human harvest*, 121.

58. Blackburn, *Human harvest*, 122.

59. Blackburn, *Human harvest*, 123.

60. Blackburn, *Human harvest*, 122, 192.

61. See Lynne Rominger, "Personality: Mike Boyd," *Sacramento Magazine*, July 2002, 2.

62. Kelleher and Kelleher, *Murder most rare*, 144.

63. Kelleher and Kelleher, *Murder most rare*, 144.

64. Kelleher and Kelleher, *Murder most rare*, 144.

65. Kelleher and Kelleher, *Murder most rare*, 144; Biography.ms, "Dorothea Puente," 2–3.

66. Biography.ms, "Dorothea Puente," 3.

67. Kelleher and Kelleher, *Murder most rare*, 144–45.

68. Blackburn, *Human harvest*, 127. The considerable public interest in this case can be evaluated in several ways. For instance, there is personal and commercial interest in

Puente memorabilia. The website Murder Auction, http://www.murderauction.com, offers a variety of serial killer artifacts and products. One such item is a letter from Puente. The auctioneer is requesting $45 for this missive, but the top bid as of August 19, 2005, was only $5.

Other serial murder-related products are available in the Puente case. A book has been written, inspired by this case. William P. Wood has written *The Bone Garden,* "based on Sacramento boardinghouse killer Dorothea Puente, who buried seven of her nine victims in her yard." The irony of Wood's authorship of this book results from his prior relationship with Puente: "Wood sent Puente to prison for earlier crimes including robbery and drugging elderly victims." See Dorchester Publishing, "William P. Wood," http://www.dorchesterpub.com, 1 (accessed August 19, 2005).

69. Blackburn, *Human harvest,* 21. Media interest in the Puente case was considerable. For instance, former Sacramento KCRA-TV news anchorperson Mike Boyd declared, "Dorothea Puente is a very big part of my career." The reason? Boyd was asked, "What was the most notorious case you covered?" He replied, "Probably, in terms of memorable, Dorothea Puente, the lady known as the 'F Street Boarding House Landlady,' who was discovered with seven bodies buried in her yard and two other murders they later pinned on her. She was eventually found guilty. She was finally tried in Monterey on a change of venue. I spent an entire summer covering that trial in Monterey." See Rominger, "Personality," 2.

70. Blackburn, *Human harvest,* 20. The Sacramento police were tiring of being asked if they had erred when Puente escaped. See Blackburn, *Human harvest,* 115.

71. Blackburn, *Human harvest,* 135.

72. Blackburn, *Human harvest,* 119.

73. Blackburn, *Human harvest,* 18, 23.

74. Blackburn, *Human harvest,* 121.

75. Blackburn, *Human harvest,* 122.

76. Blackburn, *Human harvest,* 20.

77. Blackburn, *Human harvest,* 22.

78. Blackburn, *Human harvest,* 121.

79. Blackburn, *Human harvest,* 130–31. Different serial murder stakeholders took very different positions on Puente's ride with the media. Her defense attorney complained that it was wrong for the police to have held her, especially in contact with the press, for such an extended period of time without her having had the chance to consult with counsel. The media included in the trip defended their actions. Bob Jordan, an executive at KCRA-TV, said, "Our job is to aggressively cover the news and to run after things when they happen, and frankly, I'm quite proud of what we did." See Blackburn, *Human harvest,* 131. The *Sacramento Bee* shared the expense for the trip. Managing Editor George Baker commented, "Our role was that of an observer. I think we would have betrayed our readers if we hadn't done this." See Blackburn, *Human harvest,* 132.

Incredibly, there was a second case of media misconduct through direct involvement in the Puente case. Mike Boyd himself made this claim in a recent interview with his old station, KCRA-TV in Sacramento. Boyd claimed a decisive role in "convincing Dorothea Puente to spill facts that later aided in her conviction as a serial killer." See Rominger, "Personality," 1.

80. Blackburn, *Human harvest,* 129, 177.

81. Blackburn, *Human harvest,* 129.

82. Blackburn, *Human harvest,* 29.

83. Blackburn, *Human harvest,* 129.

84. Blackburn, *Human harvest,* 114. Puente knew that she had to keep a very low profile, because of the news reports. She had read that at least seven bodies had been dug up in her yard and that the search for her was now extended nationwide. She felt vulnerable and far too visible, even in this part of town. Her photograph in the newspapers and on each television newscast increased her vulnerability. See Blackburn, *Human harvest,* 115.

85. Blackburn, *Human harvest,* 36.

86. Blackburn, *Human harvest,* 114. Ironically, her freedom lasted a total of sixty hours. See Blackburn, *Human harvest,* 120.

87. Blackburn, *Human harvest,* 119.

88. Blackburn, *Human harvest,* 131.

89. Blackburn, *Human harvest,* 117–18.

90. NNDB, "Dorothea Puente," 1.

91. Tosi, "Mr. Bizarro's sactoland tour," 1.

CHAPTER 9

1. Brady, *Gates of Janus,* 229.

2. Kings County Sheriff's Office, "Suspect Gary Leon Ridgway," http://www.metrokc.gov; Court TV, "The big break," http://www.crimelibrary.com, 1–4; and Kari and Associates, "Gary Leon Ridgway," http://www.karisable.com, 1–3 (all accessed November 10, 2005).

3. Kari and Associates, "Gary Leon Ridgway," 1.

4. Kari and Associates, "Gary Leon Ridgway," 2.

5. KATU-TV, "Are Green River killer victims still hidden in Oregon?" http://www.katu.com, 1 (accessed November 10, 2005).

6. Matthew Preusch, "Families speak as Green River killer gets 48 life terms," *New York Times,* December 19, 2003, 1. The Associated Press agreed, adding that "the King County Sheriff's Green River task force identified him as a suspect in 1984 and continued to watch him, even after he passed a polygraph test." See Associated Press, "Early tip fell short in Green River killings," *New York Times,* December 26, 2003, 2. The victim in this case was Marie Malvar. It was reported that "Gary Ridgway had been a suspect as early as 1984, when the boyfriend of Marie Malvar saw her getting into his pickup." See Gene Johnson, "Case closed: Catching the Green River killer," Associated Press, *Albuquerque Journal,* December 14, 2003, B8.

Another reporter placed Ridgway under an earlier cloud of suspicion, stating that he "first came under scrutiny as early as 1983." See Jill Smolowe, "Catching the Green River killer," *People,* November 24, 2003, 118. Still another account confirmed the 1984 date: "As long ago as 1984, Mr. Ridgway had been named a suspect in the investigation." See Sarah Kershaw, "In deal for life, man admits killing 48 women," *New York Times,* November 6, 2003, 2.

7. Smolowe, "Catching the Green River killer," 118.

8. Sarah Kershaw, "21-year hunt for killer shapes man and family," *New York Times,* November 7, 2003, 2.

9. Kershaw, "21-year hunt," 3.

10. Kershaw, "In deal for life," 2.

11. National Briefing, *New York Times,* April 4, 2003, 1.

12. Scott, *Homicide,* 250.

13. Sarah Kershaw, "New discoveries move Green River case to fore again," *New York Times,* September 22, 2003, 1.

14. Antonio Mendoza, *Killers on the loose* (London: Virgin Books, 2000), 38.

15. Mendoza, *Killers on the loose,* 39.

16. Brady, *Gates of Janus,* 217.

17. Carlton Smith and Tomas Guillen, *The search for the Green River killer* (New York: Onyx Books, 1991), 232–33.

18. Gene Johnson, "Guilty plea set in 48 Green River deaths," Associated Press, *Albuquerque Journal,* October 31, 2003, A11.

19. Hickey, *Serial murderers and their victims,* 246.

20. Gary C. King, "The Green River killer," in Art Crockett, ed., *Serial murderers* (New York: Windsor, 1990), 85–108.

21. Kershaw, "In deal for life," 2.

22. Gene Johnson, "'Green River nightmare' ends," Associated Press, *Albuquerque Journal,* November 6, 2003, A4; Gene Johnson, "Green River killer 'sorry'," Associated Press, *Albuquerque Journal,* December 19, 2003, A8; and Maria Newman, "In plea deal, man admits 48 Green River killings," *New York Times,* November 5, 2003, 1.

23. King, "Green River killer," 85–108.

24. "Bones of possible serial killer victim found," *New York Times,* September 28, 2003, 1.

25. Johnson, "Guilty plea set," A11.

26. Johnson, "Green River nightmare ends," A4.

27. Mendoza, *Killers on the loose,* 35. The size of the Green River Task Force professional staff fluctuated over time. In 2003, there were eleven full-time detectives assigned to the case. See Kershaw, "New discoveries," 1.

28. Hickey, *Serial murderers and their victims,* 254.

29. Kershaw, "New discoveries," 1–2.

30. Newman, "In plea deal," 2.

31. Hickey, *Serial murderers and their victims,* 234. There were more than 13,000 suspects in the Green River killings, according to a *New York Times* report. See Kershaw, "In deal for life," 2.

32. Smolowe, "Catching the Green River killer," 118. Brady provided a much higher estimate: "A total of 20,000 suspects had been interviewed." See Brady, *Gates of Janus,* 229.

33. Smolowe, "Catching the Green River killer," 120. Kershaw also states that the task force was a one person operation at one time, but she names a different person— Dave Reichert. She recalled that "Mr. Reichert joined the King's County Sheriff's Office in 1979. For several years he was the only full-time detective detailed to the case." See Kershaw, "21-year hunt," 2.

34. Kershaw, "21-year hunt," 2.

35. Associated Press, "Early tip fell short," 2.

36. Johnson, "Case closed," B8.

37. Johnson, "Case closed," B6.

38. Johnson, "Green River killer sorry," A8.

39. Kershaw, "In deal for life," 3.

40. Johnson, "Green River nightmare ends," A4; Kings County Sheriff's Office, "Suspect Gary Leon Ridgway," 1.

41. Johnson, "Green River nightmare ends," A4.

42. Johnson, "Green River killer sorry," A8.

43. Newman, "In plea deal," 1.

44. Kershaw, "In deal for life," 1.

45. Smith and Guillen, *Search for the Green River killer,* 345.

46. Kershaw, "New discoveries," 1.

47. Smith and Guillen, *Search for the Green River killer,* 345.

48. Brady, *Gates of Janus,* 224.

49. Publications International Ltd., *Murder and mayhem,* 108.

50. Smith and Guillen, *Search for the Green River killer,* 423. Police spokesperson Ferguson tried to explain the unhappiness of law enforcement with the media coverage: "The problem has been the aggressiveness and the competition among the news media for the stories. Some papers have their hotshot investigative reporters on this case and they think they have to come up with something big every day." See Smith and Guillen, *Search for the Green River killer,* 82–83.

51. Smith and Guillen, *Search for the Green River killer,* 40.

52. Smith and Guillen, *Search for the Green River killer,* 283.

53. Smith and Guillen, *Search for the Green River killer,* 40.

54. Smith and Guillen, *Search for the Green River killer,* 351.

55. Smith and Guillen, *Search for the Green River killer,* 348–49.

56. Johnson, "Case closed," B8.

57. Smith and Guillen, *Search for the Green River killer,* 78.

58. Smith and Guillen, *Search for the Green River killer,* 80.

59. Smith and Guillen, *Search for the Green River killer,* 64.

60. Smith and Guillen, *Search for the Green River killer,* 82.

61. Smith and Guillen, *Search for the Green River killer,* 83.

62. Smith and Guillen, *Search for the Green River killer,* 83.

63. Smith and Guillen, *Search for the Green River killer,* 56.

64. Smith and Guillen, *Search for the Green River killer,* 269.

65. Smith and Guillen, *Search for the Green River killer,* 288.

66. Scott, *Homicide,* 250.

67. Brady, *Gates of Janus,* 220.

68. Smith and Guillen, *Search for the Green River killer,* 68.

69. Smith and Guillen, *Search for the Green River killer,* 359.

70. Smith and Guillen, *Search for the Green River killer,* 355.

71. Smith and Guillen, *Search for the Green River killer,* 80. Another media zone occurred when police searched cab driver Melvyn Foster's home. According to one account, "The news media had arrived in force. Television helicopters hovered overhead, carrying live feeds back to Seattle and videotaping the events for the evening news. Scores of news media trucks jammed the narrow street." See Smith and Guillen, *Search for the Green River killer,* 148.

72. Smith and Guillen, *Search for the Green River killer,* 279.

73. Smith and Guillen, *Search for the Green River killer,* 207.

74. Smith and Guillen, *Search for the Green River killer,* 235.

75. Smith and Guillen, *Search for the Green River killer,* 174–75, 331, 436–39.

76. Wilson and Seaman, *Serial killers,* 132.

77. Publications International Ltd., *Murder and mayhem,* 197.

78. Scott, *Homicide,* 250–51.

79. Smith and Guillen, *Search for the Green River killer,* 207.

80. Smith and Guillen, *Search for the Green River killer,* 240.

81. Preusch, "Families speak," 1.

82. Preusch, "Families speak," 2.

CHAPTER 10

1. Scott, *Homicide,* 339.

2. Scott, *Homicide,* 339.

3. Scott, *Homicide,* 339. When Cunanan received a red Nissan 300ZX sportscar for his sixteenth birthday, he did not exactly respond with gratitude. He told a friend, "It just made me realize how pathetic they all were. They think that after all that's happened they can just buy back my love." See Wensley Clarkson, *Death at every stop* (New York: St. Martin's Press, 1997), 101.

4. Steven G. Michaud and Roy Hazelwood, *The evil that men do* (New York: St. Martin's Press, 1998), 25. He went on to attend the University of California, San Diego. "His coursework was sloppy or simply never handed in." See Clarkson, *Death at every stop,* 25. As an undergraduate he declared that he wanted to major in history. Cunanan was considered intelligent, and he had mastered Spanish and Italian in prep school. See Clarkson, *Death at every stop,* 22.

5. Michaud and Hazelwood, *Evil that men do,* 23.

6. Gary Indiana, *Three-month fever: The Andrew Cunanan story* (New York: Cliff Street Books, 1999), 97.

7. Michaud and Hazelwood, *Evil that men do,* 23.

8. Indiana, *Three-month fever,* 95. "Cunanan's other big problem was that he was promiscuous." See Clarkson, *Death at every stop,* 25. An old friend, Gary Danes, recalled that "Andrew had become the ultimate gay party animal." See Clarkson, *Death at every stop,* 25.

9. Indiana, *Three-month fever,* 95.

10. Scott, *Homicide,* 339–40.

11. Indiana, *Three-month fever,* 99.

12. Indiana, *Three-month fever,* 95.

13. Scott, *Homicide,* 339.

14. Maureen Orth, *Vulgar favors: Andrew Cunanan, Gianni Versace, and the largest failed manhunt in U. S. history* (New York: Delacorte, 1999), 373–75.

15. Michaud and Hazelwood, *Evil that men do,* 23.

16. Indiana, *Three-month fever,* 98.

17. Indiana, *Three-month fever,* 98.

18. Indiana, *Three-month fever,* 98.

19. Scott, *Homicide,* 341.

20. Michaud and Hazelwood, *Evil that men do,* 23. Clarkson agreed, noting that what Cunanan had concealed from his friends at his last lavish dinner party was the fact that he was flat broke. He had had to beg his credit card company to advance the payment for his one-way ticket to Minneapolis. See Clarkson, *Death at every stop,* 101.

21. Michaud and Hazelwood, *Evil that men do,* 24.

22. Michaud and Hazelwood, *Evil that men do,* 24. There is chilling evidence that Cunanan planned more murders. Police found a "handwritten list of celebrities" in Cunanan's vehicle after his death. It included Madonna, Julio Iglesias, Gordon Getty, and Harry DeWidt, among others. See Clarkson, *Death at every stop,* 174. Others who may

have been potential Cunanan targets were Elton John and actors John Travolta, Rupert Everett, and Lisa Kudrow, as well as David Hockney, an artist. Designers Giorgi Armani, Calvin Klein, and Jean-Paul Gaultier were also on the Cunanan hit list. See Clarkson, *Death at every stop,* 199. The FBI issued a warning to each of the celebrity targets on Cunanan's list two days after Versace's murder. Clarkson recalled, "The FBI refused to publicly say what had prompted the new warning but they had been talking to some of Cunanan's friends in San Diego." See Clarkson, *Death at every stop,* 199.

23. Michaud and Hazelwood, *Evil that men do,* 23.

24. Michaud and Hazelwood, *Evil that men do,* 23.

25. Michaud and Hazelwood, *Evil that men do,* 23.

26. Michaud and Hazelwood, *Evil that men do,* 24. Miglin was nearly decapitated by a wound seven-and-a-half inches long and two inches deep. See Orth, *Vulgar favors,* 275.

27. Michaud and Hazelwood, *Evil that men do,* 24.

28. Michaud and Hazelwood, *Evil that men do,* 24.

29. Scott, *Homicide,* 342. According to Matt Rodriguez, the superintendent of the Chicago Police Department, "There are some aspects of the homicide that indicate there was some torture." See Orth, *Vulgar favors,* 281.

30. Orth, *Vulgar favors,* 274.

31. Indiana, *Three-month fever,* 134–36. The Federal Bureau of Investigation document 88A-MP-47461 states that "Information had been received prior to this date from CHICAGO POLICE DEPARTMENT (CPD) Det. ——, assigned to Area Violent Crimes Unit, that an individual, ——, had contacted the CPD to advise that he was a male prostitute who had in the past had sexual relations with LEE MIGLIN and ANDREW CUNANAN." The document added, "The younger of the two occupants was driving the vehicle and would later be described by —— as ANDREW CUNANAN. The older gentleman was seated in the front passenger seat and would later be described by —— as LEE MIGLIN." See Indiana, *Three-month fever,* 134–36.

32. Michaud and Hazelwood, *Evil that men do,* 24.

33. Michaud and Hazelwood, *Evil that men do,* 24.

34. Michaud and Hazelwood, *Evil that men do,* 25.

35. Clarkson, *Death at every stop,* 233.

36. Clarkson, *Death at every stop,* 109.

37. Orth, *Vulgar favors,* 232–33, 246.

38. Orth, *Vulgar favors,* 285, 304–5.

39. Orth, *Vulgar favors,* 326–27.

40. Orth, *Vulgar favors,* 289–90; Clarkson, *Death at every stop,* 220.

41. Orth, *Vulgar favors,* 384, 465.

42. Clarkson, *Death at every stop,* 211; Orth, *Vulgar favors,* 281, 383–84.

43. Orth, *Vulgar favors,* 359, 373.

44. Orth, *Vulgar favors,* 260.

45. Orth, *Vulgar favors,* 277, 293.

46. Clarkson, *Death at every stop,* 245; Orth, *Vulgar favors,* 476.

47. Clarkson, *Death at every stop,* 247.

48. Orth, *Vulgar favors,* 427, 478, 485.

49. Indiana, *Three-month fever,* xiii. Orth added that "the media immediately leaped on the story, but Chicago police would say little." See Orth, *Vulgar favors,* 239.

50. Orth, *Vulgar favors,* 239.

51. Orth, *Vulgar favors,* 277.

52. Orth, *Vulgar favors*, 366.

53. Orth, *Vulgar favors*, 366.

54. Orth, *Vulgar favors*, 395.

55. Orth, *Vulgar favors*, 440–41.

56. Orth, *Vulgar favors*, 372.

57. Orth, *Vulgar favors*, 372–73.

58. Orth, *Vulgar favors*, 404.

59. Orth, *Vulgar favors*, 314.

60. Orth, *Vulgar favors*, 255. In a different version of the story, Douglas and Olshaker claimed that "From Chicago, then, Cunanan heads east towards Philadelphia, using Miglin's cell phone to call a friend in San Diego. But when he hears on the radio the police are after him, tracing him from the phone's signal, he pitches it out the window over a bridge." See John Douglas and Mark Olshaker, *Anatomy of motive* (New York: Scribners, 1999), 204. "On a large square projection-style TV, Andrew followed the gathering tsunami of news about himself," Indiana suggested. He added that "A few miles outside Wilmington the radio picked up a police press conference in Philly, they'd tracked signals from the Lexus cell phone to Ridley Township. . . . Andrew cut the handset wire with pliers from the Lexus tool kit and tore off the antenna on the rear window mount. Still the phone kept emitting a signal. Andrew realized he had to ditch the car." See Indiana, *Three-month fever,* 218.

61. Orth, *Vulgar favors*, 403. "Increasingly aware of the nationwide TV and newspaper coverage of his crimes, Cunanan decided that he needed to go out in disguise when he went out of the hotel. His favorite reinvention was to dress as a brunette woman," Clarkson noted. See Clarkson, *Death at every stop*, 135.

62. Orth, *Vulgar favors*, 256.

63. Orth, *Vulgar favors*, 256.

64. Orth, *Vulgar favors*, 404.

65. Orth, *Vulgar favors*, 404.

66. Orth, *Vulgar favors*, 404.

67. Orth, *Vulgar favors*, 429–30.

68. Orth, *Vulgar favors*, 381.

69. Orth, *Vulgar favors*, 340.

70. Orth, *Vulgar favors*, 340.

71. Orth, *Vulgar favors*, 431.

72. Orth, *Vulgar favors*, 381.

73. Orth, *Vulgar favors*, 378. Others profited as well. For instance, Fernando Carriera was the caretaker for the houseboat where Cunanan took his life after being surrounded by the police. He collected approximately $55,000 in reward money from the FBI, Dade County, the Greater Miami Convention and Visitors Bureau, the Miami Beach Police Department, the Gay and Lesbian Anti-Violence Project, and the Florida Department of Law Enforcement. He also sought, but was denied, a $10,000 reward offered by New York City. See Orth, *Vulgar favors*, 426.

74. Indiana, *Three-month fever,* 236.

75. Douglas and Olshaker, *Anatomy of motive*, 193.

76. Michaud and Hazelwood, *Evil that men do*, 25.

77. Douglas and Olshaker, *Anatomy of motive*, 206. Others became celebrities, as well. For instance, Fernando Carreira became a celebrity and appeared on Geraldo and Larry King Live, and then flew back to his native Portugal for the first time in forty years. He

immediately began wheeling and dealing almost upon arrival. Now he was a celebrity and he started to wear imitation silk Versace shirts. See Orth, *Vulgar favors,* 427.

78. Orth, *Vulgar favors,* 234.

79. Orth, *Vulgar favors,* 296.

80. Orth, *Vulgar favors,* 234.

81. Orth, *Vulgar favors,* 273. "Lee Miglin's elaborate funeral" was reported "as a major news event." Even magazines like *People* and *Time* covered Miglin's services. See Orth, *Vulgar favors,* 307.

82. Orth, *Vulgar favors,* 273.

83. Orth, *Vulgar favors,* 404. At the Reese crime scene, there was such a media crowd, "the scene resembled a night game in the World Series." See Orth, *Vulgar favors,* 326.

84. Orth, *Vulgar favors,* 402.

85. Orth, *Vulgar favors,* 402.

86. Orth, *Vulgar favors,* 236. "Then we are descended upon by the media," declared Miami Police Department Detective Paul Marcus. "All of a sudden they are dropping out of the sky. On the grass across the street, it grew and grew and grew. It got to the point it was overwhelming there." See Orth, *Vulgar favors,* 415.

87. Orth, *Vulgar favors,* 473.

88. Orth, *Vulgar favors,* 286.

89. Orth, *Vulgar favors,* 355.

90. Orth, *Vulgar favors,* 357.

91. Indiana, *Three-month fever,* 244–45.

92. Orth, *Vulgar favors,* 258.

93. Scott, *Homicide,* 342.

94. Orth, *Vulgar favors,* 331.

95. Orth, *Vulgar favors,* 328.

96. Orth, *Vulgar favors,* 331.

97. Scott, *Homicide,* 339. According to Orth, Cunanan was the first American serial killer to be publicized extensively on the Internet. See Orth, *Vulgar favors,* 337.

98. Orth, *Vulgar favors,* 330.

99. Orth, *Vulgar favors,* 327, 337, 393–95.

100. "Musical on serial killer criticized," *Albuquerque Journal,* January 13, 2004, B3.

101. Scott added that Cunanan seemed to remain comfortable in his twin roles of being an effeminate companion of a millionaire, while after hours he was the masculine life of the party at gay bars. See Scott, *Homicide,* 340.

CHAPTER 11

1. NNDB, "Paul Bernardo," http://www.nndb.com, 1 (accessed June 9, 2005); Scott Burnside and Alan Cairns, *Deadly innocence* (New York: Times Warner Books, 1996), 61; and Joe Chidley, "Bernardo: The untold story," Macleans, September 11, 1995.

2. Burnside and Cairns, *Deadly innocence,* 61; Chidley, "Bernardo," 3–4.

3. Chidley, "Bernardo," 4.

4. Burnside and Cairns, *Deadly innocence,* 86, 88.

5. Chidley, "Bernardo," 4–5.

6. Burnside and Cairns, *Deadly innocence,* 86, 93.

7. Chidley, "Bernardo," 1–2.

8. CBC News Online, "In-depth: Bernardo," http://www.cbc.ca, 1 (accessed June 9, 2005).

9. Chidley, "Bernardo," 1; All Serial Killers, "Paul Bernardo," http://www.allserialkillers.com, 1 (accessed June 9, 2005).

10. Freemasonry Watch, "Proof that serial killer and rapist Paul Bernardo was a Freemason in the Grand Lodge of Ontario, Canada," http://www.freemasonrywatch.org, 1–2 (accessed June 9, 2005).

11. Biography.ms, "Paul Bernardo," http://paul-bernardo.biography.ms, 1 (accessed June 9, 2005).

12. "Karla Homolka," http://www.wikipedia.org, 1 (accessed June 11, 2005); Burnside and Cairns, *Deadly innocence*, 108–9, 119.

13. Burnside and Cairns, *Deadly innocence*, 107–9.

14. Burnside and Cairns, *Deadly innocence*, 107, 111–12; "Karla Homolka," www.wikipedia.org, 1.

15. Burnside and Cairns, *Deadly innocence*, 110, 113.

16. Burnside and Cairns, *Deadly innocence*, 111, 113.

17. Burnside and Cairns, *Deadly innocence*, 116.

18. "Karla Homolka," www.wikipedia.org, 3.

19. Michaud and Hazelwood, *Evil that men do*, 234; Luann LaSalle and Nelson Wyatt, "Homolka weeps as public gets glimpse of one of Canada's most hated convicts," Canadian Press, June 2, 2005, http://news.yahoo.com, 1–2 (accessed June 11, 2005); and "Karla Homolka," www.wikipedia.org, 2, 4.

20. All Serial Killers, "Karla Homolka," http://www.allserialkillers.com, 1–2 (accessed June 11, 2005); "Karla Homolka," www.wikipedia.org, 5.

21. LaSalle and Wyatt, "Homolka weeps," 2; "Karla Homolka," www.wikipedia.org, 5.

22. Biography.ms, "Paul Bernardo," 1.

23. "Paul Bernardo," http://www.geocities.com/paedophilewatch/bernardo.html, 1 (accessed June 9, 2005).

24. "Paul Bernardo," www.geocities.com, 1; All Serial Killers, "Paul Bernardo," 1.

25. "Karla Homolka," www.wikipedia.org, 1; CBC News Online, "In-depth: Bernardo," 1–2.

26. "Karla Homolka," www.wikipedia.org, 2.

27. CBC News Online, "In-depth: Bernardo," 1.

28. Biography.ms, "Paul Bernardo," 1; Serial Killers A-Z, "Paul Bernardo," http://www.geocities.com/verbal_plainfield/a-h/bernardo.html, 1 (accessed June 9, 2005).

29. "Karla Homolka," www.wikipedia.org, 1.

30. CBC News Online, "In-depth: Bernardo," 2.

31. Serial Killers A-Z, "Paul Bernardo," 1; All Serial Killers, "Paul Bernardo," 1; "Karla Homolka," www.wikipedia.org, 1; and CBC News Online, "In-depth: Bernardo," 2.

32. Biography.ms, "Paul Bernardo," 1.

33. "Paul Bernardo," www.geocities.com, 1.

34. Serial Killers A-Z, "Paul Bernardo," 1.

35. Nationmaster.com, "Encyclopedia: Paul Bernardo," http://www.nationmaster.com, 1 (accessed June 9, 2005); All Serial Killers, "Paul Bernardo," 1.

36. "Karla Homolka," www.wikipedia.org, 1–2.

37. CBC News Online, "In-depth: Bernardo," 2.

38. Biography.ms, "Paul Bernardo," 1; "Karla Homolka," www.wikipedia.org, 2–3.

39. Biography.ms, "Paul Bernardo," 1. Wikipedia added that "it is almost absolutely certain that Paul Bernardo and Karla Homolka had other victims." See "Karla Homolka," www.wikipedia.org, 2.

40. Burnside and Cairns, *Deadly innocence*, 2, 5.

41. Burnside and Cairns, *Deadly innocence,* 36–37.

42. Burnside and Cairns, *Deadly innocence,* 43, 48.

43. Burnside and Cairns, *Deadly innocence,* 178–79, 184.

44. Burnside and Cairns, *Deadly innocence,* 56, 59, 262–63.

45. Burnside and Cairns, *Deadly innocence,* 314–16, 327.

46. Burnside and Cairns, *Deadly innocence,* 324, 333, 338.

47. Burnside and Cairns, *Deadly innocence,* 339–40.

48. Burnside and Cairns, *Deadly innocence,* 365–67, 371, 480, 504.

49. Burnside and Cairns, *Deadly innocence,* 396–97.

50. Burnside and Cairns, *Deadly innocence,* 400–401, 403–82.

51. Burnside and Cairns, *Deadly innocence,* 529, 535, 586–87.

52. Burnside and Cairns, *Deadly innocence,* 308–11, 318–19, 400–403.

53. Serial Killers A-Z, "Paul Bernardo," 1.

54. Michaud and Hazelwood, *Evil that men do,* 233.

55. Nationmaster.com, "Encyclopedia: Paul Bernardo," 1; Burnside and Cairns, *Deadly innocence,* 402. "The trial will forever be remembered due to the graphic content of the murder tapes, which were deemed so awful that the gallery was only allowed to listen while the prosecution, defense, judge and jury watched." See Serial Killers A-Z, "Paul Bernardo," 1.

56. All Serial Killers, "Paul Bernardo," 2. The same source added, "The tapes were later discovered and were nearly unbeatable evidence against the serial killer."

57. Chidley, "Bernardo," 1.

58. Chidley, "Bernardo," 3. In August 1992, Bernardo told Homolka that he wanted to "kidnap, rape and kill a woman he had spotted at Walt Disney World in Florida." See Chidley, "Bernardo," 2.

59. "Karla Homolka," www.wikipedia.org, 1.

60. "Paul Bernardo," www.geocities.com, 1.

61. CBC News Online, "In-depth: Bernardo," 4.

62. Nationmaster.com, "Encyclopedia: Paul Bernardo," 1.

63. Internet Tourbus News Service, "Paul Bernardo items on sale at eBay," http://www.tourbus.com, 1–2 (accessed June 9, 2005).

64. Burnside and Cairns, *Deadly innocence,* 58.

65. Burnside and Cairns, *Deadly innocence,* 27, 365.

66. CBC News Online, "In-depth: Bernardo," 1.

67. "Karla Homolka," www.wikipedia.org, 5; Hot News 360, "Paul Bernardo news and information," http://www.hotnews360.com, 1–2 (accessed June 9, 2005).

68. Nationmaster.com, "Encyclopedia: Paul Bernardo," 1; "Karla Homolka," www.wikipedia.org, 4.

69. Internet Tourbus News Service, "Paul Bernardo items on sale," 1–2.

70. Burnside and Cairns, *Deadly innocence,* 41.

71. LaSalle and Wyatt, "Homolka weeps," 1; CBC News Online, "In-depth: Bernardo," 1.

72. Burnside and Cairns, *Deadly innocence,* 3, 342, 398.

73. Burnside and Cairns, *Deadly innocence,* 58.

74. Burnside and Cairns, *Deadly innocence,* 40.

75. Burnside and Cairns, *Deadly innocence,* 56.

76. Burnside and Cairns, *Deadly innocence,* 355, 452.

77. Burnside and Cairns, *Deadly innocence,* 452.

78. Burnside and Cairns, *Deadly innocence*, 324–25.

79. Burnside and Cairns, *Deadly innocence*, 351.

80. Burnside and Cairns, *Deadly innocence*, 345.

81. Burnside and Cairns, *Deadly innocence*, 434, 480.

82. Burnside and Cairns, *Deadly innocence*, 49, 341.

83. Burnside and Cairns, *Deadly innocence*, 44, 52.

84. Burnside and Cairns, *Deadly innocence*, 339–41, 398–99.

85. Burnside and Cairns, *Deadly innocence*, 344–45, 365.

86. Burnside and Cairns, *Deadly innocence*, 368.

87. Serial Killers A-Z, "Paul Bernardo," 1.

88. Burnside and Cairns, *Deadly innocence*, 40, 55, 342.

89. Burnside and Cairns, *Deadly innocence*, 55.

90. Burnside and Cairns, *Deadly innocence*, 53–54.

91. Burnside and Cairns, *Deadly innocence*, 560.

92. Burnside and Cairns, *Deadly innocence*, 56–57.

93. Burnside and Cairns, *Deadly innocence*, 39.

94. Burnside and Cairns, *Deadly innocence*, 27.

95. Burnside and Cairns, *Deadly innocence*, 59.

96. Burnside and Cairns, *Deadly innocence*, 41.

97. Burnside and Cairns, *Deadly innocence*, 370, 561; "Karla Homolka," www.wikipedia.org, 3.

98. "Karla Homolka," www.wikipedia.org, 3; CBC News Online, "In-depth: Bernardo," 5. The first acts of enforcement were against the so-called "electronic ban breakers." Many of the ban violators were congregating online at alt.fan.karla.homolka. See "Karla Homolka," www.wikipedia.org, 3.

CHAPTER 12

1. Vancouver Eastside Missing Women, "Spate of charges cause experts to mull Pacific Northwest's killer record," Canadian Press, May 18, 2002, http://www.missingpeople.net, 1 (accessed May 24, 2005).

2. Shirley Lynn Scott, "Prowling at the movies," http://www.crimelibrary.com (accessed May 24, 2005).

3. Scott, "Prowling at the movies," 4.

4. Gary C. King, *Driven to kill* (New York: Pinnacle Books, 1993), 254.

5. Shirley Lynn Scott, "Molesting by thirteen," http://www.crimelibrary.com (accessed May 24, 2005).

6. Scott, "Molesting by thirteen," 2.

7. King, *Driven to kill*, 256; Scott, "Molesting by thirteen," 1.

8. Thom Spencer, "Bullies kill and kids who are bullied kill," http://www.bullypolice. org, 2 (accessed May 24, 2005).

9. Explore Dictionary of Famous People, "Westley Allan Dodd," http://www. explore-biography.com/biographies/W/Westley_Allan_Dodd.html, 1 (accessed May 24, 2005). Dodd "volunteered" to die and forego his appellate rights. See Washington Coalition to Abolish the Death Penalty, "Recent executions in Washington state," http://www.abolishdeathpenalty.org, 1 (accessed May 24, 2005).

10. Shirley Lynn Scott, "Disturbing confessions," http://www.crimelibrary.com (accessed May 24, 2005). Dodd made clear the threatening consequences if he was not

executed: "I must be executed before I have the opportunity to escape or kill someone within the prison. If I do escape, I promise you I will kill and rape and enjoy every minute of it." See Explore Dictionary, "Westley Allan Dodd," 1.

11. King, *Driven to kill,* 329.

12. Washington Coalition to Abolish the Death Penalty, "Recent executions," 1; Explore Dictionary, "Westley Allan Dodd," 1. Why did Dodd choose hanging? "Because that's the way Lee Iseli died," Dodd told reporters. See Explore Dictionary, "Westley Allan Dodd," 1.

13. Scott, "Disturbing confessions," 6.

14. King, *Driven to kill,* 196–97.

15. Scott, "Molesting by thirteen," 1.

16. Scott, "Molesting by thirteen," 1.

17. Answers.com, "Westley Allan Dodd," http://www.answers.com, 1 (accessed May 24, 2005).

18. Scott, "Molesting by thirteen," 2.

19. Scott, "Molesting by thirteen," 2.

20. King, *Driven to kill,* 210.

21. Scott, "Molesting by thirteen," 3–4.

22. Scott, "Molesting by thirteen," 3.

23. Nationmaster.com, "Encyclopedia: Westley Allan Dodd," http://www.nationmaster.com, 1 (accessed May 24, 2005).

24. Explore Dictionary, "Westley Allan Dodd," 1.

25. Answers.com, "Westley Allan Dodd," 1.

26. King, *Driven to kill,* 40.

27. Scott, "Molesting by thirteen," 6.

28. Scott, "Molesting by thirteen," 1.

29. Scott, "Molesting by thirteen," 3.

30. Scott, "Molesting by thirteen," 4.

31. Scott, "Molesting by thirteen," 6.

32. King, *Driven to kill,* 32.

33. "In memory of Cole and William Neer," http://www.free.webspace.biz, 1 (accessed May 24, 2005).

34. "In memory," www.free.webspace.biz, 1.

35. Shirley Lynn Scott, "Billy and Cole Neer," http://www.crimelibrary.com, 1 (accessed May 24, 2005).

36. "In memory," www.free.webspace.biz, 1.

37. King, *Driven to kill,* 116.

38. Shirley Lynn Scott, "Lee Iseli," http://www.crimelibrary.com, 1–6 (accessed May 24, 2005).

39. Explore Dictionary, "Westley Allan Dodd," 3; Nationmaster.com, "Encyclopedia: Westley Allan Dodd," 1.

40. Scott, "Disturbing confessions," 3.

41. Vancouver Eastside, "Spate of charges," 1.

42. Westley A. Dodd, personal communication (diary). See King, *Driven to kill,* 118–19, 176.

43. Scott, "Lee Iseli," 5.

44. Scott, "Disturbing confessions," 2.

45. Nationmaster.com, "Encyclopedia: Westley Allan Dodd," 1.

46. King, *Driven to kill,* 14, 71, 168.

47. King, *Driven to kill,* 65, 166, 168.

48. King, *Driven to kill,* 67–68, 153–54, 169–71.

49. King, *Driven to kill,* 41, 46–47.

50. King, *Driven to kill,* 46.

51. King, *Driven to kill,* 53, 64.

52. King, *Driven to kill,* 51, 55, 63.

53. King, *Driven to kill,* 53, 57.

54. King, *Driven to kill,* 94.

55. King, *Driven to kill,* 96–100.

56. King, *Driven to kill,* 100, 104.

57. King, *Driven to kill,* 139–43, 147–48.

58. King, *Driven to kill,* 148–49.

59. "In memory," www.free.webspace.biz, 1.

60. Scott, "Prowling at the movies," 2–4.

61. King, *Driven to kill,* 181–84.

62. King, *Driven to kill,* 184–85.

63. King, *Driven to kill,* 188, 242.

64. Scott, "Prowling at the movies," 3.

65. Scott, "Disturbing confessions," 1.

66. Scott, "Prowling at the movies," 4.

67. Scott, "Disturbing confessions," 1.

68. King, *Driven to kill,* 17.

69. King, *Driven to kill,* 313, 315.

70. King, *Driven to kill,* 18–19.

71. King, *Driven to kill,* 319.

72. King, *Driven to kill,* 18–20, 320.

73. Westley A. Dodd, personal communication (diary).

74. Westley A. Dodd, personal communication (diary).

75. King, *Driven to kill,* 278.

76. King, *Driven to kill,* 316.

77. Westley A. Dodd, personal communication (diary).

78. Westley A. Dodd, personal communication (diary).

79. Westley A. Dodd, personal communication (diary).

80. King, *Driven to kill,* 303–4.

81. King, *Driven to kill,* 54.

82. King, *Driven to kill,* 63–64.

83. King, *Driven to kill,* 63.

84. King, *Driven to kill,* 240.

85. King, *Driven to kill,* 115.

86. King, *Driven to kill,* 225.

87. King, *Driven to kill,* 72–73.

88. King, *Driven to kill,* 328.

89. Cyndi's Corner, Deviant Crimes, "The execution of Westley A. Dodd," http://www.deviantcrimes.com, 1, 3 (accessed May 24, 2005).

90. King, *Driven to kill,* 137–38.

91. King, *Driven to kill,* 74–75.

92. King, *Driven to kill,* 150.

93. King, *Driven to kill*, 281.
94. King, *Driven to kill*, 99.
95. King, *Driven to kill*, 158.
96. King, *Driven to kill*, 154.
97. King, *Driven to kill*, 46.
98. King, *Driven to kill*, 62.
99. Cyndi's Corner, "Execution of Westley A. Dodd," 2.
100. King, *Driven to kill*, 308–17.
101. King, *Driven to kill*, 77.

SELECTED BIBLIOGRAPHY

BOOKS AND MAGAZINES

Bardens, Dennis. *The ladykiller.* Middlesex, U.K.: Senate, 1972.

Blackburn, Daniel J. *Human harvest: The Sacramento murder story.* New York: Knightsbridge, 1990.

Brady, Ian. *The gates of Janus: Serial killing and its analysis.* Los Angeles: Feral House, 2001.

Bugliosi, Vince, and Gentry, Curtis. *Helter skelter.* New York: W. W. Norton, 1974.

Burnside, Scott, and Cairns, Alan. *Deadly innocence.* New York: Times Warner Books, 1996.

Caputi, Jane. *The age of sex crime.* Bowling Green, OH: Bowling Green State University Press, 1987.

Chidley, Joe. "Bernardo: The untold story." *Macleans,* September 11, 1995.

Clarkson, Wensley. *Death at every stop.* New York: St. Martin's Press, 1997.

Davis, Don. *The Milwaukee murders: Nightmare in apartment 213—the true story.* New York: St. Martin's Press, 1991.

Douglas, John, and Olshaker, Mark. *Anatomy of motive.* New York: Scribners, 1999.

Everitt, David. *Human monsters: An illustrated encyclopedia of the world's most vicious murderers.* Chicago: Contemporary Books, 1993.

Fisher, Joseph C. *Killer among us: Public reaction to serial murder.* Westport, CT: Praeger, 1997.

Gibson, Dirk C. *Clues from killers: Serial murder and crime scene messages.* Westport, CT: Praeger, 2004.

Hickey, Eric W. *Serial murderers and their victims.* Belmont, CA: Wadsworth, 1997.

Kelleher, Michael D., and Kelleher, C. L. *Murder most rare: The female serial killer.* New York: Dell, 1998.

King, Gary C. *Driven to kill.* New York: Pinnacle Books, 1993.

Lane, Brian, and Gregg, Wilfred. *The encyclopedia of serial killers.* New York: Berkeley Books, 1992.

Mendoza, Antonio. *Killers on the loose.* London: Virgin Books, 2000.

Michaud, Steven G., and Hazelwood, Roy. *The evil that men do.* New York: St. Martin's Press, 1998.

Newton, Michael. *The encyclopedia of serial killers: A study of the chilling criminal phenomenon, from the "Angels of Death" to the "Zodiac" killer.* New York: Checkmark Books, 2000.

Newton, Michael. *Hunting humans: The encyclopedia of serial killers.* New York: Avon Books, 1990.

O'Brien, Darcy. *Two of a kind: The Hillside Stranglers.* New York: New American Library, 1985.

Orth, Maureen. *Vulgar favors: Andrew Cunanan, Gianni Versace, and the largest failed manhunt in U. S. history.* New York: Delacorte, 1999.

Publications International Ltd. *Murder and mayhem.* Lincolnwood, IL: Publications International Ltd., 1991.

Sanders, Ed. *The family: The story of Charles Manson's dune buggy attack.* New York: E. P. Dutton, 1971.

Schechter, Harold. *Bestial: The savage trail of an American monster.* New York: Pocket Books, 1998.

Schechter, Harold, and Everitt, David. *The A-Z encyclopedia of serial killers.* New York: Simon and Schuster, 1996.

Schwartz, Anne. *The man who could not kill enough.* New York: Birch Lane Books, 1992.

Schwartz, Ted. *The Hillside Strangler: A murderer's mind.* New York: New American Library, 1981.

Scott, Gini G. *Homicide: 100 years of murder in America.* Los Angeles: Lowell House, 1998.

Smith, Carlton, and Guillen, Tomas. *The search for the Green River killer.* New York: Onyx Books, 1991.

Williams, Emlyn. *Beyond belief.* New York: Random House, 1968.

Wilson, Colin, and Wilson, Damon. *The killers among us: Sex, madness, and mass murder.* Vol. 2. New York: Warner Books, 1995.

GOVERNMENT DOCUMENTS

LaBianca Homicide Report. http://www.users.adelphia.bet. First Homicide Investigation Progress Report DR 69-586 381 (August 10, 1969).

INTERNET SOURCES

All Serial Killers.com. "Karla Homolka." http://www.allserialkillers.com (n.d.).

All Serial Killers.com. "Paul Bernardo." http://www.allserialkillers.com (n.d.).

Answers.com. "Hillside Strangler." http://www.answers.com (n.d.).

Answers.com. "Westley Allan Dodd." http://www.answers.com (n.d.).

Bardsley, Marilyn. "The Hillside Stranglers." Court TV, Crime Library. http://www.crimelibrary.com (2005).

Biography.ms. "Paul Bernardo." http://paul-bernardo.biography.ms (n.d.).

Burchill, John. "The Strangler." Winnipeg Police Service. http://www.winnipeg.ca/police (2002).

Court TV. "The Axeman of New Orleans: The Black Hand." Crime Library. http://www.crimelibrary.com (2005).

Court TV. "Henri Landru." Crime Library. http://www.crimelibrary.com (2005).

Court TV. "The Hillside Stranglers." Crime Library. http://www.crimelibrary.com (2005).

Fortune City.com. "Ian Brady and Myra Hindley: The Moors Murders." http://www.fortunecity.com (2000).

Gribben, Mark. "The Dark Strangler." Court TV, Crime Library. http://www.crimelibrary.com (2005).

Guardian Unlimited. "Timetable of Moors Murders case." http://www.guardian.co.uk (2004).

"The Hillside Strangler: Timeline of events." http://www.hillside-strangler.com (2003).

"Hillside Stranglers." http://www.geocities.com/schoolgirlsadist/hillsidestranglers. html?200523 (n.d.).

History Channel. "The Hillside Stranglers." http://www.thehistorychannel.co.uk (2004).

Kari and Associates. "The Hillside Stranglers: Kenneth Bianchi and Angelo Buono." http://www.karisable.com (n.d.).

Murder in the U.K. "Ian Brady and Myra Hindley: Moors Murderers." http://www. murderuk.com (1997–2005).

New Criminologist. "Obituary: Angelo Buono." http://www.newcriminologist.com (2005).

News of the Odd. "French Bluebeard guillotined." http://www.newsoftheodd.com (1992).

Rapid Intelligence Pty., Ltd. "Encyclopedia: Paul Bernardo." http://www.nationmaster.com (2002).

Rapid Intelligence Pty., Ltd. "Encyclopedia: Westley Allan Dodd." http://www. nationmaster.com (2002).

Rotten.com. "Henri Desire Landru: AKA the French Bluebeard." http://www.rotten.com (n.d.).

Scott, Shirley Lynn. "Molesting by thirteen." Court TV. Crime Library. http://www. crimelibrary.com (2005).

Serial Killers A-Z. "Earle Nelson." http://www.geocities.com/verbal_plainfield/i-p/ nelson.html (2003).

Serial Killers A-Z. "Paul Bernardo." http://www.geocities.com/verbal_plainfield/a-h/ bernardo.html (2003).

Summers, Chris. "The Hillside Stranglers." http://www.bbc.co.uk (2004).

Summers, Chris. "Moors Murderers." http://www.bbc.co.uk (2004).

Trivia Library.com. "Henri Desire Landru the Bluebeard: Parts 1, 2, and 3." http://www.trivia-library.com (1975–81).

Wikipedia. "Karla Homolka." http://en.wikipedia.org (2005).

INDEX

About the Author

DIRK C. GIBSON is Associate Professor of Communication and Journalism at the University of New Mexico. He has published numerous articles on a variety of topics in such journals as *Public Relations Quarterly, Public Relations Review,* and *Southern Communication Journal.* He has also published several book chapters and two books, *The Role of Communication in the Practice of Law* (1991) and *Clues from Killers* (Praeger, 2004).